Edwin Othello Excell

Gospel in song

Combining Sing the Gospel, Echoes of Eden, and other selected Songs and Solos for the Sunday school

Edwin Othello Excell

Gospel in song
Combining Sing the Gospel, Echoes of Eden, and other selected Songs and Solos for the Sunday school

ISBN/EAN: 9783337181727

Printed in Europe, USA, Canada, Australia, Japan

Cover: Foto ©Thomas Meinert / pixelio.de

More available books at **www.hansebooks.com**

THE

GOSPEL IN SONG,

COMBINING

Sing the Gospel, Echoes of Eden,

And other Selected Songs and Solos

FOR THE

SUNDAY SCHOOL.

E. O. EXCELL,

Author and Publisher,

148 MADISON STREET, CHICAGO, ILL.

PREFACE.

In response to the urgent request of many of my musical friends who have expressed a desire to have ALL my SONGS and SOLOS in one collection, I send forth "THE GOSPEL IN SONG," trusting that "he whose care is o'er us all" will use it to HIS honor and to HIS glory.

E. O. EXCELL,
Author and Publisher.

THE GOSPEL IN SONG.

No. 1. The Song of Jubilee.

Rev. L. Bacon. E. O. Excell.

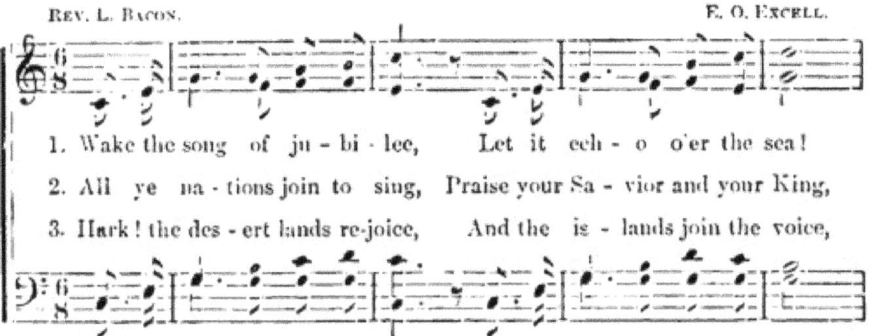
1. Wake the song of ju - bi - lee, Let it ech - o o'er the sea!
2. All ye na - tions join to sing, Praise your Sa - vior and your King,
3. Hark! the des - ert lands re-joice, And the is - lands join the voice,

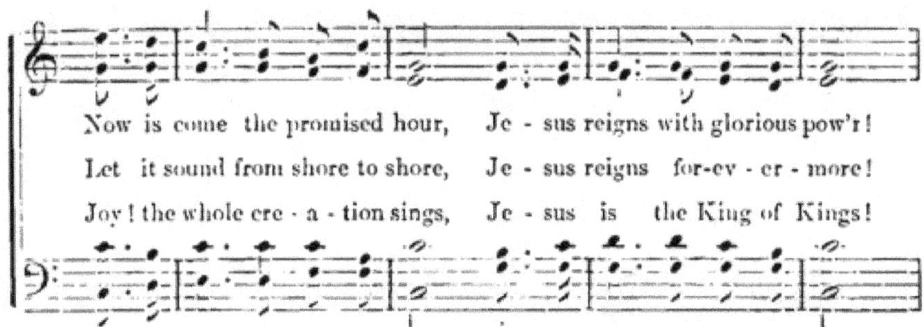
Now is come the promised hour, Je - sus reigns with glorious pow'r!
Let it sound from shore to shore, Je - sus reigns for-ev - er - more!
Joy! the whole cre - a - tion sings, Je - sus is the King of Kings!

Now is come the promised hour, Je - sus reigns with glorious pow'r!
Let it sound from shore to shore, Je - sus reigns for-ev - er - more!
Joy! the whole cre - a - tion sings, Je - sus is the King of Kings!

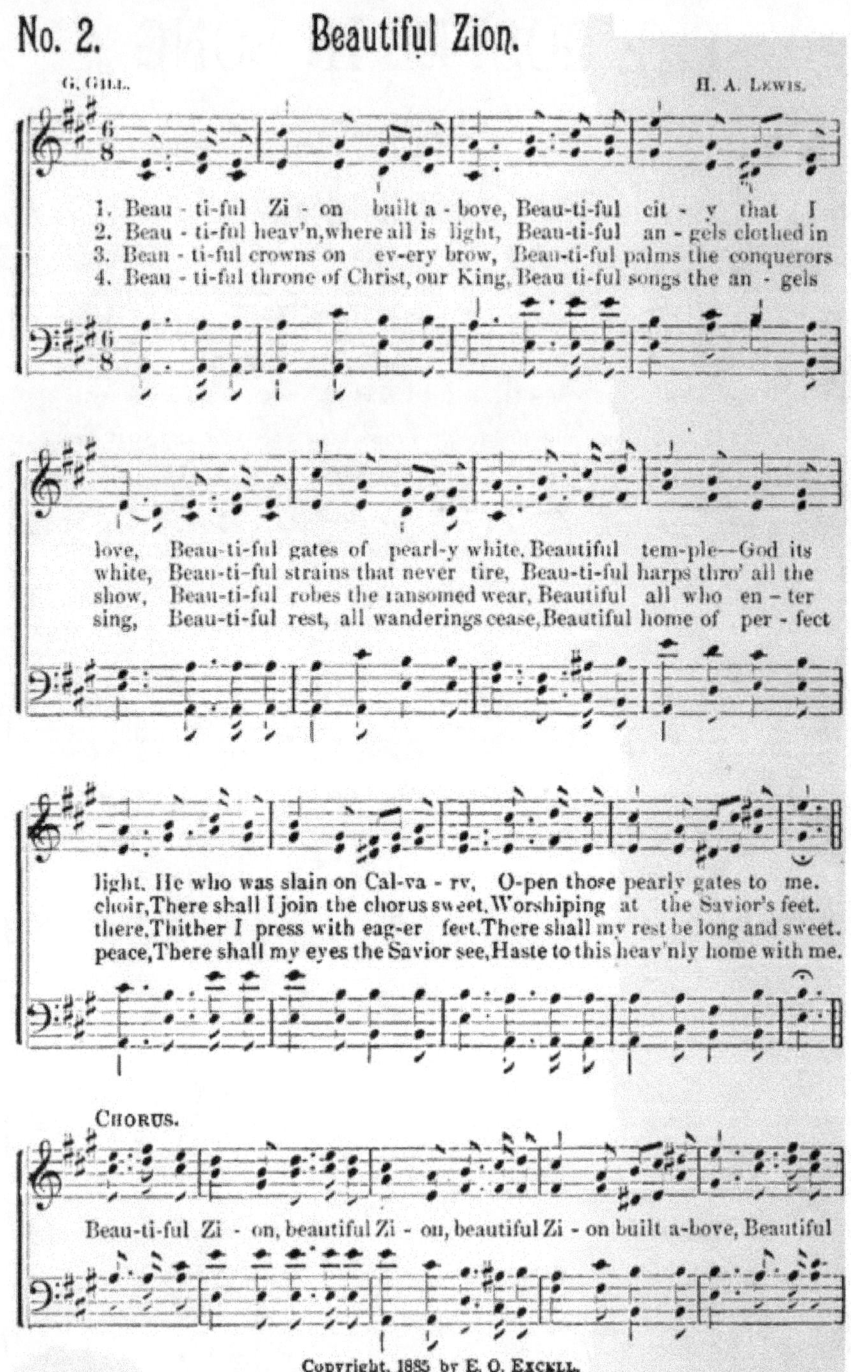
No. 2. Beautiful Zion.
G. Gill.
H. A. Lewis.
1. Beau - ti-ful Zi - on built a - bove, Beau-ti-ful cit - y that I
2. Beau - ti-ful heav'n, where all is light, Beau-ti-ful an - gels clothed in
3. Beau - ti-ful crowns on ev-ery brow, Beau-ti-ful palms the conquerors
4. Beau - ti-ful throne of Christ, our King, Beau ti-ful songs the an - gels
love, Beau-ti-ful gates of pearl-y white, Beautiful tem-ple—God its
white, Beau-ti-ful strains that never tire, Beau-ti-ful harps thro' all the
show, Beau-ti-ful robes the ransomed wear, Beautiful all who en - ter
sing, Beau-ti-ful rest, all wanderings cease, Beautiful home of per - fect
light. He who was slain on Cal-va - ry, O-pen those pearly gates to me.
choir, There shall I join the chorus sweet, Worshiping at the Savior's feet.
there, Thither I press with eag-er feet. There shall my rest be long and sweet.
peace, There shall my eyes the Savior see, Haste to this heav'nly home with me.
Chorus.
Beau-ti-ful Zi - on, beautiful Zi - on, beautiful Zi - on built a-bove, Beautiful

Beautiful Zion.—Concluded.

cit - y, beau ti - ful cit - y, beau-ti-ful cit - y that I love.

No. 3. Around the Throne of God.

ANNIE SHEPHERD. English.

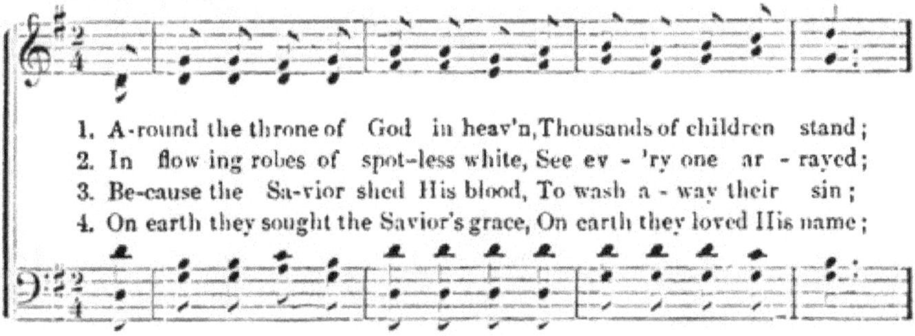

1. A-round the throne of God in heav'n, Thousands of children stand;
2. In flow ing robes of spot-less white, See ev - 'ry one ar - rayed;
3. Be-cause the Sa-vior shed His blood, To wash a - way their sin;
4. On earth they sought the Savior's grace, On earth they loved His name;

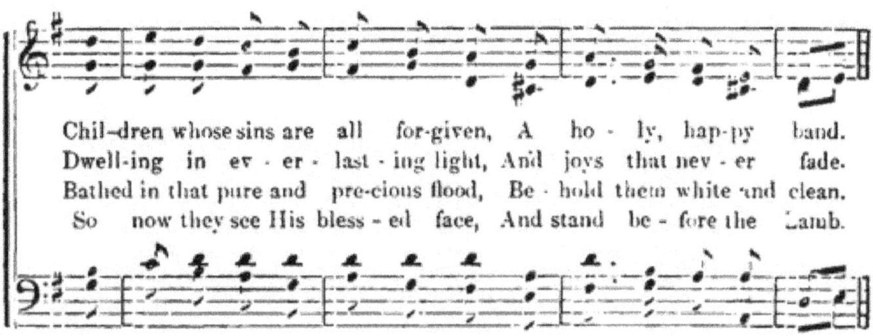

Chil-dren whose sins are all for-given, A ho - ly, hap-py band.
Dwell-ing in ev - er - last - ing light, And joys that nev - er fade.
Bathed in that pure and pre-cious flood, Be - hold them white and clean.
So now they see His bless - ed face, And stand be - fore the Lamb.

CHORUS.

Sing-ing, Glo-ry, glo - ry, glo - ry be to God on high......

No. 4. Nearer My Home.

Unknown. E. O. Excell.

1. O'er the hill the sun is set - ting, And the eve is draw-ing on; Slow-ly
2. One day nearer, sings the sail-or, As he glides the waters o'er, While the
3. Worn and weary, oft the pilgrim. Hails the setting of the sun, For the
4. Nearer home! yes, one day nearer To our Father's house on high, To the

droops the gen - tle twi-light, For an - oth-er day is gone. Gone for
light is soft - ly dy - ing On his dis-tant na - tive shore. Thus the
goal is one day near - er, And his jour-ney near-ly done. Thus we
green fields and the foun-tains Of the land be-yond the sky. For the

D.S. Chorus. *Near - er*

aye, its race is o - ver. Soon the darker shades will come; Still it's
Christian, on life's o - cean, As his light boat cuts the foam, In the
feel, when o'er life's des - ert, Heart and sandal worn, we roam; As the
heav'ns grow brighter o'er us, And the lamps hang in the dome, And our

home! yes, one day near - er To our Father's house on high; To the

D.S. for Chorus.

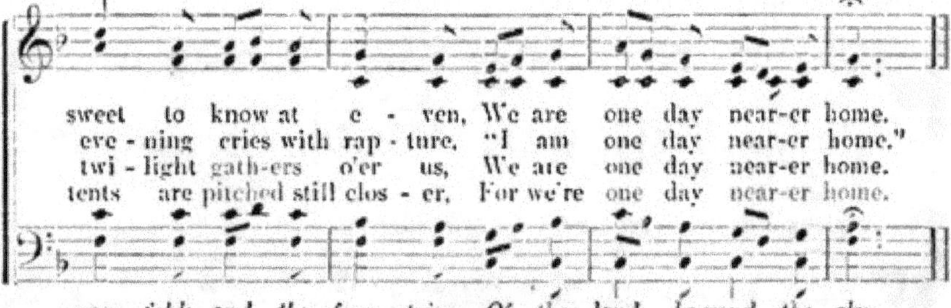
sweet to know at e - ven, We are one day near-er home.
eve - ning cries with rap - ture, "I am one day near-er home."
twi - light gath-ers o'er us, We are one day near-er home.
tents are pitched still clos - er, For we're one day near-er home.
green fields and the foun - tains Of the land be-yond the sky.

No. 5. Shall I be Saved To-Night?

"Look unto me, and be ye saved."—Isa. xlv, 22.

Fanny J. Crosby. Mrs. M. E. Willson.

1. Je - sus is plead-ing with my poor soul, Shall I be saved to-night?
2. Je - sus was nail'd to the cross for me, Shall I be saved to-night?
3. Je - sus is knock-ing at my poor heart, Shall I be saved to-night?
4. What if that voice I should hear no more, Shall I be saved to-night?
If I be-lieve, He will make me whole, Shall I be saved to-night?
How can my heart so un - grate-ful be, Shall I be saved to-night?
What if His Spir - it should now de - part? Oh! shall I be saved to-night?
Quick-ly I'll o - pen the bolt - ed door, Save me, O Lord, to-night,
Ten-der-ly, sad-ly I hear Him say, How can you grieve me from day to day,
Now He will save me by grace di-vine, Now, if I will, I may call Him mine,
O-ver and o-ver His voice I hear, Sweet-ly it falls on my list'ning ear,
Bless-ed Redeemer, come in, come in, Pit - y my sor-row, for-give my sin,
Shall I go on in the old, old way, Or shall I be saved to-night?
Can I the pleas-ures of earth re - sign, Oh, shall I be saved to-night?
Shall I re - ject Him, a friend so dear? Oh! shall I be savéd to-night?
Now let Thy work in my soul be - gin, For I will be saved to-night!

No. 6. Sinful, Weary, Heavy Laden.

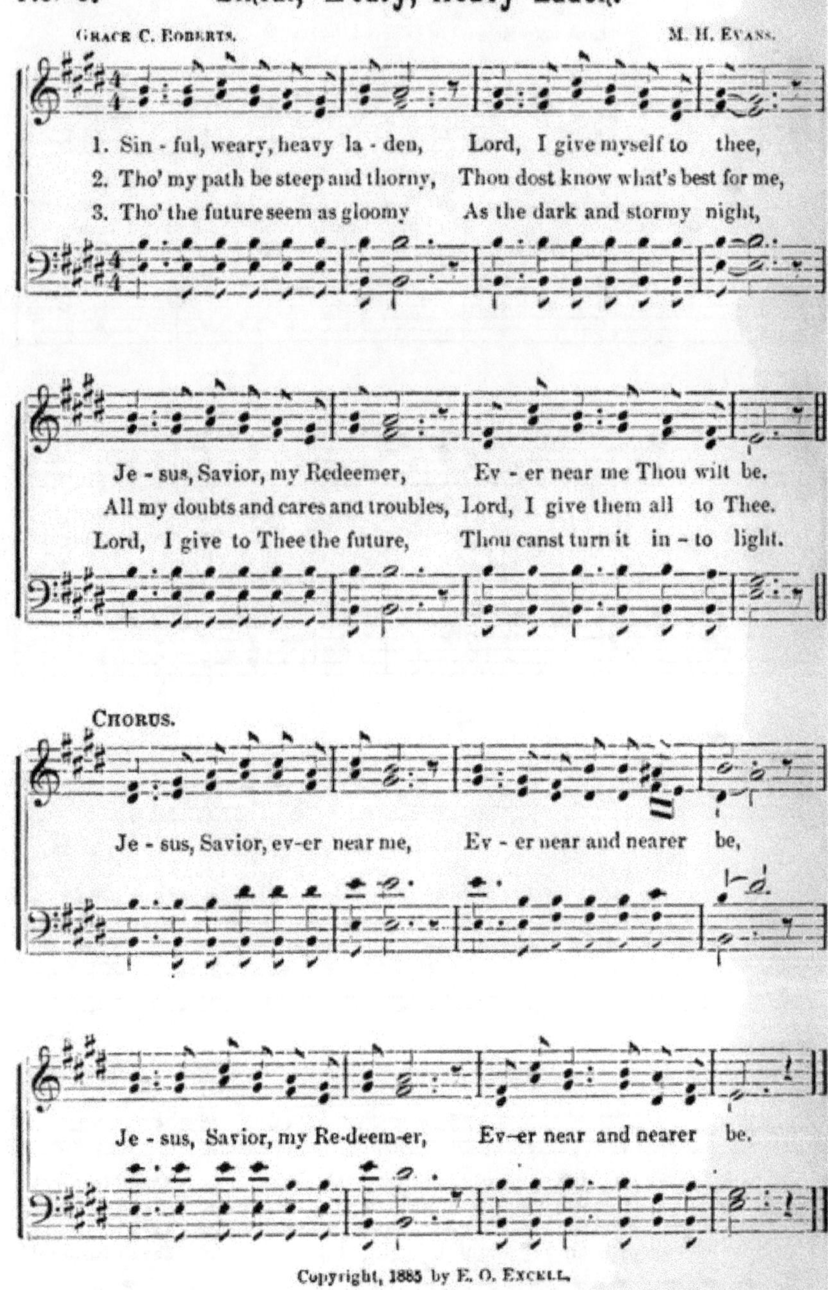
GRACE C. ROBERTS.
M. H. EVANS.
1. Sin - ful, weary, heavy la - den, Lord, I give myself to thee,
2. Tho' my path be steep and thorny, Thou dost know what's best for me,
3. Tho' the future seem as gloomy As the dark and stormy night,
Je - sus, Savior, my Redeemer, Ev - er near me Thou wilt be.
All my doubts and cares and troubles, Lord, I give them all to Thee.
Lord, I give to Thee the future, Thou canst turn it in - to light.
CHORUS.
Je - sus, Savior, ev-er near me, Ev - er near and nearer be,
Je - sus, Savior, my Re-deem-er, Ev-er near and nearer be.
Copyright, 1885 by E. O. EXCELL.

No. 7. O Zion, Zion.

L. H. Jameson. J. H. Rosecrans.

1. There is a hab - i - ta - tion, Built by the liv-ing God,
2. A ci - ty with foun-da-tions Firm as th' eternal throne;
3. No night is there, no sor - row, No death and no de - cay;
4. With-in its pearl-y por-tals An - gel - ic arm-ies sing,
For all of ev - ery na-tion, Who seek that grand a - bode.
Nor wars, nor des - o - la-tion Shall ev - er move a stone.
No yes - ter-day, no mor-row— But one e - ter - nal day.
With glo - ri - fied im - mor-tals, The prais - es of its King.
Chorus.
O Si - on, Si - on, I long thy gates to see; O
O Si - on, love-ly Si - on, O love - ly
Si - on, Si - on, When shall I dwell in thee?
Si - on, love - ly Si - on,

By permission.

No. 8. Hark the Voice of Jesus Calling.

M. B. Slight.
H. R. Palmer.
1. Hark! the voice of Je - sus call-ing, "Fol-low me, fol - low me!"
2. Who will heed the ho - ly man-date, "Fol-low me, fol - low me!"
3. Heark - en, lest he plead no long-er, "Fol-low me, fol - low me!"
Soft - ly thro' the si - lence fall - ing, "Fol-low, fol-low me!"
Leav-ing all things at his bid-ding, "Fol-low, fol-low me!"
Once a - gain, O hear him call - ing, "Fol-low, fol-low me!"
As of old he call'd the fish-ers, When he walk'd by Gal - i - lee,
Hark! that ten-der voice en-treat-ing Mar - i - ners on life's rough sea,
Turn - ing swift at thy sweet summons, Ev-er - more, O Christ, would we,
rit.
Still his pa - tient voice is plead - ing, "Fol-low, fol - low me!"
Gent - ly, lov - ing - ly re - peat - ing, "Fol-low, fol - low me!"
For thy love all else for - sak - ing, "Fol-low, fol - low me!"

By permission.

No. 9. Children's Day.

Rev. W. C. Wilbor. E. O. Excell.

1. The children's Sabbath comes a-gain, With birds and flowers bright,
2. The passing year God's love has blest, The hills with mu-sic ring,
3. Sing un-to God who made the day, Whose praise the night prolongs,
4. From sea to sea, in temples fair, To-day his children meet,

With ear-ly fruits and gen-tle rain, And floods of sun-shine light.
The pastures now with flocks are drest, The valleys shout and sing.
Win-ter and Summer own his sway The earth to him be-longs.
From north to south we breathe a prayer And worship at his feet.

CHORUS.

All na-ture's voic-es loud proclaim God's goodness great and free,

Let all the children praise his name With glad, sweet melody.

No. 10. Marching Home.
Unknown.
H. A. Lewis.
1. We are marching homeward to that land: To the region of the blest; We shall soon be with the angel band, Where our weary feet may rest.
2. In that blessed land we're nearing now, We shall see our Sa - vior's face; He will place a crown on ev-ery brow, Saved by his re-deem-ing grace.
3. Brothers will you join our happy band, Trav'ling up the shin - ing way? Je - sus is the Cap-tain in command, Will you now his call o - bey.
of the blest;
Savior's face;
shining way?
Chorus.
Marching home, marching home, We are marching to that happy, happy land, marching home, marching
marching home, marching home,
happy land, marching home,

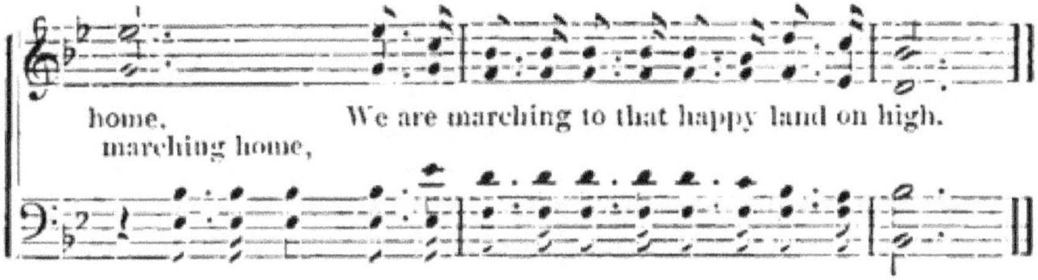

Marching Home.—Concluded.

home, We are marching to that happy land on high.
marching home,

No. 11. Close to Thee.

"I cried unto the Lord with my voice; With my voice unto the Lord did I make my supplication."
Psa. 142: 1.

Mrs. Harriet Jones. H. A. Lewis.

1. Dear Lord, to Thee I come Wea - ry, distressed; I kneel at mercy's throne, For rest, sweet rest.
2. Dear Je - sus, lend an ear While low I bow; Dis-pel my ev - ery fear, O! an - swer *now.*
3. Dear Lord, I would be thine Hence-forth for aye; O, fill with love di- vine, Just now I pray.
4. Dear Lord, for-ev-er true, Thou hearest me— Just now, like gentle dew, Grace comes from Thee.

Chorus.

Just now I'm needing Thee, Just now I'm needing Thee, O, draw me close to Thee! Close, close to Thee.

(*Chorus for last verse.*)— All praise, O Lord to Thee, Thy grace has set me free, Now keep me close to Thee! Close, close to Thee.

Rit.

No. 12. One by One.

Arr. by E. O. E.
Matt. 25; 31, 34.
E. O. Excell.
1. Gath-er-ing homeward from every land, Gath-er-ing one by one;......
2. Lov'd ones have gone to that distant shore, Gath-er-ing one by one;......
3. We, too, shall come to the riv-er-side, Gath-er-ing one by one;......
4. Je - sus, Re-deem-er, be thou our stay! Gath-er ing one by one;......
Pilgrims are join-ing, the heavenly band, Gath-er - ing one by one;
Oth - ers are go ing for ev - er more, Gath-er - ing one by one;
Near-er its wa-ters each e - ven-tide, Gath-er - ing one by one;
Cross the dark riv - er with us, we pray, Gath-er - ing one by one;
Each brow is en - closed in a gold en crown. Their travel-stained robes are
Our sis - ters so gentle, our brothers so brave, The beau-ti - ful children
O Je - sus, our faint - ing strength up-hold, The waves of that river are
Then bold ly we'll come to Jor - dan's side, And fear-less - ly breast its
all laid down, Gathering homeward from every land, Gathering one by one.
o'er the wave, Gathering homeward from every land, Gathering one by one.
dark and cold, Gathering homeward from every land, Gathering one by one.
swelling tide, Gathering homeward from every land, Gathering one by one.

One by One.—Concluded.

No. 13. A Sinner Like Me.

C. J. B. — C. J. Butler.

Repeat pp
Home, to our beautiful home, We are gathering one by one.
Home a-bove, to our beautiful home a - bove,
1. I was once far a - way from the Sa - vior, And as
vile as a sin-ner could be,...... I...... won-dered if
Christ the Re-deem-er, Could save a poor sinner like me.

2 I wandered on in the darkness,
Not a ray of light could I see,
And the thought filled my heart with sadness,
There's no hope for a sinner like me

3 And then, in that dark lonely hour,
A voice sweetly whispered to me,
Saying, Christ the Redeemer has power
To save a poor sinner like me.

4 I listened, and lo! 'twas the Savior
That was speaking so kindly to me;
I cried, I'm the chief of sinners,
Thou canst save a poor sinner like me.

5 I then fully trusted in Jesus,
And oh, what a joy came to me;
My heart was filled with his praises,
For saving a sinner like me.

6 No longer in darkness I'm walking,
For the light is now shining on me,
And now unto others I'm telling,
How he saved a poor sinner like me.

7 And when life's journey is over,
And I the dear Savior shall see,
I'll praise him forever and ever,
For saving a sinner like me.

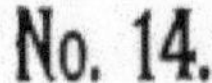

No. 14. Wonderful Love.

Anon. M. H. Evans.

1. Oh, have you not heard of that wonderful love, That flows from God's heart so free, Which led Him to give for a per - ish-ing world, His Son to be nailed to the tree?
2. Poor sinners, undone, and sinful and lost, This love of our God re-ceive; No heart is to sad for this love to make glad, When once on God's word we believe.
3. Oh, sweet is the rest to the wea-ry and worn, Who feel the great load of sin; It seeks for no mer-it, it's bliss to in-her - it, No goodness without or within.

Chorus.

Believe in that wonderful love...... Believe in that wonderful love... .. The Gos-pel is free, for God sends it to thee, Be-lieve in that won-der-ful love.

wonderful love, wonderful love.

No. 15. Glorious Fountain.

COWPER.
T. C. O'KANE.
1. { There is a fountain filled with blood, filled with blood, filled with blood, There
{ And sinners plung'd beneath that flood, beneath that flood, beneath that flood, And
2. { The dy-ing thief rejoiced to see, rejoiced to see, rejoiced to see, The
{ And there may I, tho' vile as he, tho' vile as he, tho' vile as he, And
is a foun - tain filled with blood Drawn from Immanuel's veins, }
sin - ners plung'd beneath that flood, Lose all their guilt y stains. }
dy - ing thief re-joiced to see That foun-tain in his day, }
there may I tho' vile as he, Wash all my sins a - way. }
CHORUS.
Oh, glo - ri - ous fount-ain! Here will I stay, And in thee
ev - er Wash my sins a - way.

3 Thou dying Lamb,|: thy precious blood,:|
Shall never lose its power,
Till all the ransomed |: Church of God,:|
Are saved, to sin no more.

4 E'er since by faith |: I saw the stream;:|
Thy flowing wounds supply.
Redeeming love |: has been my theme,:|
And shall be till I die.

By permission.

No. 16. While the Years are Rolling On.

HARRIET E. MCKEEVER.
JNO. R. SWENEY, by per.
Recitante.
1. In a world so full of weep-ing, While the years are roll - ing on,
2. There's no time to waste in sigh-ing, While the years are roll - ing on;
3. Let us strength-en one an-oth - er, While the years are roll - ing on;
4. Friends we love are quick-ly fly - ing, While the years are roll - ing on;
Chris-tian souls the watch are keep-ing, While the years are roll - ing on.
Time is fly - ing, souls are dy - ing, While the years are roll - ing on.
Seek to raise a fall - en broth - er, While the years are roll - ing on.
No more part - ing, no more dy - ing, While the years are roll - ing on.
While our jour-ney we pur-sue, With the ha - ven still in view, There is
Lov - ing words a soul may win From the wretched paths of sin; We may
This is work for ev - 'ry hand, Till, thro'-out cre - a - tion's land, Ar-mies
In the world be-yond the tomb Sor-row nev - er more can come, When we
work for us to do, While the years are rolling on.
bring the wand'rers in, While the years are rolling on.
for the Lord shall stand, While the years are rolling on.
meet in that blest home, While the years are rolling on.
CHORUS.
Are rolling on,
are rolling on,
Are rolling on,
are rolling on,
Oh, the joy that we may scatter, While the years are rolling on.

No. 17. Go and Gather.

Rev. J. B. Atchinson.
E. O. Excell.
1. Go and gather, go and gather, Was the or - der from the King;
2. Go and gather, go and gather, Is the or - der from our King;
3. Go and gather, go and gather, Teachers, scholars, all o - bey;
Chorus. Go and gather, go and gather, Gath-er tro-phies for our King;
Fine.
Gath - er mon-ey for the tem-ple, Tell the peo - ple all to bring;
Gath - er from the streets and al-leys, Souls im-mor-tal homeward bring;
Hear the voice of Je - sus say-ing, I am with you all the way;
Hast - en, hast-en, for the treasures Lie around you per - ish - ing.
Hast - en, hast-en for the treas-ure, For God's work must not de-lay;
Tar - ry not, for they are dy - ing, Go ye forth with - out de-lay;
Hast - en to the vine-yard, hast-en! Tell the sto - ry of his love;
Chorus, D.C.
And the peo-ple joy - ful answer'd, Bring-ing off'rings day by day.
Gath - er in the pre-cious fragments, Hour by hour, and day by day.
Gath - er treasures for the tem-ple Je - sus hath prepar'd a - bove.

No. 18. Open the Door for the Children.

E. O. Excell.

1 O - pen the door for the children, Ten-der-ly gather them in;
2 O - pen the door for the children. See, they are coming in throngs;
3 O - pen the door for the children; Take the dear lambs by the hand,

In from the highways and hedg - es, In from the places of sin;
Bid them sit down to the ban - quet, Teach them your beauti-ful songs,
Point them to truth and to good-ness, Lead them to Canaan s bright land,

Some are so young and so help - less, Some are so hun-gry and cold;
Pray you the Fa - ther to bless them, Pray you that grace may be given;
Some are so young and so help - less, Some are so hun-gry and cold;

O - pen the door for the chil - dren, Gath - er them in - to the fold.
O - pen the door for the chil - dren, Theirs is the kingdom of heaven.
O - pen the door for the chil - dren, Gath - er them in - to the fold.
D.S.-O - pen the door for the chil - dren, Gath - er them in - to the fold.

Fine.

Open the Door for the Children.—Concluded.

Chorus.
O - pen the door,......... Gath - er them in........... D.S.
O pen the door, o pen the door, Gather them in, gath-er them in.
No. 19. Jesus Loves Me.
E. O. Excell.
1. Je - sus loves me, and I know I love Him. Love brought Him down my poor
Yes, it was love made Him die on the tree, Oh, I am cer-tain that
2. If one should ask of me how I can tell, Glo - ry to Je - sus! I
God's Ho-ly Spir - it with mine doth a-gree, Con-stant - ly wit-ness-ing—
3. In this as-sur-ance I find sweetest rest, Trust-ing in Je - sus I
Sa - tan dismayed, from my soul now doth flee, When I just tell him that
1st. 2d.
soul to redeem; Jesus loves me.
know ver - y well; Jesus loves me.
know I am blest; Jesus loves me.
Chorus.
Je-sus loves me, yes, Je sus loves me,
Je-sus loves me, yes, Je sus loves me,
1st. 2d.
Oh, I am cer - tain that Je - sus loves me;
Oh, I am cer - tain that Je - sus loves me.

No. 20. There's Much We Can Do.

"Whatsoever thy hand findeth to do, do it with thy might."—Eccl. 9: 10.

MRS. E. C. ELLSWORTH. E. O. EXCELL.

1st.
1. There's much we can do if we work with a will, No time to be wast - ed to - day;
The Mas - ter is read - y our la - bors to bless, And [OMIT] wag - es he of - fers to pay.
2. So much we can do in the sow - ing of seed, Some fields are yet bar - ren and waste,
The foe will be bus - y in spreading the tares, Then [OMIT] go, and be working with haste.
3. So much we can do in the reap - ing of wheat, Some fields for the harvest are white; [
So much may be lost when the harv - est is past, If [OMIT] left to the mildew and blight.
2d.
CHORUS.
No time to be wast - ed, for man - y the fields, And laborers, as ev - er, are few; A - way to the
as ev - er, are few;
work that is need - ing a hand! So much! O so much we can do!

No. 21. In a Little While.

Geo. R. Clarke.
Heb. x. 37.
J. W. Dueffr.
1. In a lit-tle while the night of sin, Will yield to end-less day;
In a lit-tle while the Lord will come, And take his bride a - way;
2. In a lit-tle while the seed - ing time Will end, the grain be sown;
In a lit-tle while the har - vest fields, Of earth will all be mown;
3. In a lit-tle while the bel's of time, Will cease their doleful sound;
In a lit-tle while e - ter - ni - ty, Be - gins its end-less round;
In a lit - tle while the sun will set, To rise on earth no more;
In a lit - tle while the garnered sheaves, Of bright and gold-en wheat;
In a lit - tle while the pearl - y gates, Of heav'n will o - pen wide;
rit.
In a lit-tle while the judge will rise, And shut, to all, the door.
In a lit-tle while we'll lay them down, The sheaves at Je - sus' feet.
In a lit-tle while will en - ter in, The Bridegroom and the Bride.
Chorus.
E'en now we see with - in the east, The morn-ing streaks of grey,
Then roll a - long, ye wheels of time, And ush-er in the day.

No. 22. Say, is Your Lamp Burning?

(To my Co-worker W. B. Jacobs.) E. O. EXCELL.

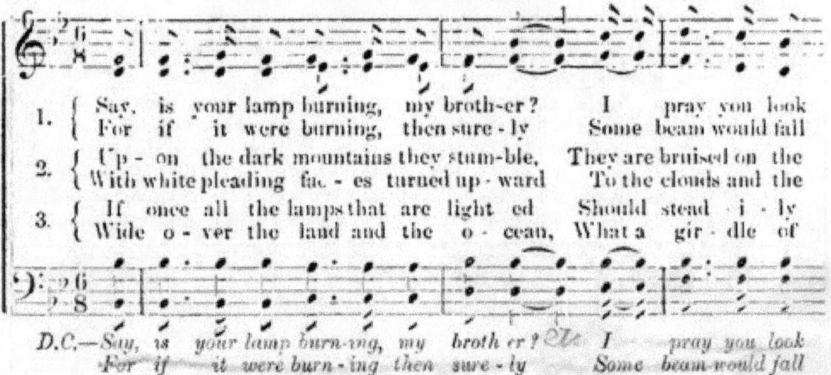
1. { Say, is your lamp burning, my broth-er? I pray you look
For if it were burning, then sure-ly Some beam would fall
2. { Up - on the dark mountains they stum-ble, They are bruised on the
With white pleading fa - es turned up - ward To the clouds and the
3. { If once all the lamps that are light ed Should stead - i - ly
Wide o - ver the land and the o - cean, What a gir - dle of
D.C.—Say, is your lamp burn-ing, my broth er? I pray you look
For if it were burn - ing then sure - ly Some beam would fall

Fine.
quick - ly and see, } { There are man - y and man - y a -
bright - ly on me. } { If you thought that they walked in the
rocks and they lie } { There is man - y a lamp that is
pit - i - ful sky, } { But not man - y a - mong them, my
blaze in a line } { How all the dark plac - es would
glo - ry would shine! } { How the earth would laugh out in her
quick - ly and see,
bright - ly on me.

1st. 2d.
round you, Who follow wherev-er you go. . . . . D.C.
shad-ow, Your . . . . lamp would burn brighter. I know.
light-ed, We behold them a-near and a-far. . . . . D.C.
broth-er, Shine . . . . stead - i - ly on like a star.
brighten. How the mists would roll up and away! . . . . D.C.
glad-ness To . . . . hail the mil-len-ni-el day.

No. 23. Welcome, Wandrer, Welcome.

Dr. H. Bonar. Ira D. Sankey.

1. In the land of strang - ers, Whith - er thou art gone,
2. "From the land of hun - ger, Faint - ing famished, lone;
3. "Quit the haunts of ri - ot, Wast - ed woe be - gone;
Hear a far voice call - ing: "My son! my son!"
Come to love and glad - ness, My son! my son!"
Sick at heart and wea - ry, My son! my son!"
Chorus.
p
Wel-come! wanderer, wel - come! Wel - come back to home!
m
Thou hast wan-dered far a - way: Come home! come home!"

4 "See the door still open!
Thou art still my own;
Eyes of love are on thee,
My son! my son!"

5 "Far off thou hast wandered:
Wilt thou further roam?
Come: and all is pardoned
My son! my son!"

6 "See the well-spread table,
Unforgotten one!
Here is rest and plenty,
My son! my son!"

7 "Thou art friendless, homeless,
Hopeless, and undone;
Mine is love unchanging,
My son! my son!"

[1] *By permission.*

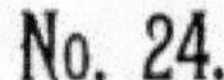

No. 24. Is it Right?

J. P. Elliott. J. H. F.

1. If you find your-self in - sult - ed, And you feel in-clined to
2. If you find you're feel-ing peev - ish, And like do - ing things for
3. If your par - ents have for - bid - den You to be out late at
4. When in an - y sort of mis - chief You be - gin to take de-

fight, Wait un - til this lit - tle ques - tion Is de - ci - ded:
spite, Lis - ten to the voice of conscience As it whis-pers,
night, And you feel like dis - o - bey - ing, Stop and pon-der:
light, Well may you re - flect, and ask Your-self the ques-tion:

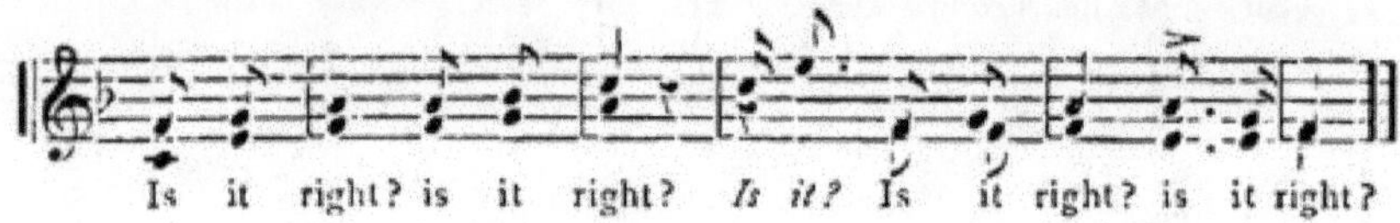

Is it right? is it right? *Is it?* Is it right? is it right?

No. 25. Which Loved Mother Best?

J. H. F.

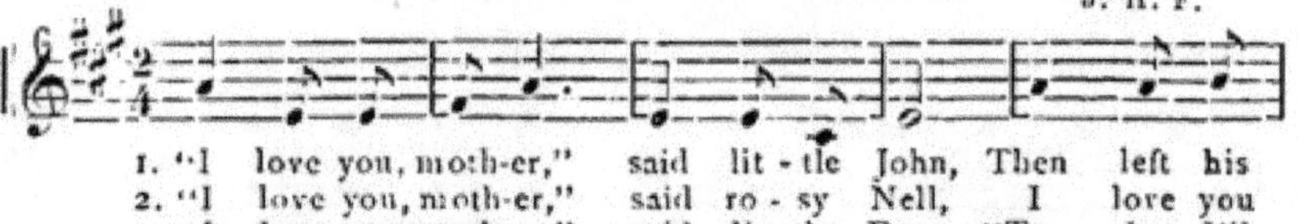

1. "I love you, moth-er," said lit - tle John, Then left his
2. "I love you, moth-er," said ro - sy Nell, I love you
3. "I love you, moth-er," said lit-tle Fan, "To - day I'll
4. Then step-ping soft - ly, bring-ing the broom, Swept up the
5. "I love you, moth-er," that night they said; Three lit - tle

work, and his cap went on; Then to the gar - den,
more than my tongue can tell; Then she went pout - ing
help you as best I can; "How glad am I that
floor and then clean'd the room; Bu - sy and hap - py
chil - dren were gone to bed; How are you think-ing

high in the swing—Left her the water and the wood to bring.
full half the day, Moth-er was glad when she'd gone to play.
school doesn't keep,"—She rock'd the baby till it fell a - sleep.
all day was she, Help-ful and happy as a child could be.
that moth-er guessed Which of her children real-ly lov'd her best?

From "Songs for the Wee Ones," by per. of Fillmore Bros.

No. 26. When I Tune My Harp in Glory.
Emma Pitt.
S. G. Smith.
1. When I tune my harp in glo - ry, When I sing the new, new song,
2. When I tune my harp in glo - ry,— O - ver on the oth - er side;
3. When I tune my harp in glo - ry,— O - ver on the golden shore;
4. When I tune my harp in glo - ry, Where the angels sing the song,
Will you join that sweet old sto - ry? Will you join that ransom'd throng?
Youth so tender—age so hoar - y,— All shall meet across the tide.
When I sing "the old, old sto - ry," Praising Je - sus ev - er-more.
Will you join with me the sto - ry, Sing with yonder shin - ing throng?
CHORUS.
Say, dear comrades, worn and weary, On that morrow bright and fair,
When we leave these scenes so dreary, Will you, ev - 'ry one, be there?

DO RE MI FA SO LA SI

No. 27. For You and For Me.

W. L. T.
Will L. Thompson.
Very slow. pp
m
1. Softly and tenderly Je-sus is calling, Calling for you and for me,
2. Why should we tarry when Jesus is pleading, Pleading for you and for me?
3. Time is now fleeting, the moments are passing, Passing from you and from me;
4. Oh! for the wonderful love he has promised, Promised for you and for me;
See on the portals he's waiting and watching, Watching for you and for me.
Why should we linger and heed not his mercies, Mercies for you and for me?
Shadows are gathering, death beds are coming, Coming for you and for me.
Tho' we have sinned he has mercy and pardon, Pardon for you and for me.
m CHORUS.
cres.
Come home, . come home, . Ye who are weary, come home, . .
Come home,
come home,
pp
ppp
rit.
pp
Earnest-ly, tender-ly Je-sus is calling, Calling, O sinner, come home!
DO RE MI FA SO LA SI

By permission.

No. 28. Wonderful Saviour.

A. B. — Alfred Beirly.

1. "I am the *Light*," says Je - sus, To the un - re - gen'-rate heart;
2. "I am the *Way*," says Je - sus, Leading to yon mansions fair,
3. "I am the *Truth*," says Je - sus, Yea, what oth - er can there be?
4. "I am the *Life*," says Je - sus, To the un - ac - cept - ed child;
"He that foll'weth me, be - hold, His darkness shall de - part."
"Come to me" and all this home Of peace and beau - ty share.
Might - y truth that shall en - dure Through all e - ter - ni - ty.
Turn thee from thine e - vil ways, Henceforth be rec - on - ciled.
CHORUS. *f*
O Sav - iour, Won - der - ful, won - der - ful Sav - iour;
Thou that dwellest in glo - ry, We would ev - er a - dore thee,
Through a long e - ter - ni - ty; Won - der - ful, wonder - ful Saviour.
DO RE MI FA SO LA SI

From "Great Joy," by per. of G. D. Newhall & Co.

No. 29. Jesus' Blood.

No. 29. Jesus' Blood.
John Mc Pherson.
E. O. Excell.
1. Je - sus' blood a- lone here frees us, From the blight of sin to - day;
2. If men knew the aw - ful end- ing That a-waits the careless one;
3. In the east the sun is ris - ing; In the west, at close of day,
Why de- lay to come to Je - sus, He will take the stain a- way.
Ear- nest prayers to God ascend - ing Would be heard ere day is done.
See it set-ting,—glow surpris- ing! May your life thus pass a- way.
CHORUS.
To this fountain then come quickly, Ere the shades of night shall fall,
And death's shadows fall so thick- ly, Hid- ing you as with a pall.
DO RE MI FA SO LA SI

No. 30. Singing with the Angels.
E. A. Hoffman.
Music and Chorus by A. S. Kieffer.
1. I have dream'd sweet dreams of a better home, Of a better home than this;
2. I have dream'd sweet dreams of a better life, Of a better life than this;
3. I have dream'd sweet dreams of a better land, Of a better land than this;
Of a home where sorrows nev-er come, Where all is per- fect bliss.
Where there is no con-flict and no strife, Where all is per- fect peace.
Where the ransom'd tread the golden strand, Where joy shall never cease.
CHORUS.
Sing - - - - - ing with the an-gels, There, there, o- ver, o- ver there;
Singing with the angels, with the an - gels,
Sing - - - - - - ing with the an - gels, In that sweet home so fair
Singing with the an- gels,

By permission.

DO RE MI FA SO LA SI

No. 31. Give Me Welcome.
E. O. E.
E. O. Excell.
1. Hear you not the voice of Je - sus, As he calls so ten - der - ly?
2. Give me welcome, I will guide you, I'm the Way, the Truth, the Light,
3. Give me welcome, wait no lon- ger, I have opened heaven's gate,
Give me welcome, give me welcome, For I would a - bide with thee.
Lead you ev - er true and faithful, To the man - y mansions bright.
And the heart that bids me welcome, Shall go in and ne'er be late.
CHORUS.
I will wel - come, I will wel - come,
Wel-come, wel-come, welcome, wel-come, wel-come, wel-come, welcome, wel-come,
Welcome Je - sus to my heart, Welcome Je - sus to my heart.
welcome to my heart,
welcome to my heart.
DO RE MI FA SO LA SI

No. 32. We'll Sing the Gospel.

Mrs. E. C. Ellsworth.
S. G. Smith.
1. Oh, joyful is the tribute we would bring Un - to thee, O our Saviour and King, Ac - cept our off - 'ring and re - veal this day Thine ac-ceptance of our humble lay.
2. Oh, joyful is the welcome Christ shall give Unto all who his promise be-lieve; Come with your songs, all ye who seek his face, Ev - er singing of his wondrous grace.
3. Oh, joyful is the triumph we shall know, With our conflicts all ended be-low, We'll join our songs with angels round the throne, Ev - er, giving praise to Christ alone.
CHORUS.
Come, join our song, come, join our song,
Sing the blessed gospel, Sing the blessed gospel, Sing the blessed gospel, Come, sing the blessed gospel,
All ye who love Christ the Lord,
Bring him praises, oh, bring him joyful praises, While we're singing in sweet accord.
DO RE MI FA SO LA SI

No. 33. Jesus is Calling for Thee.

Grace Glenn. J. H. Fillmore.

1. When, as of old, in her sad - ness Ma - ry sat weeping a - lone,
2. Oh, when thy pleasures are flowing, Fad-ing thy hope and thy trust,
3. Down by the shore of death's river, Sometime thy footsteps shall stray,
Soft- ly the voice of her sis - ter Whispered, "The Master has come."
When of the dearest earth-treasures Dust shall re-turn un - to dust.
Where waits a boatman to bear thee O - ver to in - fi - nite day.
So in the depths of thy sor - row, Gall though its fountain may be,
Then tho' the world may invite thee, Vain will its of - fer- ing be,
What then tho' dark be his sha- dow, If when his coming thou see,
List, for there cometh a whisper, Je - sus is calling for thee.
List, for there cometh a whisper, Je - sus is calling for thee.
Cometh there softly a whisper, Je - sus is calling for thee.
CHORUS.
Repeat pp.
Call - - ing, call - - ing, Je - sus is call- ing for thee.
Call-ing for thee, call-ing for thee,
DO RE MI FA SO LA SI

By permission.

No. 34. Will you and I be There?

W. F. Chute. Aldine S. Kieffer.

1. We know there's a bright and a glorious home, Away in the heav'ns on high,
2. In raiments of white, o'er the streets of gold, Beneath a fair, cloudless sky,
3. From all of the kingdoms of earth they come, To swell the triumphal cry;
4. If you come to him as your Saviour, now, Who for sinners once did die;
Where all the redeemed shall with Jesus dwell, But will you be there, and I?
They walk in the light of the Father's smile, But will you be there, and I?
They sing of the Lamb who for us was slain, But will you be there, and I?
He'll gather his own in that bright, bright home, O will you be there, and I?
CHORUS.
Will you and I be there? Will you and I be there? In that
home of love on high, Where saints redeemed shall sing Endless
praise to Christ our King, O will you be there and I?
DO RE MI FA SO LA SI

No. 35. Leaving All.
H. Lyte.
E. O. Excell.
1. Je - sus, I my cross have ta - ken, All to leave, and fol - low thee;
2. Per - ish ev - 'ry fond am - bi - tion, All I've sought, or hoped, or known;
3. Let the world despise and leave me, They have left my Saviour, too;
4. And while thou shalt smile upon me, God of wisdom, love, and might,
Nak - ed, poor, despised, for- sak - en, Thou, from hence, my all shalt be;
Yet how rich is my con - di - tion, God and heav'n are still my own!
Hu- man hearts and looks deceive me; Thou art not, like them, un-true;
Foes may hate, and friends may shun me, Show thy face and all is bright.
rit.
CHORUS.
Leaving all to fol- low thee, Leaving all to fol- low thee,
Leav-ing all, yes, all to fol - low thee, Leav- ing all, yes, all to fol - low thee,
Thou my all from hence shalt be, Thou my all from hence shalt be,
Thou my all in all, Thou my all in all,
DO RE MI FA SO LA SI

No. 36. With Jesus by and by.

EMMA PITT. L. C. THAYER.

1. Nev-er mind your earthly sorrows, Never mind your toil and care,
2. If on Christ your hopes are resting, If on him you place your trust,
3. Pilgrim, trust, 'twill soon be o - ver, Tho' the waves roll mountain high;
4. Look across yon shining riv - er, Crowns of gold the ransomed wear;

Look beyond, a bright to - morrow Waits for those who suf- fer here.
Tho' dark billows you are breasting, Conquer all you sure - ly must.
See beyond, the clouds are breaking, Beth'lem's star shines in the sky.
With the Lord you'll be for - ev - er, Loved ones too you'll welcome there.

CHORUS.

Nev-er mind the earth-born shadows, Do not fear a cloud -y sky;

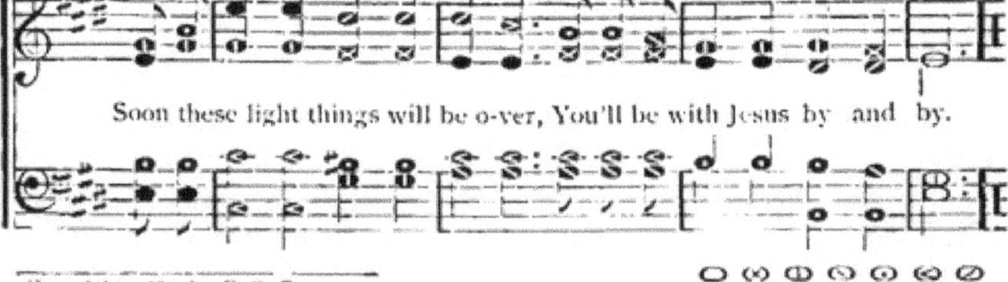

Soon these light things will be o-ver, You'll be with Jesus by and by.

DO RE MI FA SO LA SI

No. 37. They Say there's a Land.
W. L. T.
Will L. Thompson.
1. They say there's a land o'er the o - cean, Where wonders and beauties are
2. They say we shall dwell there forev - er, If we list to our Saviour's com-
3. They say we shall know all our loved ones, When we meet on that bright, golden
seen, They say it's a glo - ri - ous E - den, Where
mand, They say we shall ev - er be hap - py, When
shore, They say we shall clasp hands so glad - ly, And to-
none but the bless - ed convene. Many friends for that land have de-
safe in that beauti - ful land. 'Tis there we shall meet loving
geth- er re- joice ev- er-more. Oh, let us pre-pare for the
By permission.
DO RE MI FA SO LA SI

They Say there's a Land.—Concluded.

part - ed, They have cross'd over life's troubled sea. . . . Oh!
Je - sus, Who suffered and died, us to save, . . . He will
jour - ney, Let our hearts be kept loy- al and true, . . . Then the
let us sail o- ver and meet them, Jesus' life-boat will carry us free.
stand on the bright shore, and hail us, As we ride o'er the last broken wave.
Saviour will watch and protect us, Till the mansions of heaven are in view.
CHORUS.
Then sail away o'er the ocean, Where we'll join with the bright angel band, Then
Then sail, sail away
sail a- way o'er the o - cean, To our home in that happy, happy land.
sail, sail a- way

No. 38. Is My Name Written There?
Enid Williams.
Wm. B. Blake.
1. Is my name on the page of the Lamb's book of life, In the city of God over there? 'Tis the strongest and deepest desire of my heart! I would know: is my name written there?
2. Is the date of my birth on its mystical page, In the hand of the Lord, strong and fair? Is my cleansing from sin put in letters of light? O my Lord! is my name written there?
REFRAIN.
Is my name written there? Is my name written there?
In the Lamb's book of life, Is my name written there?
DO RE MI FA SO LA SI

From "Sweet Fields of Eden," by per.

No. 39. Go, Wash in the Stream.
R. Torrey, Jr.
"A fountain is opened for sin."—Zech. xiii. 1.
I. Baltzell.
1. I'll sing of that stream, of that beau - ti - ful stream, That flows thro' the
2. I'll sing of that stream, of that beau - ti - ful stream, Which gladdens the
3. I'll sing of that stream, of that beau - ti - ful stream, That fount God has
4. I'll sing of that stream, of that beau - ti - ful stream, That fount that is
sweet Canaan Land; Its wa- ters gleam bright in their heavenly light, And
ci - ty of God; It flows from the throne of the Father, a- lone; And
opened for sin; That stream from his side who for sinners once died: He's
flowing so free; I'll sing of that flood, which is crimsoned with blood, From
CHORUS.
rip - ple o'er sil - ver - y sand.
spreads its sweet wa - ters a - broad.
healed, who but plunges there - in.
sin that has cleansed ev - en me.
Go, wash in that beau - ti - ful
Wash in the
stream, . . Go, wash in that beau- ti - ful stream, . . Its
beau - ti - ful stream, Wash in the beau - ti - ful stream,
waters so free are flowing for thee; Go, wash in that beauti- ful stream.
DO RE MI FA SO LA SI

By permission.

No. 40. Let Him In.

Rev. J. B. Atchinson. E. O. Excell.

1. There's a stranger at the door, Let him in,
2. O-pen now to him your heart, Let him in,
3. Hear you now his loving voice? Let him in,
4. Now ad-mit the heavenly Guest, Let him in,
Let the Saviour in, let the Saviour in,
He has been there oft be-fore, Let him in;
If you wait he will de-part, Let him in;
Now, oh, now make him your choice, Let him in,
He will make for you a feast, Let him in,
Let the Saviour in, let the Saviour in,
Let him in ere he is gone, Let him in, the Ho-ly One, Je-sus
Let him in, He is your Friend, He your soul will sure de-fend, He will
He is standing at the door, Joy to you he will re-store, And his
He will speak your sins forgiven, And when earth ties all are riven, He will
Christ, the Father's Son, Let him in.
keep you to the end, Let him in.
name you will a-dore, Let him in.
take you home to heaven, Let him in.
Let the Saviour in, let the Saviour in.
DO RE MI FA SO LA SI

No. 41.

Only Waiting.

"The Lord shall direct your hearts into . . . the patient waiting for Christ."—2 Thess. iii. 5.

W. G. Ervin. J. H. Fillmore.

1. I am waiting for the morn-ing Of the blessed day to dawn,
2. I am waiting; worn and wea-ry With the battle and the strife,
3. Waiting, hoping, trusting ev-er, For a home of boundless love;
4. Hoping soon to meet the loved ones Where the "many mansions" be;
When the sorrow and the sadness Of this changeful life are gone.
Hop-ing when the warfare's ov-er To receive a crown of life.
Like a pilgrim, looking forward To the land of bliss a-bove.
List'ning for the hap-py welcome Of my Saviour call-ing me.
Chorus.
I am wait - - - - - ing on-ly waiting, Till this
waiting, waiting, waiting, on-ly waiting,
wea - - - - ry life is o'er; Only wait - - - - ing for my
weary, weary, weary—Till this wea-ry life is o'er; waiting, waiting, waiting
welcome, From my Saviour on the oth-er shore.
for my welcome,

By permission.

DO RE MI FA SO LA SI

No. 42. Wonderful Fountain.
E. A. H.
Zech. xiii. 1.
E. A. Hoffman.
1. There's a won - der - ful fount - ain of cleans - ing; All its ful - ness and pow'r we may know; 'Tis the blood, and it cleanses the vil - est, And it makes them as white as the snow; 'Tis the blood, and it cleanses the vil - est, And it makes them as white as the snow.
2. This fount - ain was o - pened for sin - ners, To re- deem them from sin and its woe; It will cleanse them from all their de- file - ment, And will make them as white as the snow; It will cleanse them from all their de-filement, And will make them as white as the snow.
3. Oh! come to this fount - ain of cleans - ing! Whith - er else to be saved can you go? Je - sus says: "Though your sins be as scar - let, I will make them as white as the snow;" Je - sus says: "Though your sins be as scarlet, I will make them as white as the snow.
4. Flow on, O ye streams of sal - va - tion! Till the earth and its peo - ple shall know In the blood there is pow - er to cleanse us, And to make us as white as the snow; In the blood there is pow - er to cleanse us, And to make us as white as the snow.
CHORUS.
White as snow! can it be so He will make me? make me?
Make me white as snow? make me white as snow?
DO RE MI FA SO LA SI

By permission.

No. 43. Will you be Washed in the Blood?
E. O. E.
Rev. i. 5.
E. O. Excell.
1. List, the Spir - it calls to thee, Will you be washed in the blood?
2. Sin - ner, now this blessing claim, Will you be washed in the blood?
3. He can wash you white as snow, Will you be washed in the blood?
4. Christ did drink that cup for all, Will you be washed in the blood?
Je - sus died to make you free, Will you be washed in the blood?
Thro' the dear Redeem - er's name, Will you be washed in the blood?
And the wit - ness you may know, Will you be washed in the blood?
Don't re - ject the Spir - it's call, Will you be washed in the blood?
Par - don free - ly giv - en, Cleans - ing you for heav - en.
Claim him as your Sav - iour, He can save for - ev - er.
You can know this hour Of his dy - ing pow - er.
Grace is all a - bound - ing, Joy thro' heav'n re - sound - ing.
Chorus.
Will you be washed, . . Washed in the blood of the Lamb,
Will you be washed in the blood of the Lamb,
Will you be washed, . . Washed in the blood of the Lamb.
Will you be washed in the blood of the Lamb,
DO RE MI FA SOL LA SI

No. 44. I've Washed My Robes.

E. O. E.
E. O. Excell.
1. My robes were once all stain'd with sin, I knew not how to make them clean;
2. That promise, "whoso - ev - er will," In-clud-ed me,—includes me still;
3. I do not doubt, nor do I say, "I hope the stains are wash'd away,"
4. Oh, who will come and wash to-day, 'Till all their stains are wash'd away;
Un - til a voice said, sweet and low, "Go wash, I'll make them white as snow."
I came and ev - er since, I know, His blood it cleanseth white as snow.
For in his Word I read it so: His blood it cleanseth white as snow.
Un - til by faith they see and know Their robes are wash'd as white as snow?
CHORUS.
I've wash'd my robes . . . in Je - sus' blood, . . . And he has
I've wash'd my robes
in Jesus' blood,
made . . . them white as snow: . . I've wash'd my robes . . in Je - sus'
And he has made
them white as snow,
I've wash'd my robes
blood, . . . And he has made . . . them white as snow.
in Jesus' blood,
And he has made them white as snow, white as snow.
DO RE MI FA SO LA SI

No. 45. Whosoever Believeth.
W. A. O.
"Whosoever believeth on me hath everlasting life."
W. A. Ogden.
1. "Who - so - ev - er be - liev - eth," Precious words I hear him say,
2. "Who - so - ev - er be - liev - eth," Once a - gain I hear him say,
3. "Who - so - ev - er be - liev - eth," Yet a - gain I hear him say,
D.C.—"Who - so - ev - er be - liev - eth," Precious words I hear him say,
Fine.
"Who - so - ev - er be - liev - eth, Hath ev - er - last - ing life."
"Who - so - ev - er be - liev - eth, Hath ev - er - last - ing life."
"Who - so - ev - er be - liev - eth, Hath ev - er - last - ing life."
"Who - so - ev - er be - liev - eth, Hath ev - er - last - ing life."
DUET.
The Lamb of God I know 'tis he, In mer - cy now in - vit - eth me, He
To Je-sus Christ I'll look and live, To Jesus Christ my heart I'll give, His
To Je - sus Christ my soul I bring, To Je - sus' cross by faith I cling, And
CHORUS.
D.C.
of - fers par - don full and free, And "ev - er - last - ing life."
blessed prom - ise I be - lieve, 'Tis "ev - er - last - ing life."
Je - sus' prom - ise now I sing, 'Tis "ev - er - last - ing life."
DO RE MI FA SO LA SI

No. 46. What must it be?

W. A. Ogden.

1. We speak of the realms of the blest, That country so bright and so fai
2. We speak of its pathways of gold, Of its walls deck'd with jewels so rare,
3. We speak of its freedom from sin, From sorrow, temptation, and care,
4. O Lord, in this val - ley of woe, Our spir - its for heaven prepare;

And oft are its glories confessed, But what must it be to be there?
Of its wonders and pleasures untold, But what must it be to be there?
From tri - als without and with - in, But what must it be to be there?
Then shortly we al - so shall know And feel what it is to be there.

CHORUS.

What must it be to be there? What must it be to be there?
be there, be there,

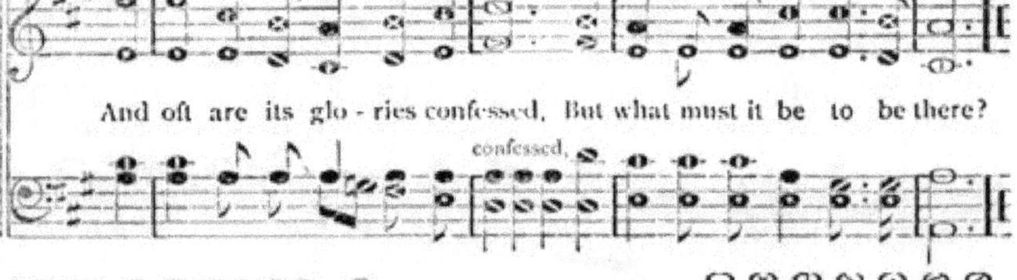
And oft are its glo - ries confessed, But what must it be to be there?
confessed,

DO RE MI FA SO LA SI

No. 47. Why I love My Jesus.

E. A. Hoffman.

1. Would you know why I love Je - sus? Why he is so dear to me?
2. Would you know why I love Je - sus? Why he is so dear to me?
3. Would you know why I love Je - sus? Why he is so dear to me?
'Tis because my blessed Je - sus From my sins has ransomed me.
'Tis because the blood of Je - sus Ful- ly saves and cleanses me.
'Tis because, a - mid tempt - a - tion, He supports and strengthens me.
CHORUS.
This is why . . . . I love my Je - - - sus, This is
This is why I love my Je - sus, This is why I love him so, This is
why . . . . I love him so, He a - toned
why I love my Je - sus, This is why I love him so, He has pardoned my trans-
. . for my transgres - sions, He has washed . . me white as snow.
gressions, He has pardoned my transgressions, He has washed me, he has washed me white as snow.
DO RE MI FA SO LA SI

Would you know why I love Jesus?
Why he is so dear to me?
'Tis because in every conflict
Jesus gives me victory.

5 Would you know why I love Jesus?
Why he is so dear to me?
'Tis because my friend and Saviour
He will ever, ever be.

By permission.

No. 48. Hail the Great Emancipation.

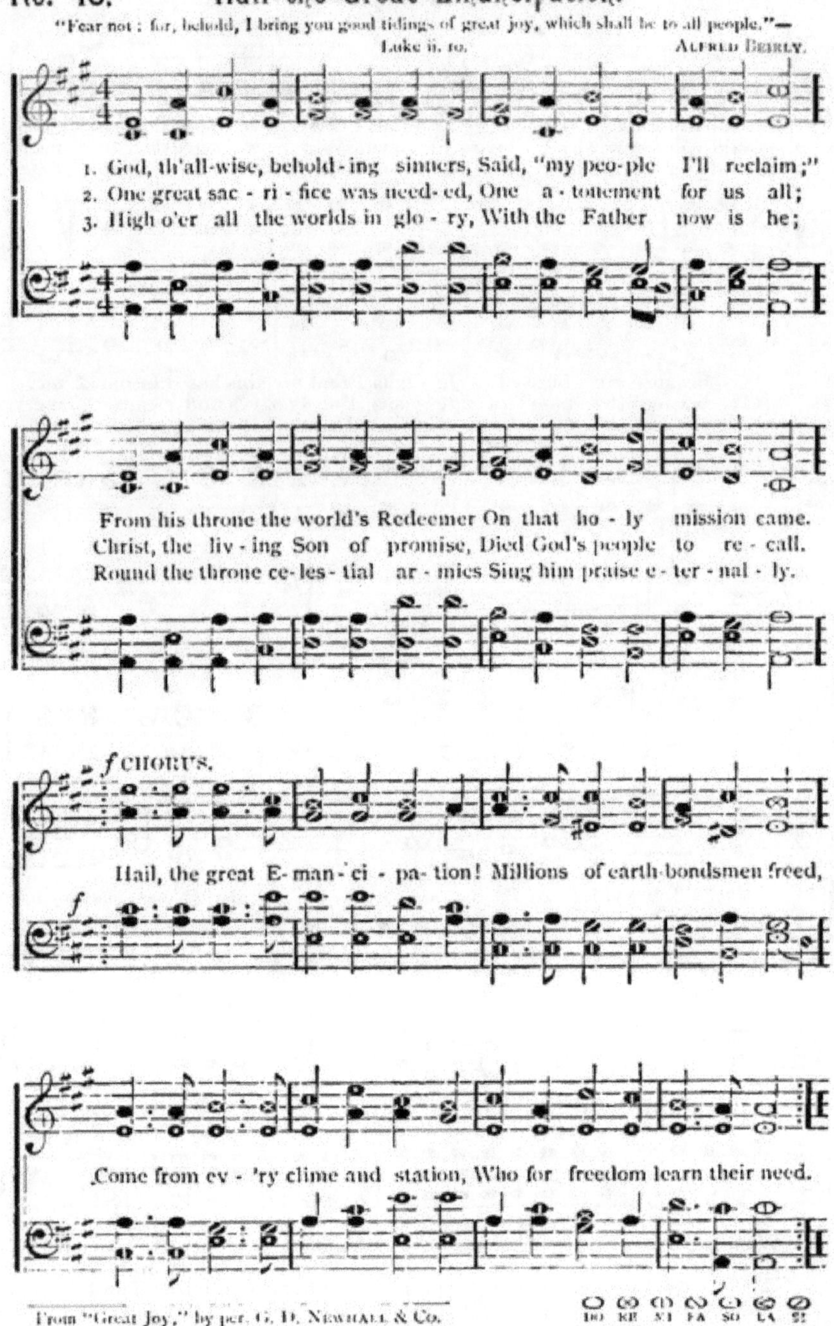
"Fear not: for, behold, I bring you good tidings of great joy, which shall be to all people."—
Luke ii. 10.
Alfred Beirly.
1. God, th'all-wise, behold-ing sinners, Said, "my peo-ple I'll reclaim;"
2. One great sac - ri - fice was need-ed, One a - tonement for us all;
3. High o'er all the worlds in glo - ry, With the Father now is he;
From his throne the world's Redeemer On that ho - ly mission came.
Christ, the liv - ing Son of promise, Died God's people to re - call.
Round the throne ce-les - tial ar - mies Sing him praise e - ter - nal - ly.
f CHORUS.
Hail, the great E - man - ci - pa - tion! Millions of earth-bondsmen freed,
f
Come from ev - 'ry clime and station, Who for freedom learn their need.
DO RE MI FA SO LA SI

From "Great Joy," by per. G. D. Newhall & Co.

No. 49. Song of Peace.

Arr. by W. A. Ogden.

1. God's Almight - y arms are round me, Peace is mine, peace di - vine,
2. Though life's ocean wild - ly roll - eth, Peace is mine, peace di - vine,
3. Wel - come ev - 'ry ris - ing sun - light, Peace is mine, peace di - vine,
Judgment scenes need not confound me, Peace is mine, a peace di - vine;
Winds and waves our God controlleth, Peace is mine, a peace di - vine;
Near - er home in ev - 'ry midnight, Peace is mine, a peace di - vine;
Je - sus came himself and sought me: Lost in sin he found and bought me;
I can sing with Christ beside me, Though a thousand ills be - tide me;
Death can nev - ermore ap - pal me, Safe in Christ, whate'er be - fall me;
Bles - sed freedom Je - sus taught me, Ev - er - last - ing peace is mine.
Safe - ly he will keep and guide me, Ev - er - last - ing peace is mine.
Calm - ly wait I 'till he call me, Ev - er - last - ing peace is mine.

DO RE MI FA SO LA SI

No. 50. My Soul doth Magnify the Lord.
J. E. H.
J. E. Hall.
1. My soul doth mag - ni - fy the Lord And praise his glo- rious name:
2. I'll praise him first, that when he saw Me lost,— by sin un - done,—
3. I'll praise him, too, my Sav- iour dear, For all his ten- der care,
4. With all my powers of voice I'll sing Of Je - sus' matchless love,
With heart and voice I will a - dore And spread abroad his fame.
He gave, to save my soul from death, His well - be - lov - ed Son.
For where I can - not see the way, He leads to past- ures fair.
Whose cleansing blood has made me mete To dwell with him a - bove.
CHORUS.
My soul . . . . doth mag - ni - fy the Lord, My
My soul doth mag - ni - fy the Lord and praise his name, My
soul . . . . doth mag - ni - fy the Lord, My
soul doth mag - ni - fy the Lord and praise his name,
soul doth mag - ni - fy the Lord And praise his glo- rious name.
Copyright, 1882, by E. O. Excell.
DO RE MI FA SO LA SI

No. 51. When the Harvest is Past.

S. F. Smith. H. H. McGranahan.

1. When the harvest is past and the summer is gone, And summons and pray'rs shall be o'er, When the beams cease to break of the blest Sabbath morn, And Jesus invites thee no more.
2. When the rich gales of mer - cy no long - er shall blow, The gos - pel no message de - clare; Sinner, how can'st thou bear the deep wailings of woe? How suf - fer the night of de - spair?
3. When the ho - ly have gone to the regions of peace, To dwell in the mansions a - bove, Where their harmony makes, in the fulness of bliss, Their song to the Sav - iour they love.
4. Say, O sin - ner that liv - eth at rest and se - cure, Who fear - est no trouble to come, Can thy spir - it the swellings of sorrow en - dure, Or bear the im - pen - i - tent's doom?
CHORUS
When the har - - - vest is past . . . . and the sum - - - mer is gone, . . . When the harvest is past and the summer is gone, And Jesus invites thee no more.
When the har - vest is past, is past, and the sum - mer is gone, is gone,
DO RE MI FA SO LA SI

By permission.

No. 52. Far up in Heaven's Blue
C. E. P.
Chas. E. Pollock.
1. There comes a time, a happy time, When all the good and true
2. Our dear ones leave us one by one, Their toilsome jour - ney through;
3. The an-gel Death, with ic - y hands, Takes little chil - dren, too;
4. Our darling pa - rents, too, are there; We miss them, it is true,
5. But oh, the thought that thrills my heart As nothing else can do,
Shall meet togeth - - er in that land, Far up in heav - en's blue.
And yet we hope to meet a-gain, Far up in heav - en's blue.
And some sweet day we hope to meet, Far up in heav - en's blue.
But happy will the meeting be, Far up in heav - en's blue.
Is this, that Christ will meet me there, Far up in heav - en's blue.
CHORUS.
What a meet - ing there will be, Of all the good and true,
In that land, that happy land, Far up in heaven's blue.

By permission.

DO RE MI FA SO LA SI

No. 53. Delightful Home.
J. J. E.
J. J. Excell.
1. There is a coun - try pure and bright, Where pleasures never die;
2. Its skies are not like earthly skies, Now clear then spread with gloom;
3. All those who reach that land of rest Shall be from sor - row freed;
4. Ah, when shall I from time remove, When reach that land so fair?
A re- gion of un - clouded light, Be - yond the star - ry sky.
The peo- ple of that clime ne'er die, In end - less life they bloom.
They'll lean up- on the Saviour's breast, On liv - ing pastures feed.
When will the gold - en char - iot come, To take me o - ver there?
REFRAIN.
O hap - py land, O ho - ly land, Land ev - er bright and fair;
When shall I join that hap - py band, Who worship ev - er there?

By permission.

DO RE MI FA SO LA SI

No. 54. O Look Above.
Jas. L. Orr.
1. Does life seem sad and gloomy now? O look a - bove! Cast
2. Do troubles gath - er like a cloud? O look a - bove! E'en
3. 'Tis Je - sus sits up - on the throne, O look a - bove! He
first thine eyes on Calvary's brow, Then look a - bove! See
when the storm is long and loud, Then look a - bove! Has
waits to make thy cause his own, Then look a - bove! Car-
where thy Saviour bore for thee Thy sins, when hanging on the tree, Think
life but lit - tle here be- low, Enjoyments few while sorrows flow, And
ry to him thy grief and care, He feels each pain the members bear, Seek
how he suf - fered then for thee, O look a - bove.
trib - u - la - tions great you know, O look a - bove.
com - fort then through ear - nest prayer, O look a - bove.
DO RE MI FA SO LA SI

No. 55. Christ is the Door.

Rev. Frank Pollock. "I am the door"—John x 9. Chas. E. Pollock.

1. Poor sin - ner, where art thou to - day? Say, whither dost thou roam?
2. The way is broad that leads to death, To darkness and un - rest:
3 'Tis Je - sus saves the soul from death; No oth - er name is given:
Art thou not lost from wisdom's way, And straying far from home?
Oh, turn and take the nar - row way To mansions of the blest!
Go, wash in Je - sus' precious blood, And fol - low him to heaven.
CHORUS.
1
Christ is the door of the beau- ti - ful home, The beau-ti - ful home, the
2
beau - ti - ful home; The beau - ti - ful, beau - ti - ful home.
DO RE MI FA SO LA SI

By permission.

No. 56. Come, Sinner, Come.

"Come unto me, all ye that labor and are heavy-laden."—Matt. xi. 28.

WILL. E. WITTER — H. R. PALMER. By per.

1. While Je - sus whispers to you, Come, sin - ner, come!
2. Are you too heav - y lad - en? Come, sin - ner, come!
3. Oh, hear his ten - der pleading, Come, sin - ner, come!
While we are pray - ing for you, Come, sin - ner, come!
Je - sus will bear your bur - den, Come, sin - ner, come!
Come and re - ceive the bless - ing, Come, sin - ner, come!
Now is the time to own him, Come, sin - ner, come!
Je - sus will not de- ceive you, Come, sin - ner, come!
While Je - sus whispers to you, Come, sin - ner, come!
Now is the time to know him, Come, sin - ner, come!
Je - sus can now re- deem you, Come, sin - ner, come!
While we are pray - ing for you, Come, sin - ner, come!

DO RE MI FA SO LA SI

No. 57. Do you Know the Wondrous Story?
J. E. H.
J. E. Hall.
1. Do you know the wondrous sto - ry? Have you ev - er heard it told?
2. Have you heard how much he suffered? Hanging on the cru - el tree?
3. Is it true that you have heard it? Have the tidings reached your ear?
How that Je - sus came from heaven, Seek - ing lost ones from the fold?
That we all might have sal - va - tion, And might live e - ter - nal - ly.
Then why not just now be - lieve it, And find com - fort, hope, and cheer
CHORUS.
Do you know the wondrous sto - ry? Have you ev - er heard it told?
Do you know the wondrous sto - ry That with tell - ing ne'er grows old?
DO RE MI FA SO LA SI

By permission.

No. 58. I'm Washed in the Blood.

J. J. E. J. J. Excell.

1. I'm washed in the blood, in the blood of the Lamb, The Spir - it the witness doth give, The blood of the Lamb washes whiter than snow, I know that by it I shall live.
2. I'm washed in the blood, I am free from the chain That bound me to Sa- tan and sin, I walk in the light of the Life of the world For Je - sus is liv- ing with - in.
3. I'm washed in the blood, I am liv - ing in sight Of my beauti - ful home in the sky; Ere long I shall go with my Saviour to live, At home in the mansions on high.
D.S.—blood of the Lamb washes whiter than snow, I know that by it I shall live.
Fine. REFRAIN.
I know that by it I shall live, I know that by it I shall live, The
D.S.
DO RE MI FA SO LA SI

By permission.

No. 59. Refuge.

J. E. H. — J. E. Hall.

1. When with clouds the sky is fill - ing, That portend the coming storm,
2. If thy hand is placed up-on me, O thou gracious Saviour dear!
Hide me, Saviour, 'neath the shelter Of thine ev - er- last- ing arm;
If thine eye is keeping vig - il, And I know that thou art near,
Fold me close when thunders rattle, Turn the lightning darts a- side,
Then, though loud the tempest rages, And though high the billows roll,
Calm my fears a - mid the tem- pest, Let me in thy care a - bide.
I am safe within thy keep- ing, Blest Redeemer of my soul.
DO RE MI FA SO LA SI

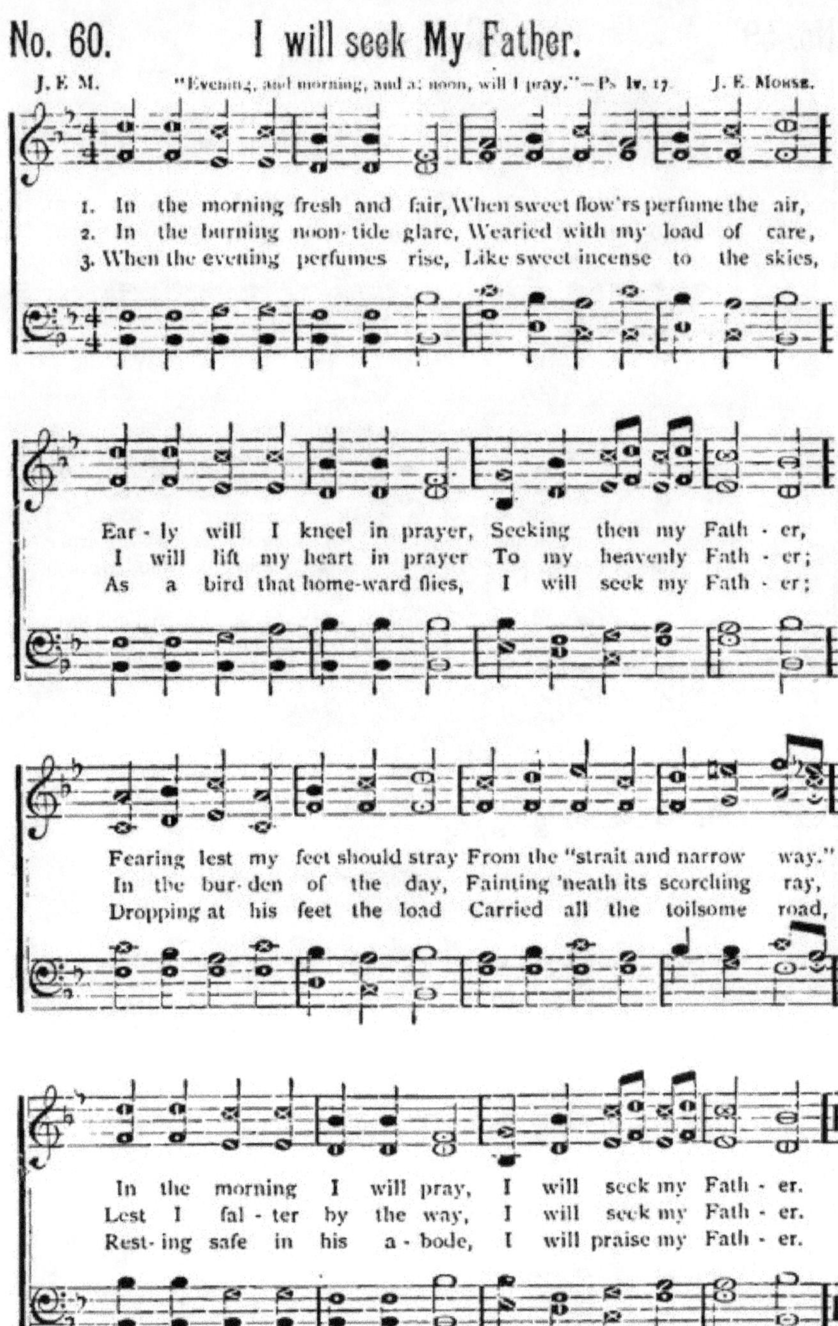
No. 60. I will seek My Father.
J. E. M.
"Evening, and morning, and at noon, will I pray."—Ps. lv. 17.
J. E. Morse.
1. In the morning fresh and fair, When sweet flow'rs perfume the air,
2. In the burning noon-tide glare, Wearied with my load of care,
3. When the evening perfumes rise, Like sweet incense to the skies,
Ear - ly will I kneel in prayer, Seeking then my Fath - er,
I will lift my heart in prayer To my heavenly Fath - er;
As a bird that home-ward flies, I will seek my Fath - er;
Fearing lest my feet should stray From the "strait and narrow way."
In the bur-den of the day, Fainting 'neath its scorching ray,
Dropping at his feet the load Carried all the toilsome road,
In the morning I will pray, I will seek my Fath - er.
Lest I fal - ter by the way, I will seek my Fath - er.
Rest-ing safe in his a - bode, I will praise my Fath - er.

DO RE MI FA SO LA SI

No. 61. I Long to be There.

Will L. Thompson.

1. My heav'nly home is bright and fair, I long to be there,
2. Its glittering tow'rs the sun out-shine, I long to be there,
3. My Father's house is built on high, I long to be there,
4. When from this earthly pris-on free, I long to be there,
No pain nor death can en-ter there, I long to be there.
That heav'nly mansion shall be mine, I long to be there.
Far, far a-bove the star-ry sky, I long to be there.
That heavenly mansion mine shall be, I long to be there.
CHORUS.
Oh, an-gels, guide me home, An-gels, guide me home,
an-gels, an-gels,
an-gels, an-gels,
Repeat Cho. pp.
An-gels, guide me home, I long to be there.
an-gels, an-gels,
DO RE MI FA SO LA SI

By permission.

No. 62. Abundantly Able to Save.

Rev. E. A. Hoffman. By per. | P. P. Bliss.

1. Who-ev-er re-ceiv-eth the Crucified One, Who-ev-er be-liev-eth on God's only Son, A free and a per-fect sal-va-tion shall have, For he is a-bun-dant-ly a-ble to save.
2. Who-ev-er re-ceiv-eth the message of God, And trusts in the pow'r of the soul-cleansing blood, A full and e-ter-nal re-demption shall have, For he is both a-ble and willing to save.
3. Who-ev-er re-pents and forsakes every sin, And opens his heart for the Lord to come in, A present and per-fect sal-va-tion shall have, For Jesus is rea-dy this moment to save.
CHORUS.
My brother, the Mas-ter is calling for thee; His grace and his mer-cy are wondrously free; His blood as a ran-som for
Brother, the Master is come and is calling for thee,
Brother, his grace and his mercy are wondrously free,
Brother, his blood as a
DO RE MI FA SOL LA SI

By permission.

Abundantly Able to Save.—Concluded.

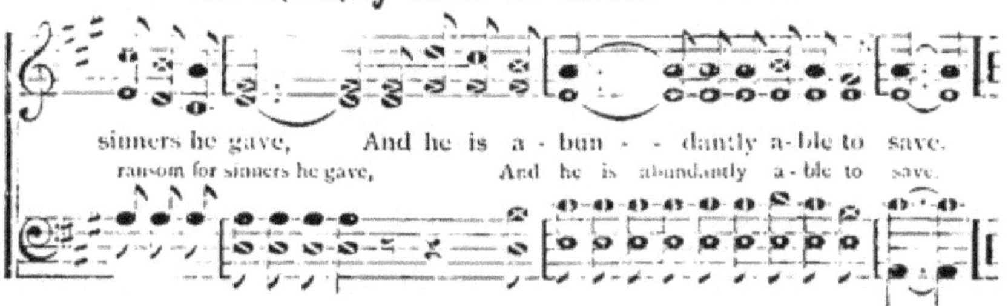
sinners he gave, And he is a - bun - - dantly a-ble to save.
ransom for sinners he gave, And he is abundantly a - ble to save.

No. 63. Nearer to Me.

E. A. Hoffman. William A. Galfin.

1. Draw near, O Christ, to me, Near - er to me, Unworth - y and un-
2. Draw near, O Christ, to me, Near - er to me, My soul with strong de-
3. Draw near, O Christ, to me, Near - er to me, Let all thy wealth of

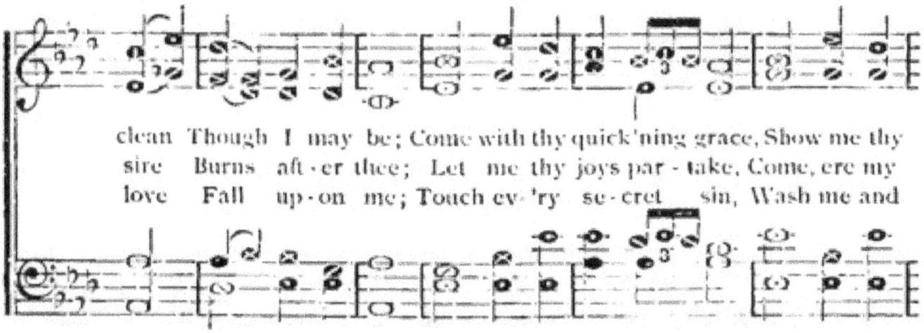

clean Though I may be; Come with thy quick'ning grace, Show me thy
sire Burns aft - er thee; Let me thy joys par - take, Come, ere my
love Fall up - on me; Touch ev - 'ry se - cret sin, Wash me and

smil - ing face, Draw near this hallowed place, Draw near to me.
spir - it break, For thy sweet mercy's sake, Draw near to me.
make me clean, Let noth - ing stand be - tween My heart and thee.

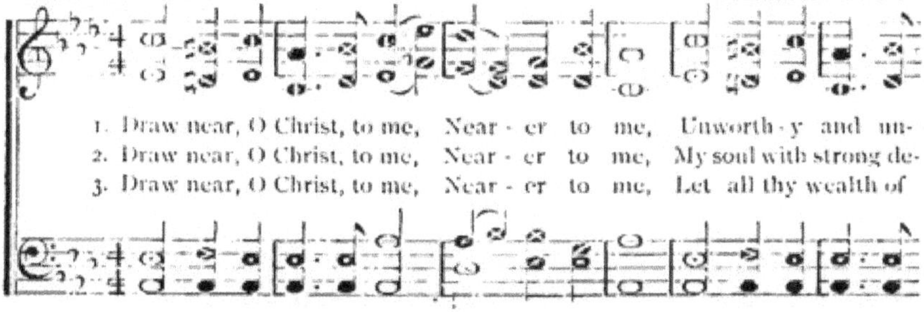

By permission

DO RE MI FA SO LA SI

No. 64. Stay, Weary Child.

R. A. Glen. Chas. E. Pollock.

1. Stay, wea - ry child, thy Saviour calls, Oh, turn and hear his gentle voice:
2. Oh, hear the lov - ing voice that calls; Forsake the desert paths of sin,
3. Then, weary child, to Je - sus come, All weak and helpless as thou art;
Come now to him, be re - conciled, And he will bid thy heart re - joice.
For at the gates of mer - cy, now, Thy Saviour waits to let thee in.
Thy burdens to the Saviour bring, And he will cheer thy drooping heart.
CHORUS.
Oh, hear . . . . the Saviour's voice, He's
Hear the Sav - iour's voice, Hear the Sav - iour's voice, He's
call - - - - ing now to thee, Oh, make . . . .
call - ing now to thee, He's call - ing now to thee; Make him now thy
. . . him now thy choice; He of - fers pardon full and free.
choice, Make him now thy choice;
DO RE MI FA SO LA SI

From "The Beauty of Praise," by per.

No. 65. I've been Washed in the Blood.
J. L. O.
Jas. L. Orr.
1. I have drank of the water of life, I've been washed in its sin cleansing flood;
2. I have tasted the pleasures of sin, But they quenched not the thirst of my soul;
3. Now at peace with my Saviour and God, I am seeking the evergreen shore,
Christ hath pi - tied my weakness and pardoned my sin, Washed me
Then I came to the stream of sal - va - tion and drank, Made my
I've been saved by his grace and redeemed by his blood, Hal - le-
white in his own precious blood.
wound-ed and brok - en heart whole.
lu - jah to God ev - er - more.
CHORUS.
I've been washed in the blood,
I've been washed in the blood, in the blood of the Lamb,
And salvation I've found through his name, He my sins though as crimson made whiter than snow, I've been wash'd in the blood of the Lamb.
Copyright, 188-, by E. O. Excell.
DO RE MI FA SO LA SI

No. 66. The Half has Never been Told.

FRANCES R HAVERGAL. 1 Cor. ii. 9. R. E. HUDSON.

1. I know I love thee bet-ter, Lord, Than an - y earthly joy, For thou hast giv - en me the peace Which noth - ing can de - stroy.
2. I know that thou art near-er still Than an - y earthly throng, And sweet - er is the thought of thee Than an - y love - ly song.
3. Thou hast put gladness in my heart; Then well may I be glad With-out the se - cret of thy love I could not but be sad.
4. O Saviour, precious Saviour mine! What will thy presence be If such a life of joy can crown Our walk on earth with thee?
CHORUS.
The half has never yet been told,
yet been told,
Of love so full and free;
The half has never yet been told,
yet been told,
The blood—it cleanseth me.
rit.
cleanseth me.
DO RE MI FA SO LA SI

From "Gems of Gospel Song," by per.

No. 67. I am Persuaded.
J. E. H.
J. E. Hall.
1. I am just now per - suad - ed, That naught can take from me
2. Should earthly friends for - sake me; Yet still for him I'd stand;
3. No power on earth can take from My heart this love di - vine,
The precious love of Je - sus, So boundless and so free;
For he will sure - ly hold me, With his most lov - ing hand;
For he has sure - ly prom - ised For - ev - er to be mine,
'Tis not in me to keep him, But he doth keep me sure;
No pre - sent things can drive me A - way from his dear face;
So I will trust him ful - ly, To keep me all the way,
Fine.
For I am now per - suad - ed His love will e'er en - dure.
Nor things to come, no! nev - er! Since I am kept by grace.
Oh, then at last he'll lead me To realms of end - less day.
D.S. - The precious love of Je - sus, So full, so rich, so free.
CHORUS.
D.S.
Yes, I am now per - suad - ed, That naught can take from me
DO RE MI FA SO LA SI

No. 68. The Child of a King.
Hattie E. Buell.
John B. Sumner.
1. My Fa - ther is rich in hous - es and lands, He holdeth the wealth of the
2. My Father's own Son, the "Saviour of men!" Once wander'd o'er earth as the
3. I once was an out- cast stranger on earth, A sin- ner by choice, an
4. A tent or a cottage, why should I care? They're building a palace for
world in his hands! Of ru - bies and diamonds, of sil - ver and gold, His
poor- est of men; But now he is reigning for - ev - er on High, And will
"al - ien" by birth! But I've been "a - dopted," my name's written down; An
me o - ver there! Tho' ex- iled from home, yet, still I may sing: All
cof - fers are full, He has rich - es un- told.
give me a Home in heaven, by and by!
heir to a mansion, a robe, and a crown.
Glo - ry to God, I'm the child of a King.
Chorus.
I'm the child of a King, The
child of a King; With Je - sus my Saviour, I'm the child of a King.

By permission.

No. 69. Love to Jesus.
M. A. Kidder.
Arranged.
1. When I think of Je - sus' love, Je - sus, bless-ed Je - sus,
2. When I feel my sins forgiven, Je - sus, bless-ed Je - sus,
3. When he sends his spir - it down, Je - sus, bless-ed Je - sus,
How he came from heav'n a - bove; Oh, how I love Je - sus.
When I read or sing of heav'n; Oh, how I love Je - sus.
When he points to harp and crown, Oh, how I love Je - sus.
When I know he died for me, On the hill of Cal - va - ry;
When he bids me come and rest On his kind and lov - ing breast,
When he tells me of the bliss, In that bet - ter world than this,
Died to set my spir - it free, Then how I love Je - sus.
Then my grateful heart is blest, Oh, how I love Je - sus.
Of the joys I would not miss, Then how I love Je - sus.

No. 70. Will You Meet Me?

E. O. E.
E. O. Excell.
1. Will you meet me in the morn - ing, On that bright and golden shore?
2. Oh, to meet on that bright morning, When the clouds have passed away;
3. When we meet our loving Sav- iour, What a hap - py hour 'twill be,
4. Oh, this thought should make us happy, And we all should love him more,
Will your lamp be trimmed and burning When he comes to take you o'er?
Oh, to walk and talk with Je - sus, There to dwell with him for aye.
When we're gathered with our loved ones, And their hap - py fa - ces see.
For he'll come, and will not tar - ry, Come to bear us safe- ly o'er.
Chorus.
Yes, I'll meet . . . you in the morn - ing, When I
I'll meet you there, that morning fair,
hear . . . the Saviour's call, . . . "Come, ye bless - - ed of my
the Saviour's call, the Saviour's call, ye blessed, come,
Fath - er, To a home . . . prepared for all." . . . . .
ye blessed, come, To a home prepared for all, prepared for all.
rit.
DO RE MI FA SO LA SI

No. 71. Yield so Meekly.

Rev. Frank Pollock. Chas. F. Pollock.

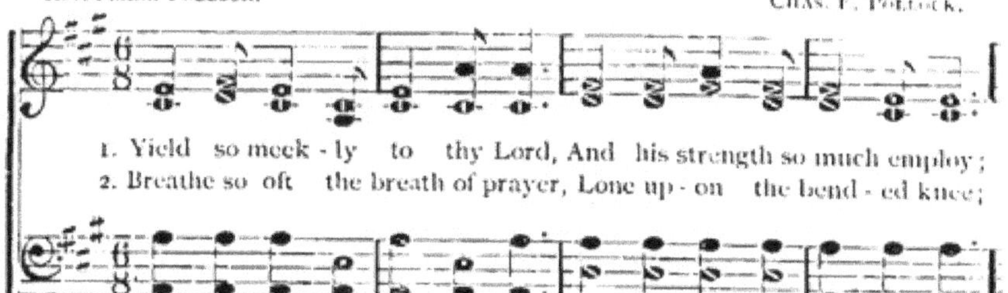
1. Yield so meek - ly to thy Lord, And his strength so much employ;
2. Breathe so oft the breath of prayer, Lone up - on the bend - ed knee;

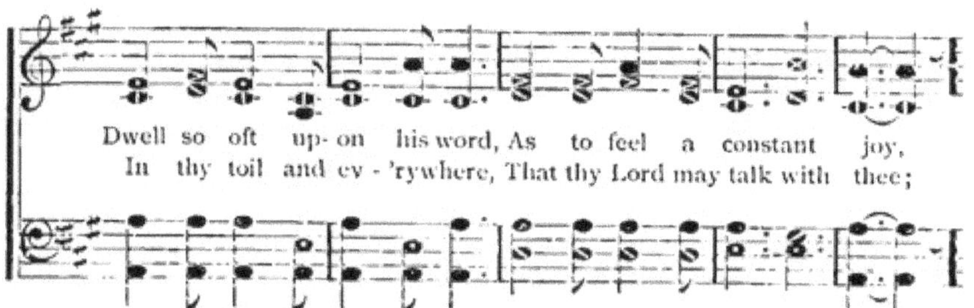
Dwell so oft up- on his word, As to feel a constant joy,
In thy toil and ev - 'rywhere, That thy Lord may talk with thee;

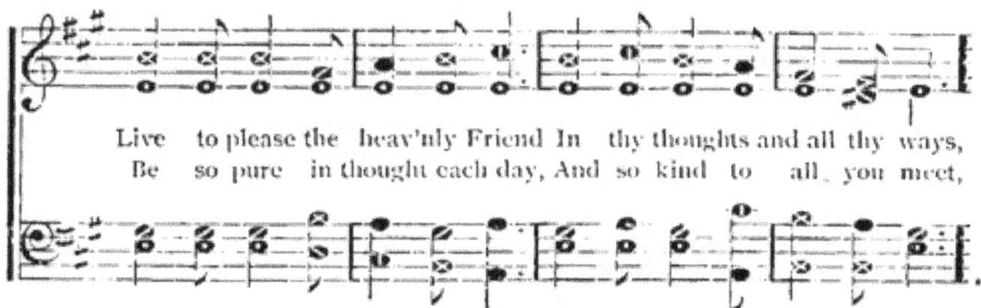
Live to please the heav'nly Friend In thy thoughts and all thy ways,
Be so pure in thought each day, And so kind to all you meet,

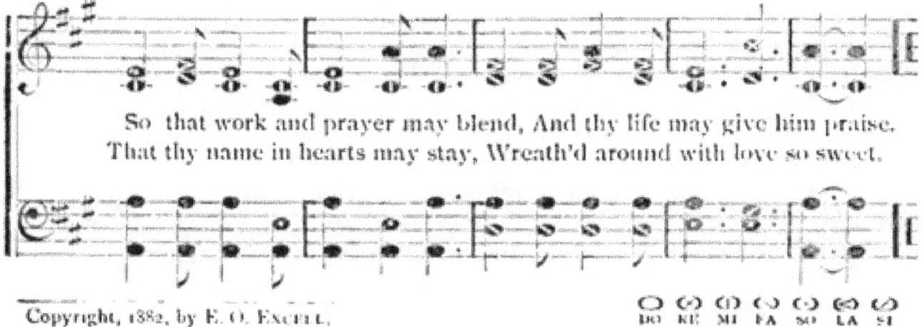
So that work and prayer may blend, And thy life may give him praise.
That thy name in hearts may stay, Wreath'd around with love so sweet.

DO RE MI FA SO LA SI

No. 72. Like the Rain.

Jno. McPherson.
Chas. E. Pollock.
DUET.
1. Gent - ly, like the summer rain, Fall the mercies of our King;
2. Ev - er soft - ly falls his love, Soothing balm for those that weep,
3. Soon we'll pass to yon - der home, Where we'll see the Saviour's face;
On sad hearts, now rent with pain, Peace and com - fort they will bring.
Falling gent - ly from a - bove, Watching o'er us while we sleep.
Soon we'll leave this world of gloom, Gain a sure, sweet rest - ing place.
CHORUS.
Like the rain, ... soft sum - mer rain, ...
Like the rain, soft sum - mer rain,
God's mercies fall, ... a sweet re - frain, O'er wea - ry
God's mercies fall,
hearts . . bent low with pain, . . . Making the soul rejoice a - gain.
O'er weary hearts bent low with pain,
DO RE MI FA SO LA SI

By permission.

No. 73. The One Thing Needful.

E. R. Latta.
Andante.
Geo. J. Kurzenknabe.
1. While up-on the earthly journey, What-so-ev - er lot be-tides,
2. In the hours of care and trou-ble, When the spir - it sinks in grief,
3. In the hours of pain and sickness, And when death is drawing near,
There is one thing that is need - ful More than all on earth besides;
There is one thing that is need - ful To af-ford the soul re-lief;
There is one thing that is need - ful The despair - ing heart to cheer;
'Tis not wealth, and 'tis not hon - or Con-stitutes the bet - ter part,
'Tis not words in kindness spo- ken, That can bid our sorrows start,
Vain is all that earth can of - fer Con-so - la - tion to im - part;
'Tis not vain and sin - ful pleasure, It is Je - sus in the heart.
'Tis not looks of pi - ty giv - en, It is Je - sus in the heart.
But there is a source of com - fort, It is Je - sus in the heart.
DO RE MI FA SO LA SI

From "Peerless Praise," by per.

No. 74. Come and be Saved.

Altered from Frances R. Havergal.
Melody by E. A. Hoffman. Har. by E. O. E.
1. Will you not come to him for *life?* Why will ye die, oh, why?
2. Will you not come to him for *peace*, Peace thro' his cross a - lone?
3. Will you not come to him for *rest?* All that are wea - ry, come!
4. Will you not come to him for *joy?* Will you not come for this?
He gave his life for you, for me! Oh, soul, why will you die?
He shed his pre- cious blood for you; Oh, make his peace your own!
The rest he gives is deep and true; Rest in his love, your home!
He gives a joy so sweet and true; Oh, taste his per - fect bliss!
CHORUS.
Come and be saved to - day, Come and be saved to - day,
Come and be saved to - day, Come and be saved to - day,
Come and be saved from all your sins to - day.
Come and be saved from all your sins to - day.

5 Will you not come to him for *love*,
Love that can fill the heart?
He loveth you, he loveth me;
Why longer stand apart?

6 Will you not come to him for *all?*
Will you not "taste and see?"
He waits to give it all to you,
And calls, "come unto me!"

DO RE MI FA SO LA SI

No. 75. Go Forward.

Mrs. E. C. Ellsworth. S. G. Smith.

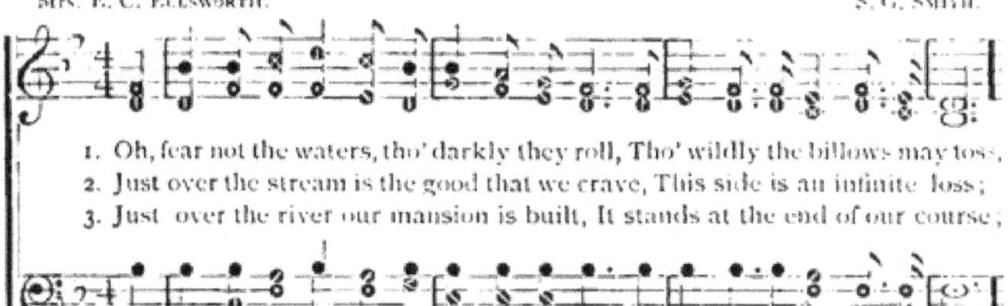
1. Oh, fear not the waters, tho' darkly they roll, Tho' wildly the billows may toss,
2. Just over the stream is the good that we crave, This side is an infinite loss;
3. Just over the river our mansion is built, It stands at the end of our course;

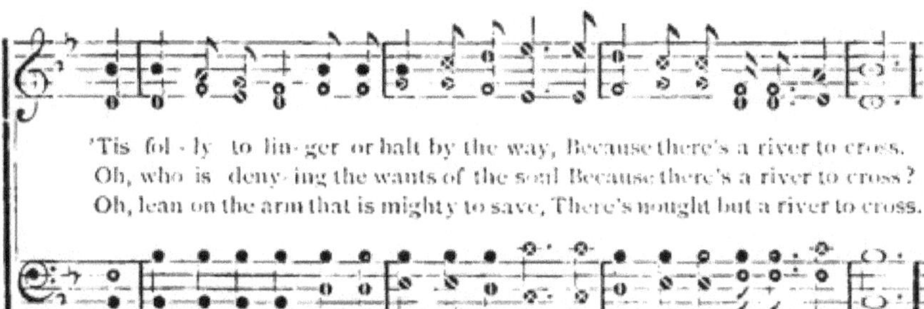
'Tis fol - ly to lin- ger or halt by the way, Because there's a river to cross.
Oh, who is deny- ing the wants of the soul Because there's a river to cross?
Oh, lean on the arm that is mighty to save, There's nought but a river to cross.

CHORUS.
Then forward, yes, forward, our motto shall be, For Jesus shall walk by our side;

His hand is preparing, in safe- ty, a path; We'll fear not the incoming tide.

DO RE MI FA SO LA SI

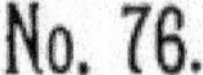

No. 76. Gathering Home.

For Male Voices, 1st tenor sings the tenor part, 2d tenor the soprano part, and first bass the alto part.

J. H. K. — J. H. Kurzenknabe.

1. We'll soon be at home from our pil - grim way, Gath - er - ing home,
2. Our sor-rows and tri - als will then be o'er, Gath - er - ing home,
3. There parents, and children, and friends will meet, Gath - er - ing home,
4. And Je - sus our Saviour will meet us there, Gath - er - ing home,

gath - er - ing home, To wake at the dawn of e - ter - nal day;
gath - er - ing home, And sigh - ing and weeping shall be no more;
gath - er - ing home, U - ni - ted and hap - py in love so sweet;
gath - er - ing home; With beau - ti - ful garments and crowns to wear,

𝄋 What a gath-er-ing that will be. *Fine.* CHORUS. Gath-er-ing home, gathering home,

Home to the mansions of glo - ry; Gath-er-ing home, gath-er-ing home, *D.S.*

From "Peerless Praise," by per.

DO RE MI FA SO LA SI

No. 77. He Saved My Soul.

Mrs. E. M. Sangster. T. C. O'Kane.

Moderate.

1. You ask me, brethren, how I know that Je - sus is di - vine;
2. A wand'rer from my Father's house, he took me by the hand;
3. He saved me! saved me from my-self, and saved me from my sins,

The rath-er ask me how I know that yonder sun doth shine; The
A mar-in-er on rag-ing seas, he guid-ed me to land; A
And here, just in that precious truth, my par - a-dise be - gins; I

rath-er bid me tell you how I know that bil-lows roll, Or winds sweep on from
weary, storm-toss'd man, he came, and made me like a child, As hungry to re-
know that Christ the blessed One is Man, and is Di-vine, I *know* because--oh!

north to south! Why, friends, "*He saved my soul,*" Glo-ry, glo-ry to Je - sus,
ceive the truth, as gen-tle and as mild.—
brethren, hear! "He saved a soul like mine."—Glo - ry, glo-ry to Je-sus,

CHORUS.

Let the chorus roll! Glo-ry, glory to Je-sus, Because "*He saved my soul.*"
Let the chorus roll!

By permission.

DO RE MI FA SO LA SI

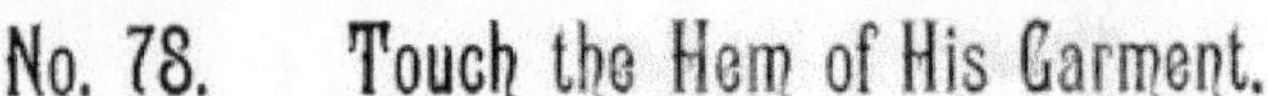
No. 78. Touch the Hem of His Garment.

E. A. H. Melody by E. A. Hoffman. Har. by E. O. E.

1. Sin- ner, press your way to Je - sus; Bring to him your burdened soul; Let the hand of faith but touch him, And the touch will make you whole.
2. Thus he saved me, hal - le - lu - jah! And I want the world to know That he can transform the sin - ner, And can wash him white as snow.
3. Are you ve - ry tired and wea - ry Of your life of guilt and sin? Do you long for peace and pardon? Do you sigh for rest within?
4. Come, then, tho' the many throng him; Make your way a- mid the press, Sure, if you but find and touch him, He your waiting heart will bless.

CHORUS.

Quickly haste, then, to the Saviour, Weary, sin-sick soul! If you touch but the hem of his garment, You shall be whole, you shall be whole!

D.S.—If you touch but the hem of his garment, You shall be . . . . whole, you shall be whole!

DO RE MI FA SO LA SI

No. 79. Waiting by the River.
Miss M. P. Griffin.
E. O. Excell.
1. We are wait-ing by the riv - er, We are watching on the shore,
2. Tho' the mists hang o'er the riv - er, And its bil-lows loud-ly roar,
3. And the bright ce - les - tial ci - ty, We have caught such radiant gleams
4. He has called for many a loved one, We have seen them leave our side;
5. When we've passed the vale of shadows, With its dark and chilling tide,
On - ly wait-ing for the boatman, Soon he'll come to bear us o'er.
Yet we hear the song of an-gels, Waft-ed from the oth - er shore.
Of its towers, like dazzling sunlight, With its sweet and peaceful streams.
With our Sav-iour we shall meet them When we too have crossed the tide.
In that bright and glo-rious ci - ty We shall ev - er-more a-bide.
CHORUS.
Wait - - - ing, watch - - ing, wait - - - ing, watch - - ing,
Wait-ing, wait-ing, watch-ing, watching, wait - ing, wait-ing, watch-ing, watching,
We are watching on the shore, . . . Wait - - ing, watch - ing,
We are watching, we are watching on the shore, Waiting, waiting, watching, watching,
wait - - ing, watch - - ing For the boatman who will bear us o'er.
waiting, waiting, watching, watching,
DO RE MI FA SO LA SI

No. 80. The Master hath need of Reapers.

Annie H. Thompson. J. H. Kurzenknabe.

1. The Master hath need of the reapers! And, mourner, he calleth for thee;
2. The Master hath need of the reapers! And, i - dler, he calleth for thee;
3. The Master hath need of the reapers! And, worker, he calleth for thee;
4. The Master hath need of the reapers! And he calleth for you and for me;
Come out from the valley of sor- row, Look up to the hill-tops and see
Come out from the mansion of pleasure, From the halls where the careless may be;
O what are thy dreams of ambition To the joys that hereafter shall be?
Oh, haste while the winds of the morning Are blowing so freshly and free:
How the fields with the harvest are whitening, How golden and full is the grain;
Soon the shadows of eve will be falling, With the mist, and the dew, and the rain;
There are tokens of storms that are coming, And summer is fast on the wane.
Let the sound of the scythe and the sickle Re - echo o'er hill-top and plain,
Oh, what are thy wants to the summons, And what are thy griefs and thy pain?
Oh, what is the world and its fol - lies, To the mold and the rust of the grain.
Then-alas for the hopes of the harvest. And a - las for the beauti- ful grain.
And gather the sheaves in the garner, For golden and ripe is the grain.
DO RE MI FA SO LA SI

From "Peerless Praise," by per.

No. 81. Sailing O'er Life's Ocean.

Chas. E. Pollock.

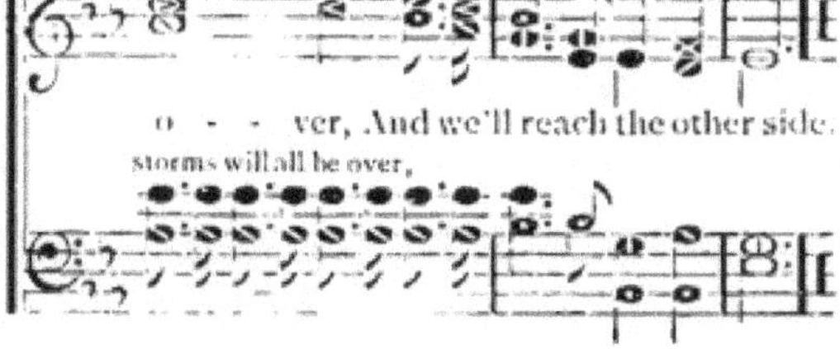

1. { We're a faith-ful pilgrim band, Sailing to the heavenly land, With a swelling sail we on-ward sweep; ‖
{ Tho' the tempest ra-ges long There is one among the throng Who will guide the sail-or o'er the deep.

CHORUS.

We are sail - - - ing o'er the o - - - cean, We are drift - - - - - - ing with the tide, Soon the storms . . . will all be o - - - ver, And we'll reach the other side.

We are sailing o'er the ocean, We are sailing o'er the ocean, We are drifting with the tide, We are drifting with the tide, Soon the storms will all be o - ver, Soon the storms will all be over,

2 Tho' the rolling billows swell,
Yet securely we may dwell,
Tho' the breakers roar upon the lea,
'Mid the storm, by day or night,
If we trust our Captain's might,
He will guide us safely o'er the sea.

3 Tho' for many ages past
She has long withstood the blast,
And in safety crossed the billows o'er
Yet, amid the rocks and shoals,
She has landed many souls [shore.
On fair Canaan's bright and peaceful

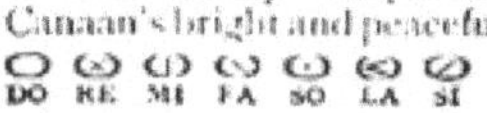

DO RE MI FA SO LA SI

No. 82. The Mansions of Love.

A. S. K.
Text—Rev. xxi. 23.
Aldine S. Kieffer.
1. There are man-sions of love In that land far a-bove, Which the Sav-iour has gone to pre-pare, And the chil-dren of day, Who de-light in his way, In those man-sions shall each have a share.
2. There's a fountain whose stream Sparkles bright in the gleam Of a day that shall not end in night, And its wa-ters make glad All the wea-ry and sad, Who have gone to that land of de-light.
3. Of that fount-ain of love, In that land far a-bove, May we drink when life's journey is o'er; And with an-gels of light Share the splen-dors so bright, In those man-sions of love ev-er-more.
CHORUS.
They shall dwell . . . . for-ev-er-more In that land . . . . so bright and fair; O-ver on . . . .
They shall dwell for-ev-ermore, They shall dwell for-ev-ermore In that land so bright and fair, In that land so bright and fair; O-ver on that hap-py
DO RE MI FA SO LA SI

By permission.

The Mansions of Love.—Concluded.

. . that happy shore, In that ci - ty of love and de - light.
shore, O - ver on that happy shore,

No. 83. Take Your Sins to Jesus.

E. A. Hoffman. FOR MALE VOICES. J. H. Tenney.

1. Take your sins to Je - sus, Weary, burdened soul; He will give you
2. Take your sins to Je - sus, He will set you free; Come, with all your
3. Take your sins to Je - sus, Give him all your heart; He will seal your

comfort, He will make you whole; Cease to look with - in you; Look to
bur - den To Mount Cal - va - ry; All your bit - ter weeping Adds but
par - don, And his love im - part; On - ly he can save you; Why so

Christ and live; Take your sins to Je - sus, Free - ly he'll for - give.
to your grief; Take your sins to Je - sus If you want re - lief.
long de - lay? Take your sins to Je - sus While 'tis called to - day.

DO RE MI FA SO LA SI

By permission.

No. 84. Music Over Yonder.
W. F. Cosner.
Chas. E. Pollock.
1. There is mu - sic o - ver yon - der, On the bright e - ter - nal shore,
2. There is mu - sic o - ver yon - der, Where the crystal wa - ters glide,
3. There is mu - sic o - ver yon - der, Where the golden lyres are swept,
4. There is mu - sic o - ver yon - der, And the songs shall nev - er cease,
Where the saints shall dwell with Jesus, All the bright for - ev - er - more;
Where the tree of life is ev - er Blooming by the sil - ver tide;
And their songs u- nite in prais- ing Him who o'er a lost world wept;
For the saints shall dwell forev - er With their Lord, in per - fect peace;
All their years of sor - row end - ed, Where no night can ev - er come,
Oh, what joy the heart is thrill - ing, O - ver on the shin - ing shore.
And we al- most think we hear them, O - ver on the gold - en strand,
Soon we hope to join their cho - rus, On the bright e - ter - nal shore,
They are sing- ing, sweetly sing - ing, In their glorious heavenly home.
Where they sing the song of Mo - ses And the Lamb for- ev - er - more.
As they sing with heavenly rapture, Crowned and robed, a glorious band.
Where the saints shall be with Je- sus All the bright for- ev - er - more.
Copyright, 1882, by E. O. Excell.
DO RE MI FA SO LA SI

No. 85. Help Each Other.
Mrs. E. C Ellsworth.
E. O. Excell.
1. Is thy brother sad and wea - ry? Wipe a brother's tear,
2. Is thy brother heav - y - lad - en? Bear a gracious part;
3. Is thy brother sad - ly fall - en? Lift with gen - tle hand,
Throw a-round his darkened spir - it All thy light and cheer.
Put thy shoulder to the bur - den, Show a brother's heart.
Thou hast had thy man - y fail- ures, Help thy broth- er stand.
CHORUS.
Oh, by help- ing each the oth - er Pathways may be bright,
Help - ing thus a need - y brother Brings to us the light.
DO RE MI FA SO LA SI

No. 86. Haste, Oh, Haste to Jesus.

Rev. J. B. Atchinson.
[FOR MALE VOICES.]
W. T. Giffe
1. O broth - er, you are help - less! With dan - ger all a - round; A - mong your boon companions No helper can be found; Heed not their proffered coun - sel, 'Twill surely lead a - stray, And in - to deep - est per - il, 'Twill wander day by day.
2. There's One who knows your per - il, He knows you're helpless, too; His might - y arm can save you, His help he offers you; He now stands near you wait - ing, In sympath - y and love, For you to call up - on him, His love and pow'r to prove.
3. This wait - ing One is Je - sus, He comes to seek and save; To save you from all e - vil, His precious life he gave; No oth - er can de - liv - er, He on - ly can re - deem; Oh, hasten now to Jesus,—Trust on - ly in his name.
4. Your weakness he re - mem - bers, That you are dust he knows, He knows that all a - round you Are many mighty foes; And he has come to help you,—All foes to o - ver - come,—And walk along be - side you, To your e - ter - nal home.
CHORUS.
Then haste, oh, haste to Je - sus; He is your tru - est Friend, He will your soul de - liv - er And help you to the end.
DO RE MI FA SO LA SI

No. 87. My God will send His Angel.

Rev. J. B. Atchisson.
FOR MALE VOICES.
W. T. Giffe.
1. Though tri - als oft be - set me, Though scorn'd by wicked men,
2. Though walk - ing in the dark - ness, Though hedg'd a - bout with sin,
3. Though wea - ry with my toil - ing, Though burdens weigh me down,
4. Though long and drear the jour - ney, We jour - ney not a - lone;
Though struggling with temp- ta - tion, Though in the li - on's den,
Though bat - tles rage a - round me, Though fightings fierce with - in,
Though doubts and fears an- noy me, Though far off seems the crown,
Though deep and dark the val - ley, The cross - ing will be soon.
CHORUS.
My God will send his an - gel,—The li - ons will not harm;
He sure - ly will de - liv - er,— I'll trust his might- y arm.
DO RE MI FA SO LA SI

No. 88. More Like Jesus.
H. H. McGranahan.
1. I want to be like Je - sus, The thought is sweet to me,
2. I want to be a wit - ness Of his life - giv - ing power,
3. Filled with his bless - ed Spir - it We shall not live in vain,
4. Whate'er we do for Je - sus Let all be done in love,
And share his lov - ing kind - ness Through all e - ter - ni - ty,
And know the grace that saves me With ev - 'ry com - ing hour,
Our tri - als, cares and cross - es Will prove e - ter - nal gain,
And when he comes to take us We'll join the saints a - bove,
REFRAIN.
Through all e - ter - ni - ty, Through all e - ter - ni - ty, And
With ev - 'ry com - ing hour, With ev - 'ry com - ing hour, And
Will prove e - ter - nal gain, Will prove e - ter - nal gain, Our
We'll join the saints a - bove, We'll join the saints a - bove, And
share his lov - ing kind - ness Through all e - ter - ni - ty.
know the grace that saves me, With ev - 'ry com - ing hour.
tri - als, cares and cross - es Will prove e - ter - nal gain.
when he comes to take us We'll join the saints a - bove.

DO RE MI FA SO LA SI

No. 89. Over the River.

I. B.
Rev. I. Baltzell.
With energy.
1. O - ver the riv - er, the riv - er of time, Lies the bright
2. O - ver the riv - er time nev - er grows old; There are en-
3. O - ver the riv - er our sor-rows will cease, Hush'd by the
land, of a ver-dure sub-lime, Val-leys of beau - ty in
joy-ments and pleasures un-told; There is a cit - y with
songs of a heav-en - ly peace; When we get there what a
splen-dor do shine; Beau - ti - ful, beau - ti - ful home!
streets of pure gold; Beau - ti - ful, beau - ti - ful home!
hap - py re-lease! Beau - ti - ful, beau - ti - ful home!
CHORUS.
O - - - ver the riv - er, The beau - - - ti - ful riv - er,
O - ver the beau - ti - ful riv - er, The beau - ti - ful, beau - ti - ful riv - er,
O - - - ver the riv - er The fields are all green.
O - ver the beau - ti - ful riv - er The beau - ti - ful fields are all green.
DO RE MI FA SO LA SI

By permission.

No. 90. Jesus, Lover of My Soul.

To Mr. and Mrs. Chas. Herr, Petrolia, Pa. — E. O. Excell.

1. Je - sus, lov - er of my soul, Let me to thy
2. Oth - er ref - uge have I none, Hangs my help - less
3. Thou, O Christ, art all I want; More than all in
8va. . .
bos - om fly, While the near - er wa - ters roll,
soul on thee: Leave, oh, leave me not a - lone,
thee I find: Raise the fal - len, cheer the faint,
CHORUS
While the temp - est still is high; Hide me, oh, my
Hide me, oh, my
Still sup - port and com - fort me. All my trust on
All my trust on
Heal the sick, and lead the blind. Just and Ho - ly
Just and Holy
8va. . .
Sav - iour, hide, Till the storm of life is past; Safe in-
Saviour, hide, Saviour, hide,
thee is stayed, All my help from thee I bring; Cov - er
thee is stayed, thee is stayed,
is thy name, I am all un - righteousness; Vile, and
is thy name, is thy name,
pp
DO RE MI FA SO LA SI

Jesus, Lover of My Soul.—Concluded.
to the hav - en guide, Oh, re - ceive my soul at last.
Safe into the haven guide, haven guide,
my de - fence - less head With the sha - dow of thy wing.
Cover my de-fenceless head, defenceless head
full of sin I am, Thou art full of truth and grace.
Vile, and full of sin I am, sin I am,
pp
No. 91. Steal Away to Jesus.
E. O. Excell.
1. Re - turn, O wand'rer, to thy home, Thy Fath - er calls for thee;
2. Re - turn, O wand'rer, to thy home, 'Tis Je - sus calls for thee;
3. Re - turn, O wand'rer, to thy home, 'Tis mad - ness to de - lay;
No long - er now an ex - ile roam In guilt and mis - er - y.
The Spir - it and the Bride say, Come: O now for ref - uge flee.
There are no par - dons in the tomb, And brief is mer - cy's day.
CHORUS. pp
Steal a - way, steal a - way, Steal a - way to Je - sus;
rit.
Steal a - way, steal a - way home, For Je - sus waits to save you.

No. 92. Throw the Door Wide Open.
Mrs. E. C. Ellsworth.
M. H. Evans.
1. Throw the door wide o-pen! One would enter in, Bringing love's sweet mes-sage, Par-don for thy sin; Hast thou not a wel-come? Shall the mes-sage stay? Life on thee is wait-ing,— Shall it wait for aye?
2. Throw the door wide o-pen! Lo, thy Lord has come; He is seek-ing en-trance To thy hum-ble home; Art thou still de-ny-ing To thy Roy-al Guest? And thy-self de-priv-ing Peace and ho-ly rest?
3. Throw the door wide o-pen! Soon he may de-part, And the lov-ing mes-sage Nev-er reach thy heart; When thou would'st receive him, And would'st glo-ry see, "I have nev-er known you," He may say to thee.
CHORUS.
Throw the door wide o-pen! Stand thyself a-side; Haste, thy heart unbarring, Throw it open wide!
DO RE MI FA SO LA SI

No. 93. Seek a Saviour's Blessing.

A. L. S. — Allie L. Smith.

1. Would you have a Saviour near? Come and seek his bless - ing;
2. When your footsteps stray from God, Come and seek his bless - ing;
3. When dark woes your heart oppress, Come and seek his bless - ing;
4. World - ly man, no long - er stray, Come and seek his bless - ing;
Would you have his love and cheer? Come, your sins con - fess - ing.
When so heav - y seems his rod, Come, your sins con - fess - ing.
When great doubts your souls distress, Come, your sins con - fess - ing.
Gain the rest now far a - way, Come, your sins con - fess - ing.
CHORUS.
He of - fers life to - day, — He is the on - ly way;
To him bow your heart and pray, — He will sure - ly bless you.
DO RE MI FA SO LA SI

No. 94. Three Warnings.

Rev. W. T. Dale. Chas. E. Pollock

1. Re - sist not the Spirit, But yield to him now; In mercy he calls thee, Come, sin - ner, and bow; No long - er re - sist him,—No longer de - lay; He pleads with thee gently, He's pleading to-day.
2. Oh, quench not the Spirit, His grace from above Will warm thy affections And cause thee to love; Thy heart which is frozen, Shall glow as the flame; Thy spirit, when ransomed, His love shall proclaim.
3. Oh, grieve not the Spirit, He stands at the door, He waits to be gracious, He'll save thee this hour; How long he's been waiting! How long must he wait? Oh, sinner, this moment May close mercy's gate.
CHORUS.
{Re - sist / Oh, quench / Oh, grieve} not the Spir - - - - it, {Re - sist / Oh, quench / Oh, grieve} him not now, In
{Re - sist / Oh, quench / Oh, grieve} not the Spir - it, {Re - sist / Oh, quench / Oh, grieve} him not now, {Re - sist / Oh, quench / Oh, grieve} not the Spir - it, {Re - sist / Oh, quench / Oh, grieve} him not now, In
DO RE MI FA SO LA SI

From "The Beauty of Praise," by per.

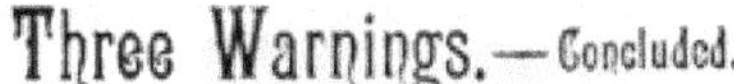

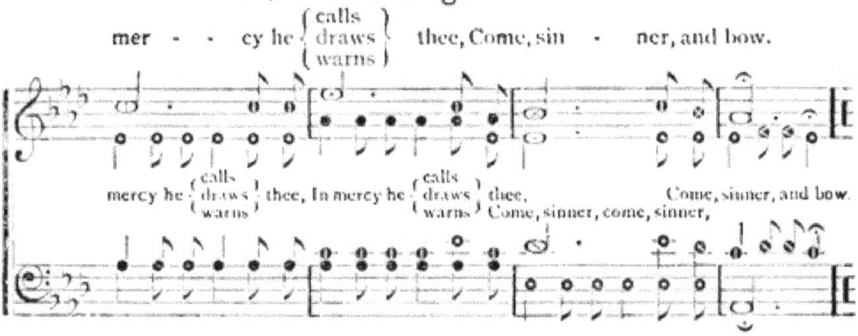

mer - - cy he {calls / draws / warns} thee, Come, sin - ner, and bow.

mercy he {calls / draws / warns} thee, In mercy he {calls / draws / warns} thee, Come, sinner, come, sinner, Come, sinner, and bow.

No. 95. Our Father.

Rev. Tryon Edwards, D. D. George Beaverson.

Slowly.

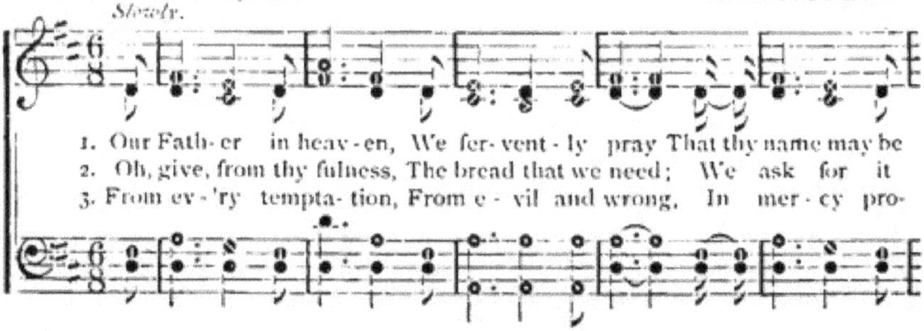

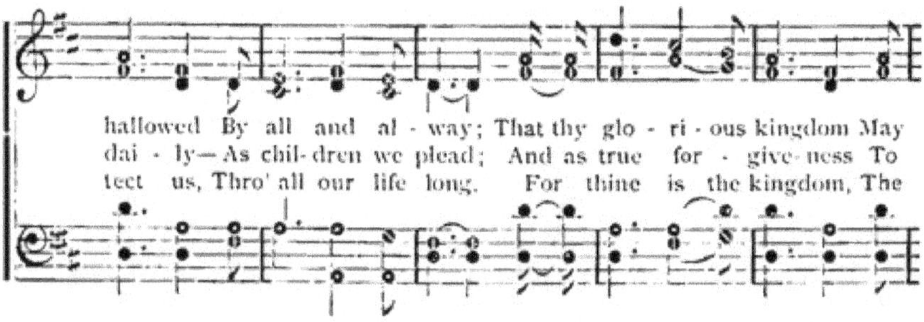

1. Our Fath- er in heav- en, We fer- vent - ly pray That thy name may be hallowed By all and al - way; That thy glo - ri - ous kingdom May speed - i - ly come, And on earth, as in heaven, Thy will may be done.
2. Oh, give, from thy fulness, The bread that we need; We ask for it dai - ly— As chil- dren we plead; And as true for - give- ness To oth - ers we show, On us, O our Father, Thy pardon be- stow.
3. From ev- 'ry tempta- tion, From e - vil and wrong, In mer - cy pro- tect us, Thro' all our life long. For thine is the kingdom, The glo - ry, the power, To shield us and guide us From ill ev - er- more.

DO RE MI FA SO LA SI

No. 96. Bright Home.
Rev. C. C. Hunt.
J. A. Dailey.
1. There's a land of wondrous beau - ty far a - way, In the splendor of its glo - ry ev - er bright; End-less bliss and love im- mor - tal ev - er stay In that fair, bright land of fadeless light.
2. Gold - en gateways, nev - er clos - ing night or day, Stand to greet the wea - ry pilgrim's homeward flight, While a throng of ho - ly an- gels lead the way To that fair, bright land of fadeless light.
3. Oh, how sweet to lay life's wea - ry bur - den down, And ex- change for it a robe of spotless white; Oh, what joy to wear a star - ry, gold - en crown In that fair, bright land of fadeless light.
4. There no toil, or pain, or sor - row ev - er come; Oh, what rap - ture! oh, what glo - ry! what de - light! We will find our bright, our bles - sed, hap - py home In that fair, bright land of fadeless light.
CHORUS.
Sweet home a - bove, Sweet home where all is love;
Sweet home a - bove, Sweet home where all is love;
There'll be joy com - plete, When in heaven we all shall meet.
DO RE MI FA SO LA SI

No. 97. The Promised Land.

W. L. T.
Will L. Thompson.
1. Oh, sing me a song of the bet - ter land, Bet - ter land, bet - ter land,
2. We'll all en - ter in at the pearly gates, Pearly gates, pearly gates,
3. We'll sing as we walk on the golden streets, Golden streets, golden streets,
4. We'll play on the harps with the angel band, An - gel band, an - gel band,
Oh, sing me a song of the bet - ter land, Where we're going by and by.
We'll all en - ter in at the pearly gates, Where we're going by and by.
We'll sing as we walk on the golden streets, Where we're going by and by.
We'll play on the harps with the angel band, Where we're going by and by.
CHORUS.
By and by, by and by, There we'll with the happy an - gels
By and by, by and by,
stand, By and by, by and by, We will meet you in the promised land.
By and by, By and by,
By permission.
DO RE MI FA SO LA SI

No. 98. I Yield to Thee.

Rev. Frank Pollock. — Chas. F. Pollock.

With expression.
1. I yield to thee, my Fath - er; O take this heart of stone,
2. I yield to thee, dear Je - sus; Thy blood can peace im - part;
3. I yield to thee, blest Spir - it, To take the full con - trol;
And give me one so ten - der That it shall be thy throne.
And write thy name most pre- cious Up - on my yield- ing heart.
Oh, sanc - ti - fy the pow - ers Of my poor, yearning soul.
REFRAIN.
I yield, I yield, I yield this heart of stone;
I yield, I yield,
O give me one so ten - der That it shall be thy throne.
DO RE MI FA SO LA SI

No. 99. Give to Jesus Glory.
W. H. Clark.
Wm. J. Kirkpatrick.
1. From mountain top and dew - y vale, From temples old and hoary, Proclaim redemption's wondrous tale, And give to Jesus glo - ry.
2. From break of day to star - ry night, Ring out sal - va - tion's story; And when returns the morning light, Still give to Je - sus glo - ry.
3. High in the heaven of heavens a - bove, Where angels hosts a - dore thee, We'll sing the Father's matchless love, And give to Jesus glory.
2. Oh, sin - ner, ere per - di - tion's waves Shall roll in fu - ry o'er thee, Come unto Jesus Christ who saves, And give to him the glo - ry.
CHORUS.
Give to Je - sus glo - ry, Give to Je - sus glo - ry, Proclaim re - demp - tion's wondrous tale, And give to Je - sus glo - ry.

From "The Wells of Salvation," by per.

DO RE MI FA SO LA SI

No. 100. City of Beauty.
M. E. Servoss.
E. O. Excell.
DUET.
1. O ci - ty of beauty, I long to behold Thy pearly white gates and thy pavement of gold; And I long for a stroll on that beau-ti-ful shore, Where earth-weary feet shall grow weary no more.
2. When sad and oppress'd with life's burdens and fears, Sweet thoughts of that city my weary heart cheers, And I feel that each bat-tle must bravely be won That I may re-joice in a Father's "well done."
3. My Saviour hath promised for me to prepare A home in that country so peaceful and fair; And I rest in this hope, till his lov - ing command Shall summon me home to that beauti - ful land.
CHORUS.
But dear - er by far than all to me Is the thought that the face of my Lord I shall see; Yes, dearer by
than all oth- er
Copyright, 1881, by John J. Hood.
DO RE MI FA SO LA SI

City of Beauty.—Concluded.
far than all to me, Is the thought that the face of the Lord I shall see.
than all oth- er
No. 101. No Matter.
J. E. Morris.
E. O. Excell.
1. What tho' the path be rugged, wild and dreary, What tho' the bur- den seems too heav - y now? Sweet-er the rest of heaven to those grown wea - ry, Brighter the crown if thorns have scerred the brow.
2. What tho' our journey lie through desert places? What tho' we plod on, heart and san-dal worn? Sure - ly the path our Father for us trac - es; Sure - ly he'll light - en ev - 'ry bur - den borne.
3. What tho' our staff seems sometimes nearly broken? What tho' we oftimes faint and near- ly fall? His mighty arm still holds us, he hath spok - en, "My grace shall prove suf - fi - cient," all in all.
4. What tho' our earthly hopes lie plucked and faded, What tho' our i - dols crumble in - to dust? We look be- yond, by heavenly vi - sion aid - ed, Where treasures grow not old, or dim with rust.
rit.
5 What though affliction's tempests beat about us,
With hope and cheer we'll breast the swelling tide;
No matter how the billows lash and move us,
We'll boldly strike out for the other side.
6 Then when we reach the shores of life eternal,
And drop our burdens all at Jesus' feet,
No matter then, in joy and peace supernal,
With labor ended, rest will be complete.
Copyright, 1882, by E. O. Excell.
DO RE MI FA SO LA SI

No. 102. Whiter than the Snow.
Mrs. M. A. Kidder.
J. A. Dailey.
1. Fear not, little flock, says the Saviour divine, The Father has willed that the kingdom be thine, O soil not your garments with sin here below,—My sheep and my lambs must be whiter than snow.
2. Far whiter than snow, and as fair as the day,—For Christ is the fountain to wash guilt away; Oh, give him, poor sinner, that burden of thine, And en - ter the fold with the ninety-and-nine.
3. Yon sheep, that was lost in the valley of sin, Was found by the Shepherd, who gathered him in; With songs of thanksgiving the hills did resound,—My friends, and my neighbors the lost sheep is found.
4. Look up, O my brother! and be not cast down While heavy the cross, you are sighting the crown; Go, wash in the fountain, while waiting below, Your sins shall, tho' scarlet, be whiter than snow.
5. Ride over temptation and cease your alarms, Your Shepherd is Jesus—your refuge his arms; He'll never forsake you—a Brother and Friend—But love you and save you in worlds without end.
CHORUS.
Whit - - - - er than snow,
Whiter than the snow,
I long to be, dear Saviour,
Whit - - - - er than snow,
Whiter than the snow,
I long to be
Whit - - - - er than
Whiter than the snow,
DO RE MI FA SO LA SI

Whiter than the Snow.—Concluded.
Repeat Chorus pp.
snow, Whit - - - - - er than snow.
I long to be, dear Saviour, Whiter than the snow, Whiter than the snow.
No. 103. Come to Me.
Mrs. J. C Yule.
E. O. Excell.
DUET.—Soprano and Tenor.
1. Wea - ry soul, by care oppressed, Would'st thou find a place of rest?
2. Hun-gry soul, why pine and die, With ex-haustless stores so nigh?
3. Thirs - ty soul, earth's sweetest rill Mocks thee with its promise still;
4. Homeless soul, thy path is drear, Ang - ry tempests gath - er near,
5. Heavenly bread, and heavenly wine, Liv - ing wa - ters, all are mine,
Lis - ten, Je - sus calls to thee, Come and find thy rest in me.
Lo, the board is spread for thee, Come and feast to - day with me.
Hark, the Sav - iour calls to thee, Here is wa - ter, come to me.
Night is dark'ning o - ver thee; Here is shel - ter, come to me.
Mine they are and thine may be; Wea - ry wand'rer, come to me.
CHORUS.
Repeat p.
Come to me, come to me, Come and find thy rest in me.
Come to me, come to me, Come and feast to - day with me.
Come to me, come to me, Here is wa - ter, come to me.
Come to me, come to me, Here is shel - ter, come to me.
Come to me, come to me, Wea - ry wand'rer, come to me.
DO RE MI FA SO LA SI

F

No. 104. How I Wish I Knew.
Grace Glenn.
J. H. Fillmore.
1. Lit - tle stars that twin - kle in the heav - ens blue,
2. Did you see the cost - ly pre - sents they had brought?
3. Did you hear the moth - ers' plead - ing through their tears
4. Did you watch the Sav - iour all those years of strife?
I have oft - en won - dered if you ev - er knew
Did you see the sta - ble they in won - der sought?
For the babes that Her - od slew the com - ing years?
Did you know for sin - ners how he gave his life?
How there rose one like you, lead - ing wise old men
Did you see the wor - ship ten - der - ly they paid
Did you see how Jo - seph, warned of God in dreams,
Lit - tle stars that twin - kle in the heav - ens blue,
From the East, through Ju - dah, down to Beth - le - hem?
To that stran - ger ba - by in the man - ger laid?
Hur - ried in - to E - gypt, guid - ed by your beams.
All you saw of Je - sus how I wish ' knew.

By permission.

DO RE MI FA SO LA SI

No. 105. That Sweet Story.

JEMIMA LUKE. E. O. EXCELL.

1. I think, when I read that sweet sto - ry of old,—
D. C.—How he called lit - tle chil - dren as lambs to his fold;

Fine.
When Je - sus was here a - mong men,—
I should like to have been with him then,

D. C.
I should like to have been with him then. . . .

2 I wish that his hands had been placed on my head,
That his arms had been thrown around me,
And that I might have seen his kind look when he said,
Let the little ones come unto me.

3 Yet still to his footstool in prayer I may go,
And ask for a share in his love;
And if I thus earnestly seek him below,
I shall see him and hear him above.

4 In that beautiful place he has gone to prepare
For all who are washed and forgiven,
And many dear children are gathering there,
For of such is the kingdom of heaven.

DO RE MI FA SO LA SI

No. 106. Blessed Jesus.
J. H. Fillmore.
DUET.
SEMI-CHORUS.
1. Who was in the man - ger laid? Je - sus, bles - sed Je - sus;
2. Who can rob the grave of gloom? Je - sus, bles - sed Je - sus;
3. Who will give us sweet - est rest? Je - sus, bles - sed Je - sus;
DUET.
SEMI-CHORUS.
Who, for mon - ey, was betrayed? Je - sus, bles - sed Je - sus.
Who can raise us from the tomb? Je - sus, bles - sed Je - sus.
Who, in heaven, shall we love best? Je - sus, bles - sed Je - sus.
DUET.
Who up Cal - va - ry was led? Who for us his life-blood shed?
When be- fore the Judge we wait, Who will o - pen heav - en's gate?
At his feet our crowns we'll fling, While with rapturous songs we sing,
CHORUS.
Je - sus Christ, cre - a- tion's head, Je - sus, bles - sed Je - sus.
Je - sus Christ, our Ad - vo- cate, Je - sus, bles - sed Je - sus.
Je - sus Christ, our Sav - iour, King, Je - sus, bles - sed Je - sus.
No. 107. Jesus, Bless the Children.
E. R. Latta.
J. H. Fillmore.
1. Jesus, come and bless the children That are gathered here to - day;
2. Jesus, come and bless the children, Just as tender - ly a - gain,
3. Jesus, come and bless the children, Keep their spirits, Lord, from ill;
Now thy hand up- on their foreheads With a lov- ing pressure lay.
As be- fore thy cru - ci - fix - ion, When up- on the earth with men.
And up- on their earthly jour- ney, Let them feel thy presence still.
CHORUS.
Jesus, come and bless the chil- dren With a blessing all di- vine;
Shield them from the wiles of Sa- tan, Make and keep them ever thine.
By permission.
DO RE MI FA SO LA SI

No. 108. Let Them Come to Me.

A. H. Adams. E. O. Excell.

1. { Hear the gen - tle Shep - herd Call - ing lambs like me, }
{ In his sweet - est ac - cents, Let them come to me. }

REFRAIN.

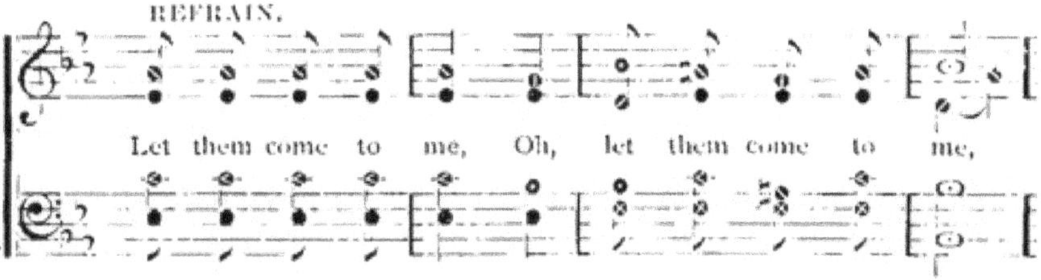

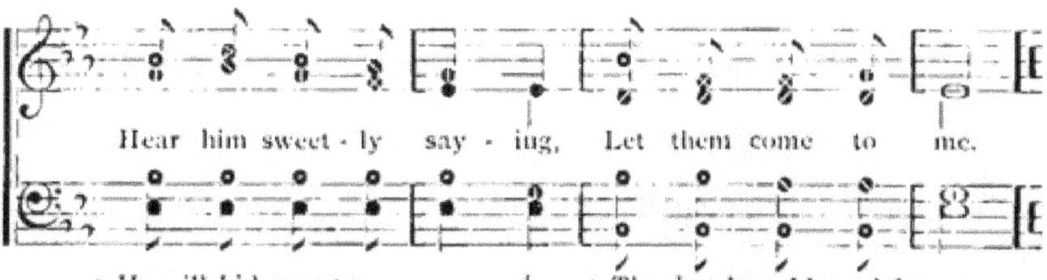

Let them come to me, Oh, let them come to me,
Hear him sweet - ly say - ing, Let them come to me.

2 He will bid us enter;
When our tired feet
Reach the golden city
He'll be there to greet.

3 Thanks, dear, blessed Jesus,
For thy words of love,
Bidding children enter
Thy bright courts above.

No. 109. The Happy Land.

1. { There is a hap - py land, Far, far a - way, } Oh, how they
{ Where saints in glo - ry stand, Bright, bright as day; } Loud let his
1
2
sweet- ly sing, "Worthy is our Saviour King;"
prais - es ring, ... Praise ev - er- more.

2 Come to that happy land,
Come, come away;
Why will ye doubting stand?
Why still delay?
Oh, we shall happy be,
When from sin and sorrow free,
Lord, we shall dwell with thee,
Blest evermore.

3 Bright, in that happy land,
Beams every eye;
Kept by a Father's hand,
Love cannot die.
Oh, then to glory run;
Be a crown and kingdom won;
And bright, above the sun,
Reign evermore.

No. 110. Before the Cross.

1 My faith looks up to thee,
Thou Lamb of Calvary,
Savior divine:
Now hear me while I pray,
Take all my guilt away,
O let me from this day
Be wholly thine.

2 May thy rich grace impart
Strength to my fainting heart,
My zeal inspire;
As thou hast died for me,
O may my love to thee
Pure, warm, and changeless be,—
A living fire.

3 While life's dark maze I tread,
And griefs around me spread,
Be thou my guide;
Bid darkness turn to day,
Wipe sorrow's tears away,
Nor ever let me stray
From thee aside.

No. 111. The Home Over There.

1 Oh, think of the home over there,
By the side of the river of light,
Where the saints, all immortal and fair,
Are robed in their garments of white.
Ref.—Over there, over there,
Oh, think of the home over there.

2 Oh, think of the friends over there,
Who before us the journey have trod,
Of the songs that they breathe on the air,
In their home in the palace of God.
Ref.—Over there, over there,
Oh, think of the friends over there.

3 My Savior is now over there,
There my kindred and friends are at [rest;
Then away from my sorrow and care,
Let me fly to the land of the blest.
Ref.—Over there, over there,
My Savior is now over there.

4 I'll soon be at home over there,
For the end of my journey I see;
Many dear to my heart, over there,
Are watching and waiting for me.
Ref.—Over there, over there,
I'll soon be at home over there.

No. 112. Come, Ye Sinners.

1 Come, ye sinners, poor and needy,
Weak and wounded, sick and sore;
Jesus ready stands to save you,
Full of pity, love, and power.

Cho. Turn to the Lord and seek salvation;
Sound the praise of his dear name;
Glory, honor, and salvation!
Christ, the Lord, has come to reign.

2 Now, ye needy, come and welcome;
God's free bounty glorify;
True belief and true repentance,—
Every grace that brings you nigh.

3 Let not conscience make you linger;
Nor of fitness fondly dream;
All the fitness he requireth
Is to feel your need of him!

4 Come, ye weary, heavy-laden,
Bruised and mangled by the fall;
If you tarry 'till you're better,
You will never come at all.

No. 113. Marching to Zion.

1 Come, we that love the Lord,
And let our joys be known,
Join in a song with sweet accord,
And thus surround the throne.

Cho.—We're marching to Zion,
Beautiful, beautiful Zion,
We're marching upward to Zion,
The beautiful city of God.

2 Let those refuse to sing
Who never knew our God;
But children of the heavenly King
May speak their joys abroad.

3 The hill of Zion yields
A thousand sacred sweets,
Before we reach the heavenly fields,
Or walk the golden streets.

4 Then let our songs abound,
And every tear be dry; [ground,
We're marching through Immanuel's
To fairer worlds on high.

No. 114. Even Me.

1 Lord, I hear of showers of blessing
Thou art scattering full and free;
Showers, the thirsty land refreshing;
Let some drops now fall on me,
Even me.

2 Pass me not, O God, my Father,
Sinful though my heart may be:
Thou might'st leave me, but the rather
Let thy mercy light on me,
Even me.

3 Pass me not, O gracious Savior,
Let me live and cling to thee;
I am longing for thy favor;
Whil'st thou'rt calling, O call me,
Even me.

4 Pass me not, O mighty Spirit,
Thou canst make the blind to see;
Witnesser of Jesus' merit,
Speak the word of power to me,
Even me.

No. 115. He Leadeth Me.

1 He leadeth me! oh, blessed thought,
Oh, words with heavenly solace fraught!
Whate'er I do, where'er I be,
Still 'tis God's hand that leadeth me!

Cho.—He leadeth me, he leadeth me,
By his own hand he leadeth me;
His faithful follower I would be,
For by his hand he leadeth me.

2 Sometimes mid scenes of deepest gloom,
Sometimes where Eden's bowers bloom,
By waters still, o'er troubled sea,—
Still 'tis his hand that leadeth me!

3 Lord, I would clasp thy hand in mine,
Nor ever murmur nor repine,
Content, whatever lot I see,
Since 'tis my God that leadeth me!

No. 116. At the Mercy Seat.

1 Jesus, thine all victorious love
Shed in my heart abroad:
Then shall my feet no longer rove,
Rooted and fixed in God.

Cho. ‖: We're kneeling at the mercy-seat,:‖
Where Jesus answers prayer.

2 O that in me the sacred fire
Might now begin to glow,
Burn up the dross of base desire
And make the mountains flow!

3 O that it now from heaven might fall,
And all my sins consume!
Come, Holy Ghost, for thee I call;
Spirit of burning, come!

4 Refining fire, go through my heart;
Illuminate my soul;
Scatter thy life through every part,
And sanctify the whole.

No. 117. The Shining Shore.

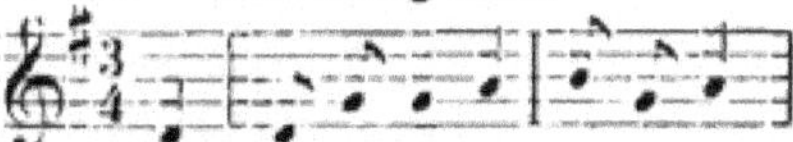

1 My days are gliding swiftly by,
And I a pilgrim stranger,
Would not detain them as they fly,—
Those hours of toil and danger.

Cho.—For now we stand on Jordan's strand,
Our friends are passing over;
And, just before, the shining shore
We may almost discover.

2 Our absent King the watchword gave,
"Let every lamp be burning;"
We look afar, across the wave,
Our distant home discerning.

3 Should coming days be dark and cold,
We will not yield to sorrow,
For hope will sing, with courage bold,
"There's glory on the morrow."

No. 118. Sweet Hour of Prayer.

1

Sweet hour of prayer, sweet hour of prayer,
That calls me from a world of care,
And bids me at my Father's throne
Make all my wants and wishes known!
In seasons of distress and grief
My soul has often found relief,
And oft escaped the tempter's snare
By thy return, sweet hour of prayer.

2

Sweet hour of prayer, sweet hour of pray'r,
Thy wings shall my petition bear
To him, whose truth and faithfulness
Engage the waiting soul to bless:
And since he bids me seek his face,
Believe his word, and trust his grace,
I'll cast on him my every care,
And wait for thee, sweet hour of prayer.

No. 119. Fountain.

1 THERE is a fountain filled with blood
Drawn from Immanuel's veins;
And sinners, plunged beneath that flood,
Lose all their guilty stains.

2 The dying thief rejoiced to see
That fountain in his day;
And there may I, though vile as he,
Wash all my sins away.

3 Thou dying Lamb! thy precious blood
Shall never lose its power,
Till all the ransomed Church of God
Are saved to sin no more.

4 E'er since, by faith, I saw the stream
Thy flowing wounds supply,
Redeeming love has been my theme,
And shall be till I die.

No. 120. Dennis.

1 How gentle God's commands!
How kind His precepts are!
Come, cast your burdens on the Lord,
And trust his constant care.

2 Beneath his watchful eye
His saints securely dwell;
That hand which bears all nature up
Shall guard his children well.

3 Why should this anxious load
Press down your weary mind?
Haste to your heavenly Father's throne,
And sweet refreshment find.

4 His goodness stands approved,
Unchanged from day to day:
I'll drop my burden at his feet,
And bear a song away.

No. 121. For Victorious Faith

1 O FOR a faith that will not shrink,
Though pressed by every foe,
That will not tremble on the brink
Of any earthly woe!

2 That will not murmur nor complain
Beneath the chastening rod,
But, in the hour of grief or pain,
Will lean upon its God.

3 A faith that keeps the narrow way
Till life's last hour is fled,
And with a pure and heavenly ray
Illumes a dying bed.

4 Lord, give us such a faith as this,
And then, whatever may come,
We'll taste, e'en here, the hallowed bliss
Of an eternal home.

No. 122. Title Clear.

1 WHEN I can read my title clear
To mansions in the skies,
I'll bid farewell to every fear,
And wipe my weeping eyes.

Cho.—We will stand the storm,
We will anchor by and by.

2 Should earth against my soul engage,
And fiery darts be hurled,
Then I can smile at Satan's rage,
And face a frowning world.

3 Let cares like a wild deluge come,
Let storms of sorrow fall,
So I but safely reach my home,
My God, my heaven, my all.

4 There I shall bathe my weary soul
In seas of heavenly rest,
And not a wave of trouble roll
Across my peaceful breast.

No. 123. I am Saved.

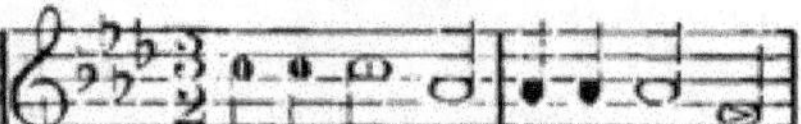

1 I AM saved! the Lord hath saved me,
Help me shout the glorious news!
I have tasted God's salvation,
And 'tis sweet as honeyed dews.

Cho.—Glory, glory, hallelujah,
I rejoice salvation came;
Glory, glory, hallelujah,
I am saved in Jesus' name.

2 Loud I sing my exultation,
Hoping it will reach the skies,
Keep, dear Lord, my soul forever
Under thy protecting eyes.

3 Free salvation! glad salvation!
Let us shout from pole to pole,
Until each diseased nation
Feels that God hath made it whole.

4 When at last the days are gathered
Into thy great judgment one,
May I find my name deep written
In the records of thy Son.

No. 124. Heaven is My Home.

1 I'm but a stranger here,—
Heaven is my home;
Earth is a desert drear,—
Heaven is my home:
Danger and sorrow stand
Round me on every hand;
Heaven is my fatherland,—
Heaven is my home.

2 What though the tempest rage?
Heaven is my home;
Short is my pilgrimage,
Heaven is my home:
Time's cold and wintry blast
Soon will be over-past,
I shall reach home at last,—
Heaven is my home.

3 There at my Savior's side,—
Heaven is my home;
I shall be glorified,—
Heaven is my home:
There are the good and blest,
Those I love most and best,
There, too, I soon shall rest,
Heaven is my home!

No. 125. I Hear Thy Welcome Voice.

1 I hear thy welcome voice,
That calls me, Lord, to thee,
For cleansing in thy precious blood,
That flowed on Calvary.

Cho.—I am coming, Lord,
Coming now to thee!
Wash me, cleanse me in the blood
That flowed on Calvary.

2 Though coming weak and vile,
Thou dost my strength assure;
Thou dost my vileness fully cleanse,
Till spotless all and pure.

3 'Tis Jesus calls me on
To perfect faith and love,
To perfect hope, and peace, and trust,
For earth and heaven above.

4 All hail, atoning blood!
All hail, redeeming grace!
All hail, the gift of Christ our Lord,
Our Strength and Righteousness!

No. 126. We Shall Walk Through the Valley.

Cho.—We shall walk thro' the valley and the shadow of death,
We shall walk thro' the valley in peace;
If Jesus himself shall be our leader,
We shall walk thro' the valley in peace.

1 We shall meet those Christians there,
We shall meet those Christians there;
If Jesus himself shall be our leader,
We shall walk thro' the valley in peace.

2 We shall wear a crown of life,
We shall wear a crown of life;
If Jesus himself shall be our leader,
We shall walk thro' the valley in peace.

3 There will be no sorrow there,
There will be no sorrow there;
If Jesus himself shall be our leader,
We shall walk thro' the valley in peace.

No. 127. GLORIA PATRI.

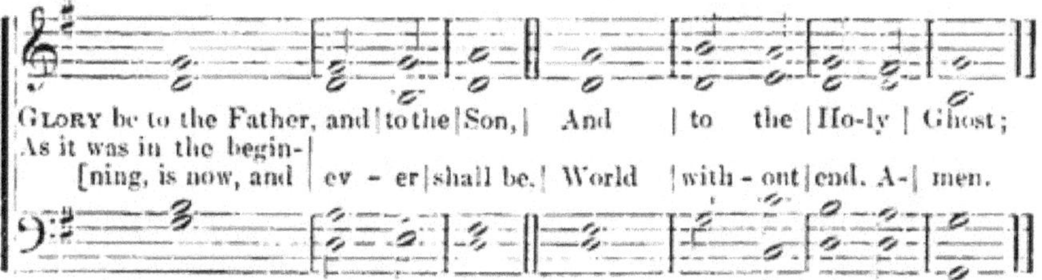
GLORY be to the Father, and | to the | Son, | And | to the | Ho-ly | Ghost;
As it was in the begin- | ning, is now, and | ev - er | shall be, | World | with - out | end. A- | men.

No. 128. Depth of Mercy.

1 DEPTH of mercy! can there be
Mercy still reserved for me?
Can my God his wrath forbear?
Me, the chief of sinners, spare?

Cho.—God is love! I know, I feel;
Jesus lives, and loves me still;
Jesus lives,
He lives and loves me still.

2 I have long withstood his grace,
Long provoked him to his face:
Would not hearken to his calls;
Grieved him by a thousand falls.

3 Now incline me to repent;
Let me now my sins lament;
Now my foul revolt deplore,
Weep, believe, and sin no more.

No. 129. Walk in the Light.

1 CHILDREN of the heavenly King,
In the light, in the light,
As we journey, sweetly sing,
In the light of God;
Sing our Saviour's worthy praise,
In the light, in the light,
Glorious in his works and ways,
In the light of God.

Cho.—Let us walk in the light,
In the light, in the light,
Let us walk in the light,
In the light of God.

2 We are trav'ling home to God,
In the light, in the light,
In the way our fathers trod,
In the light of God;
They are happy now, and we,
In the light, in the light,
Soon their happiness shall see,
In the light of God.

No. 130. Jesus is Mine.

1 FADE, fade, each earthly joy, Jesus is mine!
Break, every tender tie, Jesus is mine!
Dark is the wilderness,
Earth has no resting place,
Jesus alone can bless, Jesus is mine!

2 Farewell, ye dreams of night, Jesus is mine!
Lost in this dawning light, Jesus is mine!
All that my soul has tried,
Left but a dismal void,
Jesus has satisfied, Jesus is mine!

3 Farewell, mortality Jesus is mine!
Welcome, eternity, Jesus is mine!
Welcome, O loved and blest,
Welcome, sweet scenes of rest,
Welcome, my Saviour's breast, Jesus is mine!

No. 131. JESUS, LOVER OF MY SOUL.

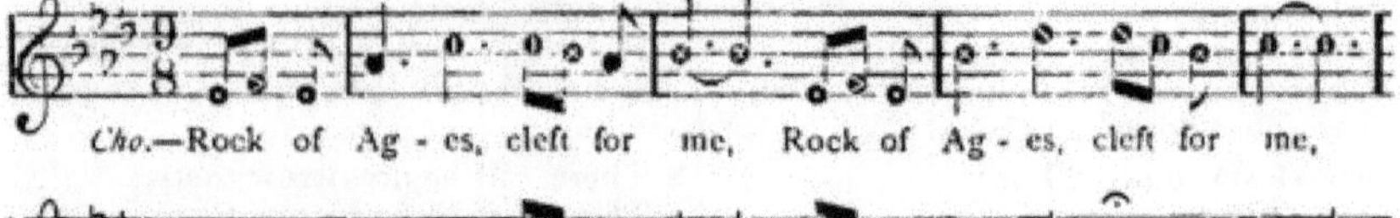
Cho.—Rock of Ag - es, cleft for me, Rock of Ag - es, cleft for me,

Rock of Ag - es, cleft for me, Let me hide my- self in thee.

1 JESUS, lover of my soul,
Let me to thy bosom fly,
While the nearer waters roll,
While the tempest still is high;
Hide me, oh, my Saviour, hide,
Till the storm of life is past;
Safe into the haven guide,
Oh, receive my soul at last.

2 Other refuge have I none,
Hangs my helpless soul on thee:
Leave, oh, leave me not alone,
Still support and comfort me.
All my trust on thee is stayed,
All my help from thee I bring;
Cover my defenceless head
With the shadow of thy wing.

3 Thou, O Christ, art all I want;
More than all in thee I find:
Raise the fallen, cheer the faint,
Heal the sick and lead the blind.
Just and holy is thy name,
I am all unrighteousness;
Vile and full of sin I am,
Thou art full of truth and grace.

No. 132. THE ROAD TO HEAVEN.

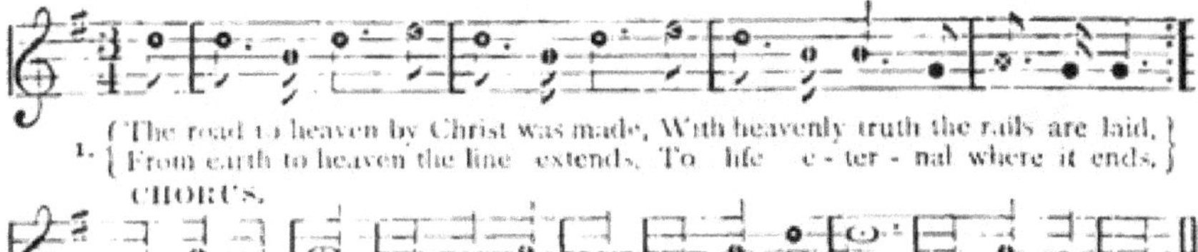

1. { The road to heaven by Christ was made, With heavenly truth the rails are laid, }
{ From earth to heaven the line extends, To life e - ter - nal where it ends. }

CHORUS.

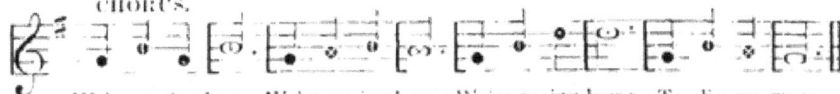

We're go - ing home, We're go - ing home, We're go - ing home To die no more.

2 Repentance is the station, then,
Where passengers are taken in;
No fee for them is there to pay,
For Jesus is himself the way.

3 The Bible is the engineer—
It points the way to heaven so clear,
Through tunnels dark and dreary here—
It does the way to glory steer.

4 God's love the fire, his truth the steam
Which drives the engine and the train;
All you who would to glory ride,
Must come to Christ—in him abide.

5 Come, then, poor sinner, now is the time
At any station on the line;
If you repent and turn from sin,
The train will stop and take you in.

No. 133. I'M GLAD SALVATION'S FREE.

Cho.—I'm glad sal - va - tion's free, I'm glad sal - va - tion's free;
Sal - va - tion's free for you and me, I'm glad sal - va - tion's free.

1 I'm glad salvation's free,
And without price or cost,
For had it been for me to buy,
My soul must have been lost.

2 In this cold world below,
With none to care for me,
A pilgrim lone, without a home—
I'm glad salvation's free.

3 Once I was blind and lost,
Of sin and sorrow full;
But now I'm saved thro' Jesus' blood,
I feel it in my soul.

4 And now I'm on the way
To brighter world's above;
I hope to triumph evermore
Through the Redeemer's love.

No. 134. AT THE FOUNTAIN.

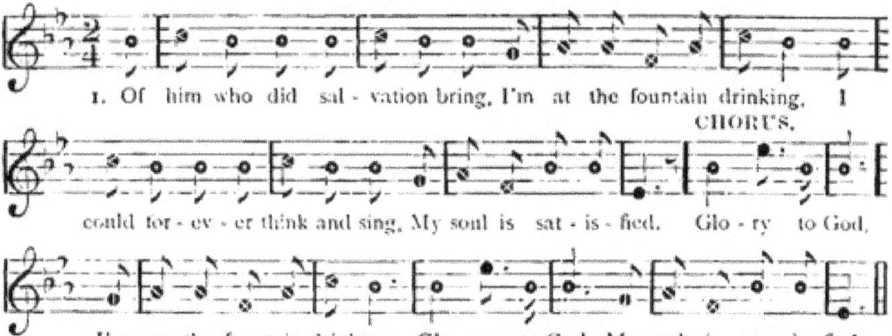
1. Of him who did sal - vation bring, I'm at the fountain drinking. I
CHORUS.
could for - ev - er think and sing, My soul is sat - is - fied. Glo - ry to God,
I'm at the fountain drinking, Glo - ry to God, My soul is sat - is - fied.

2 Lo! glad I come; and thou, blest Lamb,
Shalt take me to thee as I am:
Nothing but sin have I to give,—
Nothing but love shall I receive.

3 Then will I tell to sinners round,
What a dear Saviour I have found;
I'll point to thy redeeming blood,
And say, Behold the way to God.

No. 135. Opening Service, No. 1.

FOR

SUNDAY-SCHOOLS AND DIVINE WORSHIP.

Leader.—Make a joyful noise unto God, all ye lands: Sing forth the honor of his name.

ALL SING: DUANE STREET, L.M., D.

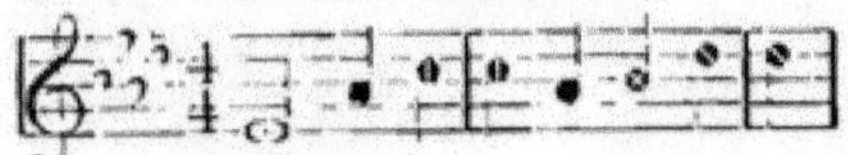

PRAISE God, from whom all blessings flow;
Praise him, all creatures here below;
Praise him above, ye heavenly host;
Praise Father, Son, and Holy Ghost.

L.—O give thanks unto the Lord, for he is good:

Congregation.—For his mercy endureth forever.

L.—To him who alone doeth great wonders:

C.—For his mercy endureth forever.

L.—Who remembered us in our low estate:

C.—For his mercy endureth forever.

L.—And hath redeemed us from our enemies:

C.—For his mercy endureth forever

ALL SING: FOUNTAIN, C.M.

E'ER since, by faith, I saw the stream,
Thy flowing wounds supply.
Redeeming love has been my theme,
And shall be till I die.

L.—I will lift up mine eyes unto the hills, from whence cometh my help.

C.—My help cometh from the Lord, which made heaven and earth.

L.—Bless the Lord, O my soul: and all that is within me, bless his holy name.

C.—Bless the Lord, O my soul, and forget not all his benefits.

ALL SING: CORONATION, C.M.

LET every kindred, every tribe,
On this terrestrial ball,
To him all majesty ascribe,
And crown him Lord of all.

L.—For his mercy endureth forever.

ALL SING: GLORIA.

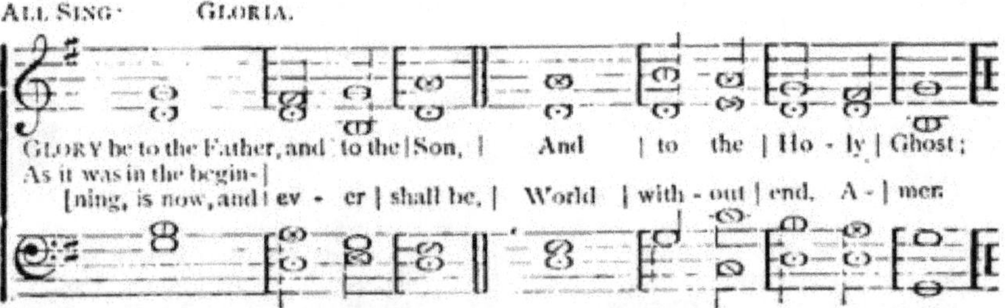
GLORY be to the Father, and to the | Son, | And | to the | Ho - ly | Ghost;
As it was in the begin- |
[ning, is now, and | ev - er | shall be, | World | with - out | end. A - | men.

No. 136. Opening Service, No. 2.

Leader.—O Lord my God, I cried unto thee, and thou hast heard me.

Congregation.—Unto thee, O Lord, do I lift up my soul.

ALL SING: BETHANY.

NEARER, my God, to thee,
Nearer to thee;
E'en though it be a cross
That raiseth me,
Still all my song shall be,
Nearer, my God, to thee,
Nearer to thee.

L.—Hear my cry, O God: attend unto my prayer.

C.—From the ends of the earth will I cry unto thee: Lead me to the Rock that is higher than I.

ALL SING: TOPLADY.

ROCK of Ages, cleft for me,
Let me hide myself in thee;
Let the water and the blood,
From thy wounded side which flowed,
Be of sin the double cure,
Save from wrath and make me pure.

L.—For thou hast been a shelter for me, and a strong tower from the enemy.

C.—Evening, and morning, and at noon, will I pray, and cry aloud: and he shall hear my voice.

ALL SING: WHAT A FRIEND.

WHAT a friend we have in Jesus,
All our sins and griefs to bear!
What a privilege to carry
Everything to God in prayer!
Oh, what peace we often forfeit,
O what needless pain we bear,
All because we do not carry
Everything to God in prayer!

L.—Casting all your care upon him, for he careth for you.

C.—How precious also are thy thoughts unto me, O God. How great is the sum of them.

L.—If I should count them, they are more in number than the sand: when I awake I am still with thee.

All.—Hear my prayer, O Lord: give ear to my supplications.

ALL SING: THE LORD'S PRAYER.

Our Father, etc.
A - men.

OUR Father which art in heaven,
Hallowed be thy name.
Thy kingdom come.
Thy will be done in earth as it is in heaven.
Give us this day our daily bread.
And forgive us our debts, as we forgive our debtors.
And lead us not into temptation, but deliver us from evil.
For thine is the kingdom, and the power, and the glory, for ever. Amen.

No. 137. Praise Service.

BY E. O. EXCELL

Congregation standing sing.

ALL HAIL THE POWER. See No. 228.

1 All hail the power of Jesus' name!
Let angels prostrate fall;
Bring forth the royal diadem,
And crown him Lord of all.

2 Let every kindred, every tribe,
On this terrestial ball,
To him all majesty ascribe,
And crown him Lord of all.

3 Oh, that with yonder sacred throng
We at his feet may fall;
We'll join the everlasting song,
And crown him Lord of all.

PRAYER.

Congregation seated.

Leader.—I will extol thee, my God, O King; and I will bless thy name for ever and ever.

Congregation.—Every day will I bless thee; and I will praise thy name for ever and ever.

L.—Great is the Lord, and greatly to be praised; and his greatness is unsearchable.

C.—One generation shall praise thy works to another, and shall declare thy mighty acts.

L.—I will speak of the glorious honour of thy majesty, and of thy wondrous works.

C.—And men shall speak of the might of thy terrible acts: and I will declare thy greatness.

L.—They shall abundantly utter the memory of thy great goodness, and shall sing of thy righteousness.

LOVING-KINDNESS. See No. 139.

1 Awake, my soul, in joyful lays,
And sing thy great Redeemer's praise;
He justly claims a song from thee,
His loving-kindness, oh, how free!
Loving-kindness, loving-kindness,
His loving-kindness, oh, how free!

2 He saw me ruined in the fall,
Yet loved me notwithstanding all;
He saved me from my lost estate,
His loving-kindness, oh, how great!
Loving-kindness, loving-kindness,
His loving-kindness, oh, how great!

3 Tho' num'rous hosts of mighty foes,
Tho' earth and hell my way oppose,
He safely leads my soul along,
His loving-kindness, oh, how strong!
Loving-kindness, loving-kindness,
His loving-kindness, oh, how strong!

C.—The Lord is gracious, and full of compassion; slow to anger, and of great mercy.

L.—The Lord is good to all: and his tender mercies are over all his works.

C.—All thy works shall praise thee, O Lord; and thy saints shall bless thee.

L.—They shall speak of the glory of thy kingdom, and talk of thy power;

Praise Service.—Concluded.

C.—To make known to the sons of men his mighty acts, and the glorious majesty of his kingdom.

L.—Thy kingdom is an everlasting kingdom, and thy dominion endureth throughout all generations.

C.—The Lord upholdeth all that fall, and raiseth up all those that be bowed down.

ROCK OF AGES. See No. 255.

1 Rock of ages, cleft for me,
Let me hide myself in thee;
Let the water and the blood,
From thy wounded side which flowed,
Be of sin the double cure,
Save from wrath and make me pure.

2 Could my tears forever flow,
Could my zeal no languor know,
These for sin could not atone;
Thou must save, and thou alone:
In my hand no price I bring;
Simply to thy cross I cling.

3 While I draw this fleeting breath,
When my eyes shall close in death,
When I rise to worlds unknown,
And behold thee on thy throne,
Rock of ages, cleft for me,
Let me hide myself in thee.

L.—The eyes of all wait upon thee: and thou givest them their meat in due season.

C.—Thou openest thy hand, and satisfiest the desire of every living thing.

L.—The Lord is righteous in all his ways, and holy in all his works.

C.—The Lord is nigh unto all them that call upon him, to all that call upon him in truth.

L.—He will fulfil the desire of them that fear him: he also will hear their cry, and will save them.

C.—The Lord preserveth all them that love him: but all the wicked will he destroy.

L.—My mouth shall speak the praise of the Lord: and let all flesh bless his holy name for ever and ever. Psalm cxlv.

Congregation standing.

OH, COULD I SPEAK. See No. 262.

1 Oh, could I speak the matchless worth,
Oh, could I sound the glories forth
Which in my Saviour shine.
I'd soar and touch the heavenly strings,
And vie with Gabriel while he sings,
In notes almost divine.

2 I'd sing the precious blood he spilt,
My ransom from the dreadful guilt,
Of sin and wrath divine!
I'd sing his glorious righteousness,
In which all perfect heavenly dress
My soul shall ever shine.

3 Well—the delightful day will come,
When my dear Lord will bring me home,
And I shall see his face:
Then with my Saviour, Brother, Friend,
A blest eternity I'll spend,
Triumphant in his grace.

PRAYER.

L.—Now unto him that is able to do exceeding abundantly above all that we ask or think, according to the power that worketh in us,

C.—Unto him be glory in the church by Christ Jesus throughout all ages, world without end. Amen. Eph. iii. 20, 21.

No. 138. Concert Reading, No. 1.

PSA. 23.

All read.—1. The Lord is my shepherd; I shall not want.

2. He maketh me to lie down in green pastures: he leadeth me beside the still waters

3. He restoreth my soul: he leadeth me in paths of righteousness for his name's. sake.

4. Yea, though I walk through the valley of the shadow of death, I will fear no evil: for thou art with me; thy rod and thy staff they comfort me.

5. Thou preparest a table before me in the presence of mine enemies: thou anointest my head with oil; my cup runneth over.

6. Surely goodness and mercy shall follow me all the days of my life; and I will dwell in the house of the Lord forever.

All Sing. ST. THOMAS.

1. The Lord my Shepherd is,
   I shall be well supplied;
   Since he is mine, and I am his,
   What can I want beside?

2. In spite of all my foes,
   Thou dost my table spread,
   My cup with blessings overflows,
   And joy exalts my head.

3. The bounties of thy love
   Shall crown my future days,
   Nor from thy house will I remove,
   Nor cease to speak thy praise.

No. 139. Concert Reading, No. 2.

PSA. 122.

All read.—1. I was glad when they said unto me, let us go into the house of the Lord.

2. Our feet shall stand within thy gates, O Jerusalem.

3. Jerusalem is builded as a city that is compact together:

4. Whither the tribes go up, the tribes of the Lord, unto the testimony of Israel, to give thanks unto the name of the Lord.

5. For there are set thrones of judgment, the thrones of the house of David.

6. Pray for the peace of Jerusalem: they shall prosper that love thee.

7. Peace be within thy walls, and prosperity within thy palaces.

8. For my breathren and companion's sakes, I will now say, peace be within thee.

9. Because of the house of the Lord our God I will seek thy good.

All Sing. DENNIS.

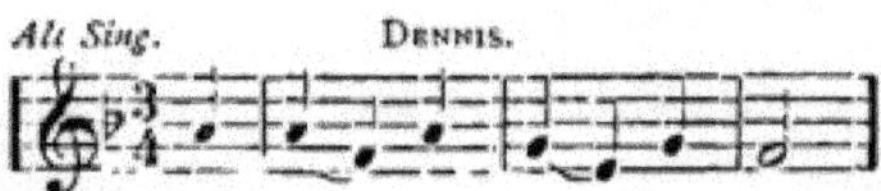

1. I love thy kingdom, Lord—
   The house of thine abode,
   The church our blest Redeemer saved
   With his own precious blood.

2. I love thy church, O God!
   Her walls before thee stand,
   Dear as the apple of thine eye,
   And graven on thy hand.

3. For her my tears shall fall,
   For, her my prayers ascend;
   To her my cares and toils be given,
   Till toils and cares shall end.

4. Beyond my highest joy
   I prize her heavenly ways,
   Her sweet communion, solemn vows,
   Her hymns of love and praise.

ECHOES OF EDEN.

No. 140. Loving Kindness.

MEDLEY.
Western Air.
1. A-wake, my soul, in joy - ful lays, And sing thy great Redeemer's praise;
2. He saw me ru - ined in the fall, Yet loved me not withstanding all;
3. Tho' num'rous hosts of might-y foes, Tho' earth and hell my way oppose,
4. When troub-le, like a gloomy cloud, Has gather'd thick, and thunder'd loud,
He just-ly claims a song from me, His loving kindness, oh, how free!
He saved me from my lost es - tate, His loving kindness; oh how great!
He safe-ly leads my soul a - long, His loving kindness, oh, how strong!
He near my soul has al-ways stood, His loving kindness, oh, how good!
Lov - ing kind-ness, lov-ing kindness, His lov - ing kindness, oh, how free!
Lov - ing kind-ness, lov-ing kindness, His lov - ing kindness, oh, how great!
Lov - ing kind-ness, lov-ing kindness, His lov - ing kindness, oh, how strong!
Lov - ing kind-ness, lov-ing kindness, His lov - ing kindness, oh, how good!

No. 141. Call Them In.

E. O. E. — E. O. Excell

1. Hear the Sav - ior sweet-ly say-ing, Call them in, make no de - lay;
2. Hear him say, let no one lin - ger, Call them in from out the cold,
3. Call them in, I can - not leave them, Call them in, I can not go;

Call them in, say *all* are wel-come, Bid them come to me to - day.
Call them in, the lit - tle chil-dren, Bid them come with-in the fold.
Oh, make haste, for souls are dy - ing, Snatch them from the brink of woe.

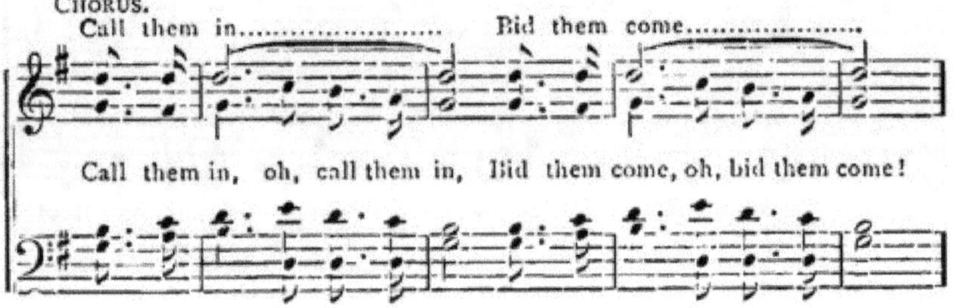

CHORUS.
Call them in........................ Bid them come......................
Call them in, oh, call them in, Bid them come, oh, bid them come!

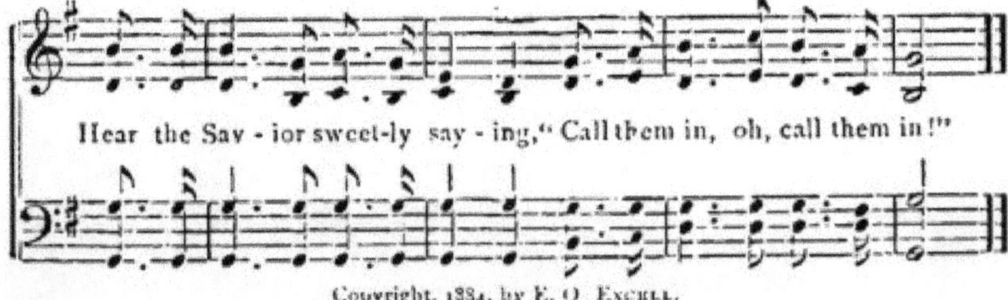

Hear the Sav - ior sweet-ly say - ing, "Call them in, oh, call them in!"

No. 142. Over on the Hills of Glory.

J. E. M. — J. E. Morse.

1. Look, ye saints, and see the light, Over on the hills of glo - ry,
2. We shall meet on that bright shore, O-ver on the hills of glo - ry,
3. We shall see our Sav - ior there, O-ver on the hills of glo - ry,
4. Oh, the rest will be so sweet, O-ver on the hills of glo - ry,

Lo the dawn is break-ing bright, O-ver on the hills of glo - ry.
Meet with loved ones gone be-fore, O-ver on the hills of glo - ry.
And a crown of life shall wear, O-ver on the hills of glo - ry.
When our jour-ney is com-plete, O-ver on the hills of glo - ry.

Chorus.

Tho' the feet have wea - ry grown, In the des - ert - path rock-strown,
We shall walk no more a - lone, O-ver on the hills of glo - ry.

No. 143. Rock of Ages.

(Dedicated to Trinity Choir, Oil City, Pa.)

Soprano prominent. E. O. Excell.

1. Rock of A - - ges, cleft for me,
2. Could my tears for - ev - er flow,
3. While I draw this fleet - ing breath,
1. Rock of A - ges cleft for me, Blest Rock of A - ges cleft for me,
2. Could my tears for - ev-er flow, Oh! Could my tears for - ev - er flow,
3. While I draw this fleeting breath, Yes, While I draw this fleet-ing breath,
Let me hide my - self in thee;
Could my zeal no lan - guor know.
When mine eyes shall close in death,
Let me hide my - self in thee, Oh! Let me hide my - self in thee!
Could my zeal no lan-guor know, Oh! Could my zeal no lan-guor know,
When my eyes shall close in death, Yes, When my eyes shall close in death,
Let the wa - ter and the blood,
These for sin could not a - tone;
When I rise to worlds un - known,
Let the wa - ter and the blood, Oh! Let the wa - ter and the blood,
These for sin could not a - tone, No, These for sin could not a - tone,
When I rise to worlds unknown, Yes, When I rise to worlds un-known,

Rock of Ages.—Concluded.

From thy wound - ed side which flow'd,
Thou must save and thou a - lone;
And be - hold thee on thy throne;
From thy wounded side which flow'd, Yes, From thy wounded side which flow'd,
Thou must save and thou a - lone, Yes, Thou must save and thou a-lone,
And be - hold thee on thy throne, Yes, And be - hold thee on thy throne,

Be of sin the dou - ble cure,
In my hand no price I bring;
Rock of A - ges cleft for me,
rit.
Be of sin the dou-ble cure, Yes, Be of sin the dou-ble cure,
In my hand no price I bring, Lord, In my hand no price I bring,
Rock of A - ges cleft for me, Blest, Rock of A - ges cleft for me,

Save from wrath and make me pure.
Sim - ply to thy cross I cling.
Let me hide my - self in thee.
Repeat pp
Save from wrath and make me pure, Yes, Save from wrath and make me pure.
Sim-ply to thy cross I cling, Lord, Sim-ply to thy cross I cling.
Let me hide my - self in thee, Oh, Let me hide my - self in thee.

No. 144. Father, Lead Me.

F. A Evans. Chas. Edw. Pollock.

1. Fa-ther, lead me, gent-ly lead me, Keep me ev - er near to thee;
2. Lord of mercy, strengthen weakness, Cheer the heart bow'd down with care;
3. Fa-ther, when the clouds grow hea-vy, Hov'ring thick up - on the way;
Friends I love may oft deceive me, Thou shalt still my com-fort be,
Make my life a life of meekness, Make my soul a soul of pray'r,
Oh, do Thou in love be-friend me, All my night will then a - way,
Oh, do Thou in love be-friend me, Let thine arms around me twine;
Dark-er days may yet be - tide me; Cheerless hours may yet sur-round;
Fa-ther, lead me, gent-ly lead me; Keep me ev - er near to Thee;
Grace and faith, O Fa-ther, lend me, Let thy light a - round me shine.
Tho' world's rich-es are de-nied me, Yet in Thee I will a - bound.
Tho' my ways may oft times grieve Thee, Fa-ther bless me e - ven me.

No. 145. Jesus Christ is Passing By.
J. E. H.
Acts. ix. 34.
J. E. Hall.
1 "In the name of Christ my Sav-ior, Now to thee, a - rise, I say,"
2. Je - sus Christ to - day is pass-ing; Hail him, sick and dy-ing soul,
3. Stay no long - er in thy sinning, Haste thee, while there yet is room,
And the pal-sied man tho' dy - ing, Ris - es up and goes his way.
Life and health He's free - ly giv - ing, Ask, and you shall be made whole.
Seek the lov - ing Lord of mer - cy, Find at last, a wel-come home.
Chorus.
Ask in faith O, ask for mer - cy, Lost one He will hear thy cry,
Ask for par-don, pleading earn-est, Je - sus Christ is pass-ing by.

No. 146. Awakening Hymn.

"It is high time to awake out of sleep." PHILIP PHILLIPS, by per.

1. Let the na - tions a-wake to the signs, of the times, A
2. Let the Chris-tian a-wake to the signs of the times, For
3 Let the young men a-wake to the signs of the times, God
4. Care-less sin - ner, a-wake to the signs of the times, Give

voice that is might-y and strong, Like the thun - der of wa - ters, pro-
long at the post some have slept; A - rise, for the Mas - ter may
calls you, because ye are strong; You can work in the vine-yard with
Je - sus your heart while you may; Oh, be wash'd in His blood-He will

claims to the world, Je - ho - vah is march - ing a - long.
sud - den - ly come, And frown at the watch you have kept.
ar - dor and zeal, For Him who is march - ing a - long.
make you his child, And take your trans-gress-ions a - way

CHORUS.

Then wake, let us stand with our face to the right, And tread 'neath our feet ev'ry wrong;

The kingdoms of darkness are trembling with fear, Jehovah is marching along

No. 147. Bringing in the Sheaves.

"The harvest is the end of the world"—Matt. xiii. 39.

Words from "Songs of Glory." Geo. A. Minor, by per.

1. Sow-ing in the morn ing, sowing seeds of kindness, Sowing in the noon-tide,
2. Sow-ing in the sunshine, sow-ing in the shadows, Fearing neither clouds nor
3. Go, then, ev-er weeping, sowing for the Mas-ter, Tho' the loss sustain'd our
and the dew - y eves; Wait-ing for the har-vest, and the time of reaping,
win-ter's chilling breeze; By and by the har-vest, and the la - bor end-ed,
spir - it of-ten grieves; When our weeping's o-ver, He will bid us welcome,
We shall come re-joic-ing, bring-ing in the sheaves.
CHORUS.
Bring-ing in the sheaves, bringing in the sheaves.
We shall come re-joic- ing, bring-ing in the sheaves,
Omit second time.
-ing, bring-ing in the sheaves.
1
2

No. 148. NOW BE THE GOSPEL BANNER.

1. Now be the gospel banner,
In every land unfurled:
And be the shout, Hosanna!
Re-echoed through the world:
Till every isle and nation,
Till every tribe and tongue
Receive the great salvation,
And join the happy throng.

2. What though the battled legions,
Of earth and hell combine?
His arm throughout their regions,
Shall soon resplendent shine;
Ride on, O Lord, victorious:
Immanuel, Price of Peace.
Thy triumph shall be glorious;
Thy empire shall increase.

No. 149. I'm Coming Back To-Night.

"Him that cometh unto me I will in no wise cast out."
Emma Pitt.
H. A. Lewis.
Duet.
1. I'm com-ing back to Je - sus, Guilt-y and full of sin, I've wan-der'd so far from His mer - cy, Still He will take me in.
2. I'm com-ing back to Je - sus, Back to the arms of love, I'll come and all bro-ken with sor - row, His sweet for-give-ness prove.
3. I'm com-ing back to Je - sus, Leav-ing all else be - hind, Fare-well to the sins that be-guile me, Now I shall par-don find.
Refrain.
I'm com-ing back to Je - sus, Back to the truth and right, I know it will cost me a strug - gle, But I'm com - ing back to-night; I'm com-ing back to Je - sus, I'm com-ing back to - night.
cres.
Repeat. pp

No. 150. A Little Talk with Jesus.

Chas. Edw. Pollock.

1. A lit - tle talk with Je - sus, How it smooths the rug - ged road,
2. I tell Him I am wea - ry, And I fain would be at rest,
3. Ah, this is what I'm want - ing, His love - ly face to see,
4. So I'll wait a lit - tle long - er, Till His ap - point - ed time,
How it seems to help me on - ward, When I faint be - neath my load.
That I'm dai - ly, hour - ly long - ing, For a home a - mong the blest,
And I'm not a - fraid to say it, For I know He's want - ing me,
And glo - ry in the knowl - edge, That such a hope is mine,
When my heart is crushed with sor - row, And my eyes with tears are dim,
And He an - swers me so sweet - ly, In tones of ten - d'rest love—
He gave His life a ran - som, To make me all His own,
Then in my Fa - ther's dwell - ing, Where "ma - ny man - sions" be,
There is naught can yield me com - fort, Like a lit - tle talk with Him.
"I am com - ing soon to take thee, To my hap - py home a - bove."
And will not for - get His prom - ise, To me His pur - chased one.
I'll sweet - ly talk with Je - sus, And He will talk with me.

No. 151. Onward, Christian Soldiers.

Rev Sabine Baring Gould.
Jos. Haydn.
1. On-ward, Christian Sol - diers, Marching as to war, With the Cross of
2. Like a might-y ar - my Moves the Church of God; Brothers, we are
3. Crowns and thrones may perish, Kingdoms rise and wane, But the Church of
4. On-ward, then, ye peo - ple, Join our hap - py throng; Blend with ours your
Je - sus Go-ing on be-fore; Christ, the Royal Mas - ter, Leads a-gainst the
treading Where the saints have trod; We are not di - vi - ded, All one bod-y
Je - sus Constant will re-main; Gates of hell can nev-er 'Gainst that Church pre-
voic - es In the tri-umph song, Glo-ry, laud, and hon - or Un-to Christ the
Chorus.
foe, Forward in- to bat - tle, See, His banners go. Onward, Christian
we; One in hope and doc - trine, One in char-i - ty. Onward, etc.
vail; We have Christ's own promise, And that cannot fail. Onward, etc.
King! This thro' countless a - ges Men and angels sing. Onward, etc.
sol - diers, Marching as to war, With the Cross of Je-sus, Go-ing on be-fore.

No. 152. My Jesus, I Love Thee.
Unknown.
To J. S. Meyer.
E. O. Excell.
1. My Je - sus, I love Thee, I know thou art
2. I love Thee be - cause Thou Hast first lov - ed
3. I will love Thee in life, I'll love Thee in
4. In man-sions of glo - ry And end - less de-
mine, For Thee all the fol - lies Of sin I re-
me, And pur-chas'd my par - don On Cal - va - ry's
death, And praise Thee as long as Thou lend - est me
light, I'll ev - er a - dore Thee, In heav - en so
sign; My gra-cious Re-deem - er, My Sav-ior art
tree; I love Thee for wear - ing The thorns on thy
breath; And say, when the death-dew Lies cold on my
bright; I'll sing, with the glit - ter ing Crown on my
Thou, If ev - er I lov'd Thee, My Je - sus, 'tis now.
brow, If ev - er I lov'd Thee, My Je - sus, 'tis now.
brow, If ev - er I lov'd Thee, My Je - sus, 'tis now.
brow, If ev - er I lov'd Thee. My Je - sus, 'tis now.

No. 153. In Heavenly Love Abiding.

He that abideth in me, and I in him, the same bringeth forth much fruit.—JOHN xv. 5.

A. L. WARING. MENDELSSOHN.

1. In heav'n-ly love a - bid - ing, No change my heart shall fear;
2. Wher-ev - er he may guide me, No want shall turn me back;
3. Green pastures are be - fore me, Which yet I have not seen;
And safe in such con - fid - ing, For noth - ing chang - es here,
My Shep-herd is be - side me, And noth - ing can I lack,
Bright skies will soon be o'er me, Where dark-est clouds have been,
The storm may roar with-out me, My heart may low be laid,
His wis - dom ev - er wak - eth, His sight is nev - er dim,
My hope I can-not meas - ure, My path to life is free,
But God is round a - bout me, And can I be dismayed?
He knows the way he tak - eth, And I will walk with him.
My Sav - ior has my treas-ure, And he will walk with me.

No. 154. Be Up and Doing.

Chas. H. Gabriel. Frank M. Davis. By per.

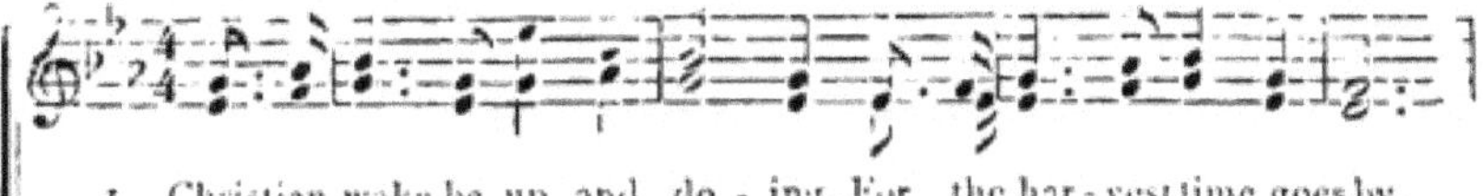

1. Christian, wake, be up and do - ing, For the har - vest time goes by,
2. Gath-er in the wea - ry wand'rers, To the ser - vice of the Lord,
3. When the last sheaf home is gathered, And the reap-ers' work is done,

See, the fields are white al - read - y, And the reap - ers loi - ter by.
Faint not, Christian, be not wea - ry, Work, and great your last re-ward.
Great will be their joy and glad - ness, Round the Master's snow white throne.

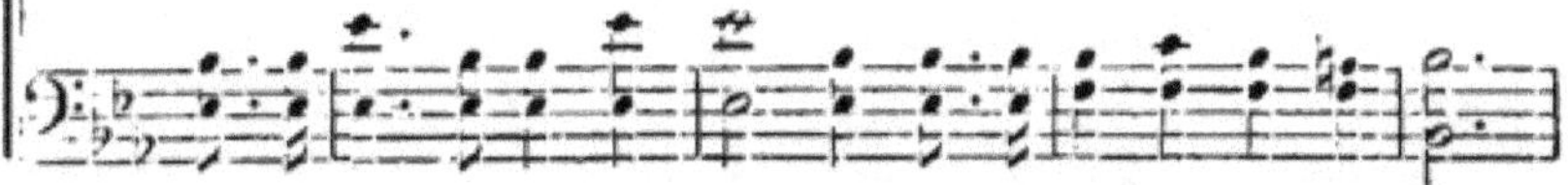

Chorus.

Go reap, go reap, The harvest of the Lord is great;
Go reap, go reap,

Go reap, go reap, No lon-ger i dle, stand and wait.
Go reap, go reap,

No. 155. The Beacon Light.

"A sure word of prophecy; where unto ye do well that ye take heed, as unto a light that shineth in a dark place." 2 Pet. i 19.

MRS. E. C. ELLSWORTH. H. A. LEWIS.

BASE SOLO.

1. Where art thou stee-ring broth-er, While sail-ing o'er life's sea? Be-fore thee are the break-ers, And dan-ger there may be.
2. Oh, man-y barks have strand-ed, Where quick-sands hidden lie! Then keep with-in the chan-nel, The Light be-fore thine eye.
4. For ves-sels large and no-ble, Up-on the rocks will break! And oft the strongest na-tures, Be-fore temp-ta-tions shake.

CHORUS.

The Light, The Light, my brother! It stands on yon-der height.

rit.

Christ marks the path of dan-ger, His word the Beacon Light

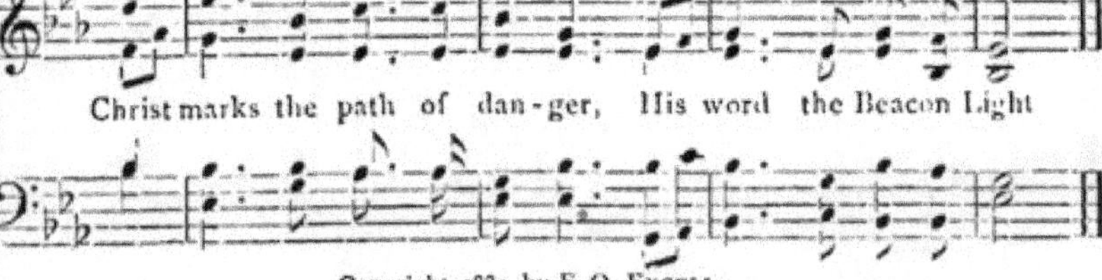

No. 156. My Faith Looks up to Thee.

Ray Palmer.
To W. B. Jacobs.
E. O. Excell.
1. My faith looks up to Thee, Thou Lamb of
2. May Thy rich grace im - part Strength to my
3. While life's dark maze I tread, And griefs a-
4. When ends life's tran - sient dream, When death's cold,
Cal - va - ry, Sav - ior di - vine! Now hear me
faint - ing heart; My zeal in - spire; As Thou hast
round me spread, Be thou my guide; Bid dark - ness
sul - len stream Shall o'er me roll, Blest Sav - ior!
while I pray, Take all my guilt a - way;
died for me, Oh, may my love to Thee
turn to day, Wipe sor - row's tears a - way,
then, in love, Fear and dis - trust re - move;
Oh, let me from this day Be whol - ly Thine.
Pure, warm, and change - less be— A liv - ing fire.
Nor let me ev - er stray From Thee a - side.
Oh, bear me safe a - bove— A ran - som'd soul!

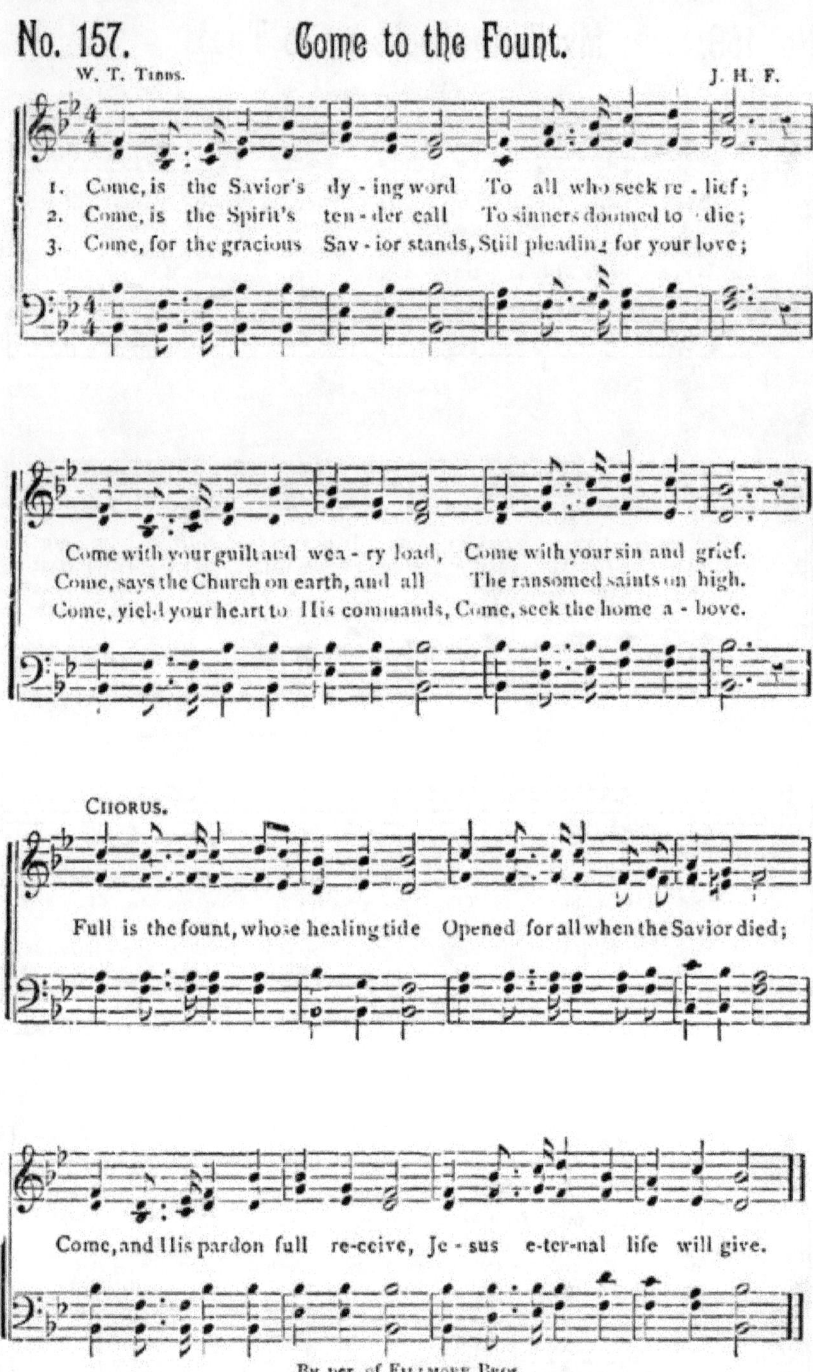
No. 157. Come to the Fount.
W. T. Tibbs.
J. H. F.
1. Come, is the Savior's dy - ing word To all who seek re - lief;
2. Come, is the Spirit's ten - der call To sinners doomed to die;
3. Come, for the gracious Sav - ior stands, Still pleading for your love;
Come with your guilt and wea - ry load, Come with your sin and grief.
Come, says the Church on earth, and all The ransomed saints on high.
Come, yield your heart to His commands, Come, seek the home a - bove.
Chorus.
Full is the fount, whose healing tide Opened for all when the Savior died;
Come, and His pardon full re-ceive, Je - sus e-ter-nal life will give.

By per. of Fillmore Bros.

No. 158. Oh, Tell it All Abroad.

"Neither is there Salvation in any other," — Acts. 4 : 12.

Mrs. E. C. Ellsworth.
H. A. Lewis.
1. We come to thee dear Sav - ior, Be-cause we need thee so,
2. We come to thee dear Sav - ior, Thy word is all our plea,
3. We come to thee dear Sav - ior, We oft have tried be - fore,
None hath a need that's great-er, None hath so far to go,
Since we are need-y help-less, None bids us come but thee,
But now we come more ful - ly, For now we love thee more,
Chorus.
Re - demp - - tion, sweet re - demp - tion! Oh
Re-demp-tion, sweet re-demp-tion! Re - demp-tion sweet, re-demp-tion! Oh
Pre - cious, pre-cious blood! Sal - va - tion, oh sal-
precious, precious blood! Oh precious, precious blood! Sal-va-tion, oh salvation! Sal-
va - - tion! Oh tell......... it all a-broad.
va-tion, oh sal-va-tion, Oh tell it, tell it all a-broad, all a-broad.
Copyright, 1884, by E. O. Excell.

No. 159. Go Tell Them.

Mrs E. C. Ellsworth.
H. A. Lewis.
1. Oh ye who fol - low Je - sus, While men in ru - in lie,
2. Oh ye who fol - low Je - sus, Shall soul's in dark - ness stray.
3. Oh ye who fol - low Je - sus, Just look on eith - er side,
Will no one haste and tell them, That Je - sus pass - eth by?
When dai - ly one is pass - ing, Who turns the night to day?
Shall an - y soul be beg - ging, And ev - er be de - nied?
Chorus.
Oh tell them, tell them quickly, Go bear the Savior's call;
There may be ma-ny wait-ing, Go quick - ly, tell them all.

No. 160. Fountain.

Cowper. To Charles Herald. E. O. Excell.

1. There is a foun-tain filled with blood, Drawn from Im-man-uel's veins;
2. The dy - ing thief re-joiced to see That foun-tain in his day;
3. Thou dy - ing Lamb! thy pre-cious blood Shall nev - er lose its pow'r,
4. E'er since by faith, I saw the stream Thy flow-ing wounds sup-ply,

And sin-ners, plunged be-neath that flood, Lose all their guil - ty stains.
And there may I, though vile as he, Wash all my sins a - way.
Till all the ransomed church of God, Are saved to sin no more.
Re - deem-ing love has been my theme, And shall be till I die.

Lose all their guil - ty stains, Lose all their guilt-y stains,
Wash all my sins a - way, Wash all my sins a - way,
Are saved to sin no more, Are saved to sin no more,
And shall be till I die, And shall be till I die,

And sin-ner's plunged beneath that flood, Lose all their guilt - y stains.
And there may I, though vile as he, Wash all my sins a - way.
Till all the ran-som'd church of God, Are saved to sin no more.
Re - deem - ing love has been my theme, And shall be till I die.

No. 161.
From Death Unto Life.
Alice Cary.
Wm. J. Kirkpatrick
1. Till I learned to love thy name, Lord, thy grace de - ny - ing,
2. Noth-ing could the world im - part, Dark - ness held no mor - row;
3. When I learned to love thy name, O thou meek and low - ly,
4. Henceforth shall cre - a - tion ring, With Sal - va - tion's sto - ry,
I was lost in sin and shame, Dy-ing, dy-ing, dy - ing!
In my soul and in my heart, Sor-row, sor-row, sor - row!
Rap - ture kind-led to a flame, Ho-ly, ho-ly, ho - ly!
Till I rise with thee to sing, Glo-ry, glo-ry, glo - ry!
This is now my con-stant theme, This my fav- 'rite sto - ry,
This is now my con-stant theme, This my fav- 'rite sto - ry,
Hal - le - lu - jah, grace is free, I will tell the sto - ry,
Hal - le - lu - jah, grace is free, I will tell the sto - ry,
Je - sus' blood a - vails for me, Glo-ry, glo-ry, glo - ry!
Je - sus' blood a - vails for me, Glo-ry, glo-ry, glo - ry!
Je - sus' blood hath made me free, Glo-ry, glo-ry, glo - ry!
Je - sus' blood hath made me free, Glo-ry, glo-ry, glo - ry!
By permission.

No. 162. Memories of Galilee.

"Jesus walked in Galilee "—John vii. 1.

Robert Morris, LL. D.
H. R. Palmer.
1. Each coo-ing dove......... and sigh-ing bough...... That makes the
2. Each flow-ery glen......... and moss - y dell........ Where hap-py
3. And when I read......... the thrill-ing lore........ Of him who
eve......... so blest to me,......... Has some thing far... ..... di-vi-ner
birds........ in song a - gree,........ Thro' sun-ny morn........ the praises
walked...... up-on the sea,......... I long, oh, how.........I long once
now,.......... It bears me back. .... to Gal - i - lee ....
tell.......... Of sights and sounds....... in Gal - i - lee............
more......... To fol - low him........... in Gal - i - lee............
Chorus.
O Gal - i-lee! sweet Gal - i-lee! Where Je-sus loved so much to be; O
Gal - i lee! blue Gal - i-lee! Come, sing thy song a - gain to me!

By permission.

No. 163. Since I Have Been Redeemed.
E. O. E.
To Geo. T. Howser.
E. O. Excell.
1. I have a *song* I love to sing, Since I have been re-deem'd,
2. I have a *Christ* that sat-is-fies, Since I have been re-deem'd,
3. I have a *Witness*, bright and clear, Since I have been re-deem'd,
4. I have a *joy* I can't ex-press, Since I have been re-deem'd,
5. I have a *home* pre-par'd for me, Since I have been re-deem'd,
Of my Re-deem-er, Sav-ior, King, Since I have been re-deem'd.
To do His will my high-est prize, Since I have been re-deem'd.
Dis-pell-ing ev-'ry doubt and fear. Since I have been re-deem'd.
All through His blood and righteousness, Since I have been re-deem'd.
Where I shall dwell e-ter-nal-ly, Since I have been re-deem'd.
Chorus.
Since I........................ have been re-deem'd,
Since I have been re-deem'd, Since I have been re-deem'd, Since
I have been rede m'd, I will glory in his name, I will glory in my Savior's name.

No. 164. Dennis.

Obligato Solo
(Quintet.)
Arr. by E. O. Excell.
1. How gen - tle God's com - mands, How kind his pre - cepts are; Come cast your bur - dens on the Lord, And trust his con - stant care.
Chorus.
2. His boun - ty will pro - vide, His saints se - cure - ly dwell; That hand which bears cre - a - tion up, Shall guard his chil - dren well.
3. Why should this anx - ious load, Press down your wea - ry mind? Oh, seek your heav'n - ly Fa - ther's throne, And peace and com - fort find.
4. His good - ness stands ap - proved, Un - changed from day to day; I'll drop my bur - den at his feet, And bear a song a - way.

No. 165. Sailing O'er the Sea.
I. B.
I. Baltzell.
1. We're a hap-py pil-grim band, Sail-ing to the good-ly land; With a swell-ing sail we on-ward sweep;
Tho' the temp-est rag-es long, There is One a-mong the throng, Who will guide us safe-ly o'er the deep.
2. When the might-y bil-lows swell, With the saved it shall be well. Tho' the break-ers roar up-on the lea.
Rolling waves shall not o'erwhelm, For we've Jesus at the helm, And he'll guide us safe-ly o'er the sea,
Chorus.
We are sail - ing o'er the sea, We are sail - ing o'er the sea, We are sail - ing o'er the sea; Praise the Lord,...... we'll soon be free.
We are sail-ing, we are sail-ing o'er the sea, We are sail-ing, we are sail-ing o'er the sea, We are sailing, we are sailing o'er the sea, Praise the Lord, soon be free.

From "Golden Songs," by per.

No. 166. Is My Name Written There?

M. A. K.
Frank M. Davis.
1. Lord, I care not for rich-es, Neither silver nor gold; I would make sure of heaven, I would en-ter the fold; In the book of thy kingdom, With its pag-es so fair, Tell me, Je-sus, my Sav-ior, Is my name written there?
2. Lord, my sins they are many, Like the sands of the sea, But thy blood, O my Sav-ior, is suf-fi-cient for me; For thy promise is written, In bright letters that glow, "Tho' your sins be as scarlet, I will make them like snow."
3. Oh! that beauti-ful cit-y, With its mansions of light, With its glo-ri-fied be-ings, In pure garments of white; Where no e-vil thing cometh, To de-spoil what is fair; Where the angels are watching, Is my name written there?
Refrain.
Is my name writ-ten there, On the page white and fair? In the book of thy king-dom, Is my name writ-ten there?

By permission.

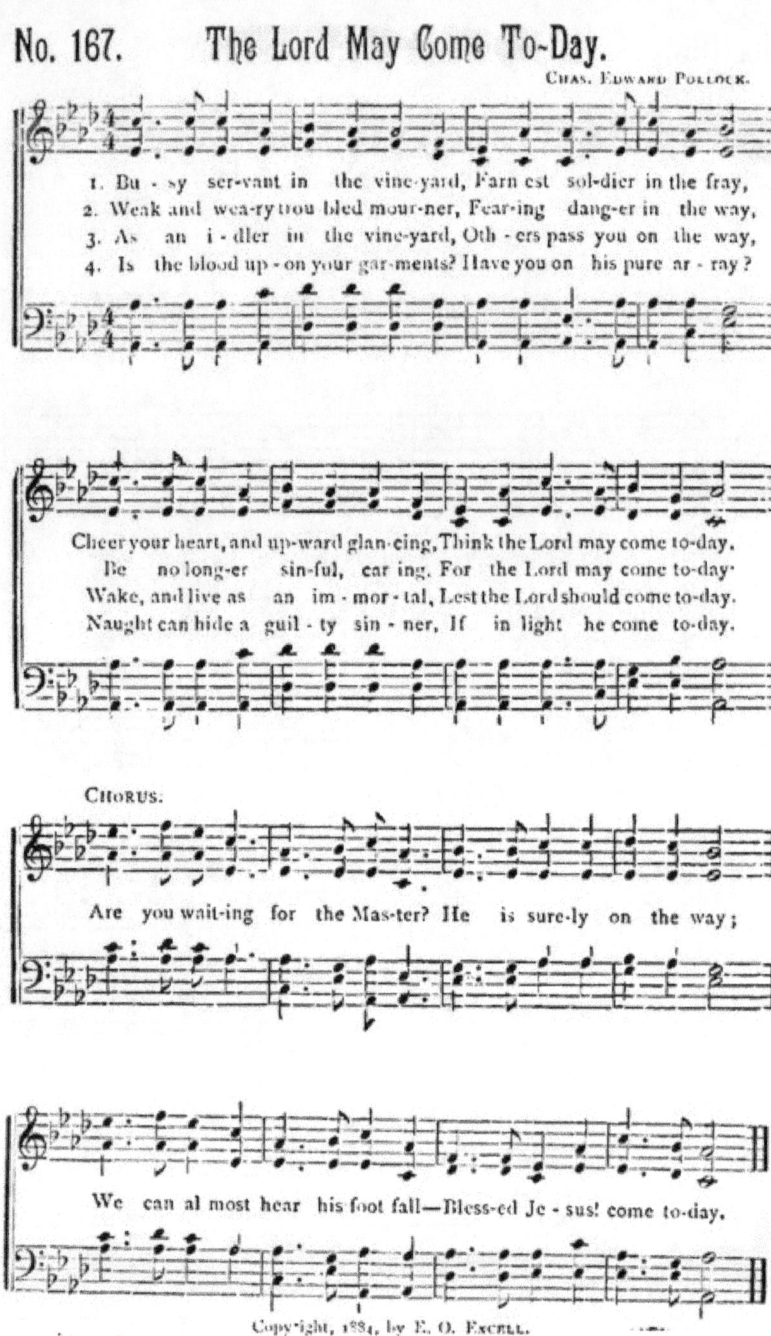
No. 167. The Lord May Come To-Day.
Chas. Edward Pollock.
1. Bu - sy ser-vant in the vine-yard, Earn-est sol-dier in the fray,
2. Weak and wea-ry trou-bled mourn-er, Fear-ing dang-er in the way,
3. As an i - dler in the vine-yard, Oth - ers pass you on the way,
4. Is the blood up - on your gar-ments? Have you on his pure ar - ray?
Cheer your heart, and up-ward glan-cing, Think the Lord may come to-day.
Be no long-er sin-ful, car-ing, For the Lord may come to-day.
Wake, and live as an im - mor - tal, Lest the Lord should come to-day.
Naught can hide a guil - ty sin - ner, If in light he come to-day.
Chorus.
Are you wait-ing for the Mas-ter? He is sure-ly on the way;
We can al-most hear his foot-fall—Bless-ed Je - sus! come to-day.

No. 168. I have Work for Thee.

Alfred J. Begbie.
Chas. Herald.
1. At the feet of Je - sus, freed from sa - tan's chain,
2. At the feet of Je - sus, weep - ing would I stand,
3. On the breast of Je - sus, I would lay my head,
4. By the cross of Je - sus, sure - ly I may stay,
Day and night re - joice - ing fain would I re - main,
Pour - ing pre - cious oint - ment with a - dor - ing hand;
But the Sav - ior whis - pers, "Do my work in - stead,"
Still the plead-ing spir - it sum - mons me a - way,
But my Lord for - bids it, "I have work for thee,"
"Go," the Mas - ter an - swers, "Make the fee - ble strong,
Sin - ners hearts are ach - ing, pil - grim's feet are sore,
Tell man-kind He loves them, spread the sto - ry wide,
Seek the groan-ing cap - tives bid them come to me.
Guide the wea - ry wan d'rer cheer the sad with song."
Rest when time is end - ed, rest for - ev - er more.
Till to reign in glo - ry comes the Cru - ci - fied.

No. 169. On the Other Side.

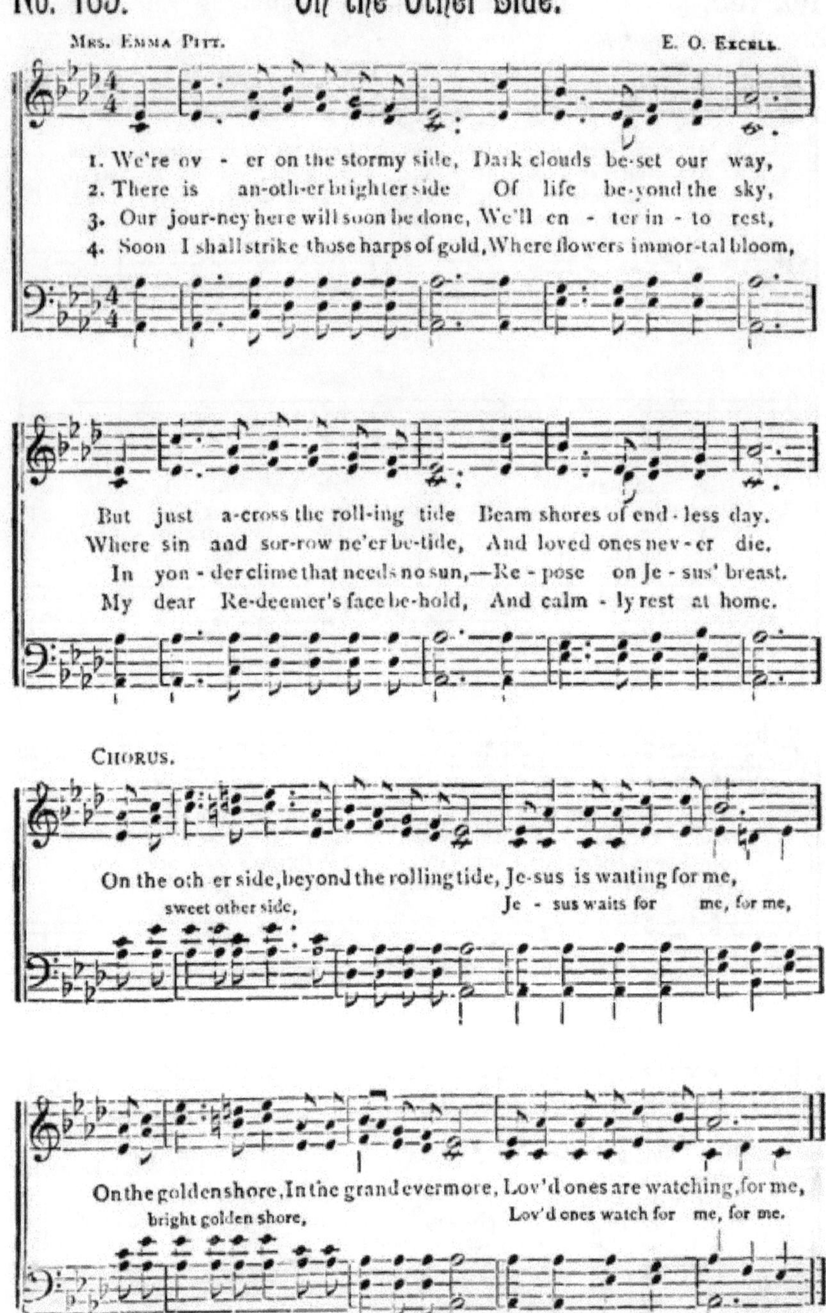
Mrs. Emma Pitt.
E. O. Excell.
1. We're ov - er on the stormy side, Dark clouds be-set our way,
2. There is an-oth-er brighter side Of life be-yond the sky,
3. Our jour-ney here will soon be done, We'll en - ter in - to rest,
4. Soon I shall strike those harps of gold, Where flowers immor-tal bloom,
But just a-cross the roll-ing tide Beam shores of end - less day.
Where sin and sor-row ne'er be-tide, And loved ones nev - er die.
In yon - der clime that needs no sun,—Re - pose on Je - sus' breast.
My dear Re-deemer's face be-hold, And calm - ly rest at home.
Chorus.
On the oth-er side, beyond the rolling tide, Je-sus is waiting for me,
sweet other side,
Je - sus waits for me, for me,
On the golden shore, In the grand evermore, Lov'd ones are watching, for me,
bright golden shore,
Lov'd ones watch for me, for me.

From "Songs of my Redeemer," by per.

No. 170. Glory to His Name.

"I will glorify thy name forever."—Ps. lxiii. 4.

Rev. E. A. Hoffman.
Rev. J. H. Stockton.
1. Down at the cross where my Sav-ior died, Down where for cleansing from sin I cried; There to my heart was the blood ap-plied; Glo-ry to his name.
2. I am so won-drous-ly sav'd from sin, Je-sus so sweet-ly a-bides with-in; There at the cross where he took me in; Glo-ry to his name.
3. Oh, pre-cious foun-tain, that saves from sin, I am so glad I have en-ter'd in; There Je-sus saves me and keeps me clean, Glo-ry to his name.
4. Come to this foun-tain, so rich and sweet; Cast thy poor soul at the Sav-ior's feet; Plunge in to-day, and be made com-plete; Glo-ry to his name.
Chorus.
Glo-ry to his name, Glo-ry to his name; There to my heart was the blood ap-plied; Glo-ry to his name.

By permission.

No. 171. The Lord's Prayer.

Andante. E. O. EXCELL.

Our Father who art in heaven, Hallowed be thy name, Thy kingdom come Thy
will be done, in earth as it is in heaven, Give us this day our dai-ly bread
And forgive us our debts, as we forgive our debtors, And lead us not in-
Cres.........
to temptation; but de-liv-er us from e-vil, For thine is the kingdom,
And the pow-er, and the glo-ry, for-ev-er, A - - men.

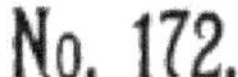

I Will Tell Jesus.

JULIA H. JOHNSTON.

LUCY J. RIDER.

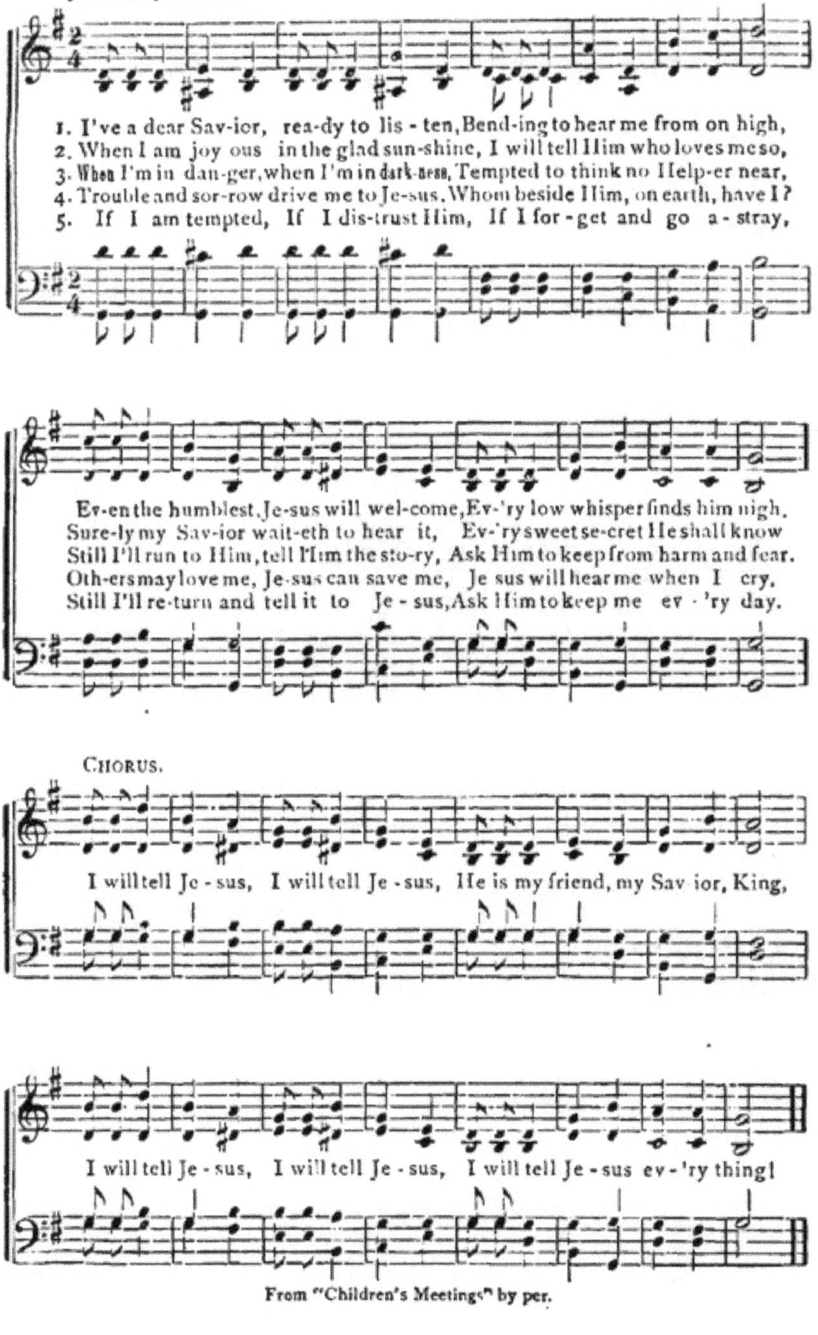

1. I've a dear Sav-ior, rea-dy to lis - ten, Bend-ing to hear me from on high,
2. When I am joy ous in the glad sun-shine, I will tell Him who loves me so,
3. When I'm in dan-ger, when I'm in dark-ness, Tempted to think no Help-er near,
4. Trouble and sor-row drive me to Je-sus, Whom beside Him, on earth, have I?
5. If I am tempted, If I dis-trust Him, If I for - get and go a - stray,

Ev-en the humblest, Je-sus will wel-come, Ev-'ry low whisper finds him nigh.
Sure-ly my Sav-ior wait-eth to hear it, Ev-'ry sweet se-cret He shall know
Still I'll run to Him, tell Him the sto-ry, Ask Him to keep from harm and fear.
Oth-ers may love me, Je-sus can save me, Je sus will hear me when I cry.
Still I'll re-turn and tell it to Je - sus, Ask Him to keep me ev - 'ry day.

CHORUS.

I will tell Je - sus, I will tell Je - sus, He is my friend, my Sav ior, King,
I will tell Je - sus, I will tell Je - sus, I will tell Je - sus ev - 'ry thing!

From "Children's Meetings" by per.

No. 173. The True Easter.

Mrs. E. C. Ellsworth.
E. O. Excell.
1. Ring on, ring on, ye bells, Peal forth a glad-some sound,
Ring on, ring on, a gladsome sound,
2. Ring on, ring on, ye bells, Your sil-v'ry tones as - cend,
Ring on, ring on, your tones as-cend,
3. Ring on, ring on, ye bells, Till dawns the glo-rious day,
Ring on, ring on, the glorious day,
4. Ring on, ring on, ye bells, Your tones of praise di - vine,
Ring on, ring on, of praise divine,
Je - sus, the vic - tor, lives to-day, His name with hon-ors crown'd.
Mingling with strains of sweet per-fume, Where flow'rs and mu-sic blend.
Earth join with heav'n, one song shall sing, And chant one com-mon lay.
Burst-ing in one tri-umph-ant song, Shall be true Eas-ter sign.
Chorus.
Ring, ring, Ring, ring on, A joy - ful an-them raise,
Ring on, ring on, ye bells, Ring, ring, ring, ring on,
Ring on, ring on, ye bells, Till earth is full of praise.
Ring, ring, ring, ring on.
Copyright, 1884, by E. O. Excell.

No. 174. In the Shadow of His Wings.

Rev. J. B. Atchinson.
E. O. Excell.
1. In the shadow of his wings There is rest, sweet rest; There is rest from care and
2. In the shadow of his wings There is peace, sweet peace, Peace that passeth under-
3. In the shadow of his wings There is joy, glad joy, There is joy to tell the
la-bor, There is rest for friend and neighbor, In the shadow of his wings,
standing, Peace, sweet peace that knows no ending, In the shadow of his wings,
sto - ry Joy ex - ceed-ing, full of glo - ry; In the shadow of his wings,
There is rest, sweet rest, In the shadow of his wings There is rest, sweet rest.
There is peace, sweet peace, In the shadow of his wings There is peace, sweet peace.
There is joy, glad joy, In the shadow of his wings There is joy, glad joy.
Chorus.
There is rest, There is peace, There is joy In the shadow of his wings;
sweet rest, sweet peace, glad joy,
There is rest there is peace, There is joy, In the shadow of his wings.
sweet rest, sweet peace, glad joy,
"From Sacred Echoes and Songs of My Redeemer." By per.

No. 175. Ho! Every One that is Thirsty.
L. J. R.
Isa., 44—3.
Lucy J. Rider.
1. Ho! ev - 'ry one that is thirst - y in spir - it,
2. Child of the world, are you tired of your bond - age?
3. Child of the king-dom, be filled with the Spir - it,
Ho! ev - 'ry one that is wea - ry and sad, Come to the fountain, there's
Wea - ry of earth-joys, so false, so un-true; Thirst-ing for God and his
Noth-ing but full-ness thy long - ing can meet, 'Tis the enduement for
full - ness in Je - sus, All that you're long - ing for,
full - ness of bless - ing; List to the prom - ise— a
life and for ser - vice; Thine is the prom-ise, so
Chorus.
come and be glad. I will pour wa - ter on him that is thirst - y,
mess-age for you. I will pour wa - ter, etc.
cer - tain, so sweet. I will pour wa - ter, etc.
I will pour floods up - on the dry ground; O - pen your heart for the

Ho! Every One that is Thirsty.—Concluded.
gifts I am bring-ing; While ye are seek - ing me, I will be found.
No. 176. I'm Nearer My Home.
Duet.
H. A. Lewis.
1. One sweet-ly, sol-emn thought, Comes to me o'er and o'er, I'm
2. I'm near-er my Father's house, Where heav'nly mansions be; I'm
3. I'm near-er the bound of life, Where we lay our burdens down; I'm
near-er my home to day Than ev - er I've been be - fore.
near-er the great white throne, Near-er the Jas - per sea.
near-er the time to leave The cross and wear the crown.
Chorus.
I'm near - er my home, I'm near - er my home, I'm
I'm near-er my home, my heav-en-ly home, I'm near-er my home, my heavenly home, I'm
Repeat Chorus last time pp.
Rit.
near - er my home to - day than ev - er I've been be - fore.
near - er my home,
Copyright, 1884, by E. O. Excell.

No. 177. Are You Washed in the Blood?

E. A. H.
Rev. E. A. Hoffman.
1. Have you been to Je - sus for the cleans-ing pow'r? Are you washed in the blood of the Lamb? Are you ful - ly trust-ing in his grace this hour? Are you washed in the blood of the Lamb?
2. Are you walk - ing dai - ly by the Sav - ior's side? Are you washed in the blood of the Lamb? Do you rest each mom-ent in the Cru - ci - fied? Are you washed in the blood of the Lamb?
3. When the Bride-groom com-eth, will your robes be white, Pure and white in the blood of the Lamb? Will your soul be read-y for the mansions bright? And be washed in the blood of the Lamb?
4. Lay a - side the garments that are stained with sin, And be washed in the blood of the Lamb; There's a foun-tain flow-ing for the soul un-clean, Oh, be washed in the blood of the Lamb?
Chorus.
Are you washed in the blood, In the soul-cleansing blood of the Lamb?
Are you washed in the blood of the Lamb?
Are your garments spotless? Are they white as snow? Are you washed in the blood of Lamb?
By permission.

No. 178. I Will Follow Thee.

E. A. H. Rev. E. A. Hoffman.

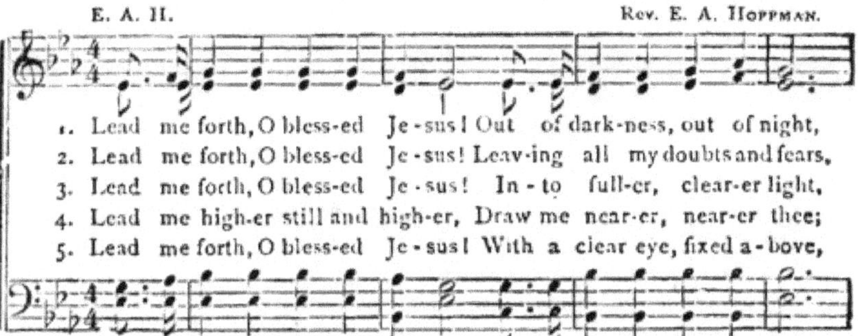
1. Lead me forth, O bless-ed Je-sus! Out of dark-ness, out of night,
2. Lead me forth, O bless-ed Je-sus! Leav-ing all my doubts and fears,
3. Lead me forth, O bless-ed Je-sus! In-to full-er, clear-er light,
4. Lead me high-er still and high-er, Draw me near-er, near-er thee;
5. Lead me forth, O bless-ed Je-sus! With a clear eye, fixed a-bove,

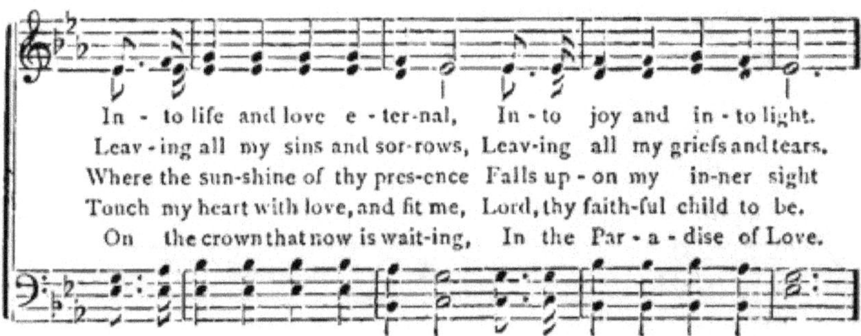
In-to life and love e-ter-nal, In-to joy and in-to light.
Leav-ing all my sins and sor-rows, Leav-ing all my griefs and tears.
Where the sun-shine of thy pres-ence Falls up-on my in-ner sight
Touch my heart with love, and fit me, Lord, thy faith-ful child to be.
On the crown that now is wait-ing, In the Par-a-dise of Love.

Chorus.

I will take my cross and fol-low, I will take my cross and

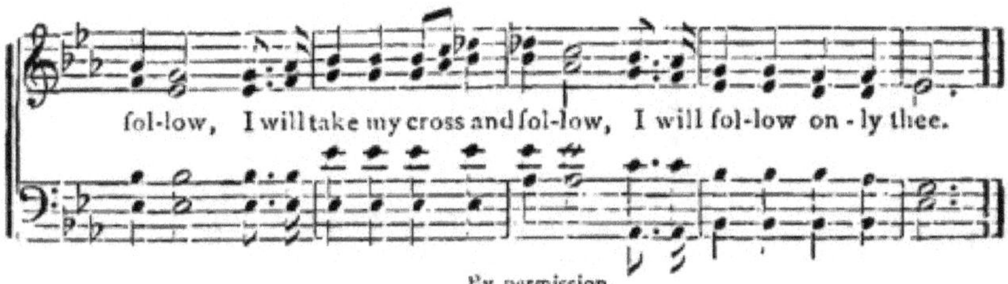
fol-low, I will take my cross and fol-low, I will fol-low on-ly thee.

By permission.

No. 179. Watch and Pray.

Rev J. B. Atchinson. Frank M. Davis. By per.

1. When the shad-ows round you gath-er, Shut-ting out the light of God,
2. When as-sailed by fierce temp-ta-tions, Then the Sav-ior's word o - bey,
3. Watch and pray thro' all life's jour-ney, Till you reach e - ter - nal day,

When the darkness hides the path-way, Which your wea-ry feet have trod.
It will sure-ly give you tri-umph, He com-mand-ed watch and pray.
In the shad-ow in the sun-shine, Dai - ly, hour-ly, watch and pray.

Chorus.

O re-mem-ber, O re-mem-ber,
O re-mem-ber Christ is near you, O re-mem-ber Christ will cheer you,

O re - mem - ber Christ is near.......... you, Call up-
Christ is near you,

on him he will hear you, watch and pray, watch and pray.

No. 180. Have You Heard?

"Behold I bring you tidings of great joy."—Luke ii. 10.

Mrs. C. L. Shacklock. Frank M Davis, by per.

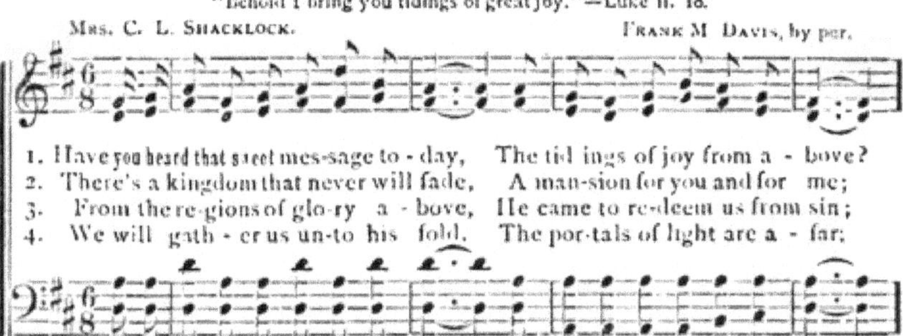
1. Have you heard that sweet mes-sage to - day, The tid-ings of joy from a - bove?
2. There's a kingdom that never will fade, A man-sion for you and for me;
3. From the re-gions of glo-ry a - bove, He came to re-deem us from sin;
4. We will gath - er us un-to his fold, The por-tals of light are a - far;

There is par-don for all who will pray, And peace in the in - fi-nite love.
For the Sav-ior our ran-som has paid, His mer-cy is bound-less and free.
Let us trust in His won-der-ful love, Our heav-en-ward jour-ney be-gin.
And we see like the wise men of old, The rays of the mys-ti - cal star.

Chorus.
Have you heard the sweet message to - day? The Sav-ior has bid-den us come,

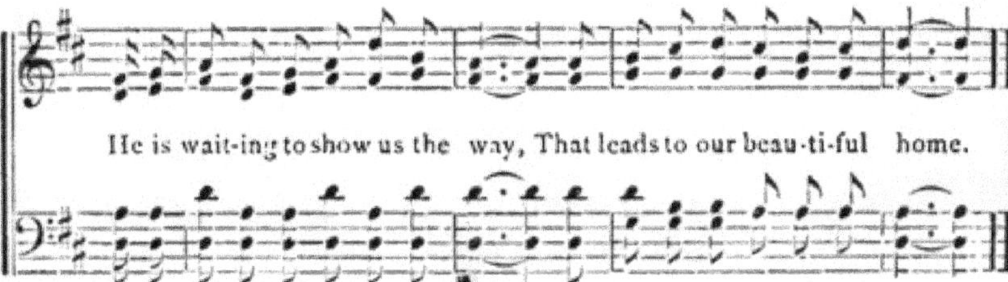
He is wait-ing to show us the way, That leads to our beau-ti-ful home.

No. 181. Out With the Life Boats.

Mrs. E. C. Ellsworth. E. O. Excell.

1. Yon-der a ves - sel is breasting the gale, Lost is her rud-der, and
2 See she has stranded! a wreck she must be, Yes, she is break-ing, so
3 Life has its o-cean, and out on its sea, Sin spreads its dangers, tho'

rent ev' ry sail; Heavily lad-en, there's nought can prevail,
wild is the sea; Sig - nals are waving, and cries may be heard,
hid - den they be, Souls there are stranded, and loud is the cry,

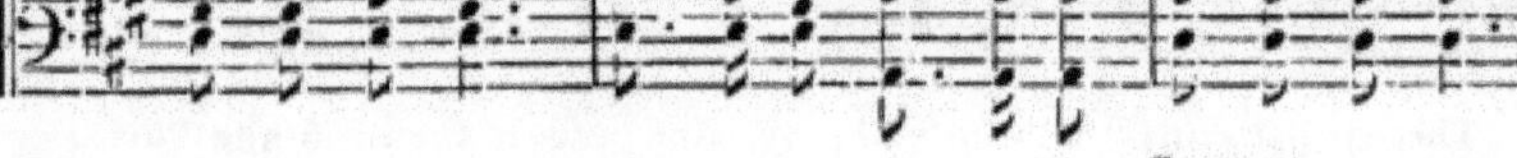

Chorus.

O'er her the wa - ters must rush with a wail. Out!...............
Sure ly a - mong us some hearts must be stir'd. Out!...............
Help now is need - ed, or else they must die. Out!...............

Out with the life - boats!

Out with the life boats! Yon-der are per - ish-ing souls in their need;

Out! out with the life-boats! Over the waters be fly-ing with speed.

Out with the life-boats!

From "Songs of my Redeemer" by per.

No. 182. **Treasures of Heaven.**

T. C. O'K. T. C. O'Kane.

1. There's a crown in heav'n for the striving soul, Which the blessed Jesus him-
2. There's a joy in heav'n for the mourning soul, Tho' the tears may fall all the
3. There's a home in heav'n for the faithful soul, In the ma-ny man-sions pre-
self will place On the head of each who shall faith-ful prove, E-ven
earth-ly night; Yet the clouds of sad-ness will break a-way, And re-
pared a-bove, Where the glo-ri-fied shall for-ev-er sing, Of a
un-to death, in the heav'n-ly race.
joic-ing come with the morning light.
Sav-ior's free and un-bound-ed love.
Refrain.
Oh, may that crown in heav'n be
Oh, may that crown
Oh, may that joy in heav'n be
Oh, may that joy
Oh, may that home in heav'n be
Oh, may that home
mine, And I a-mong the an-gels shine; Be thou, O
in heav'n be mine,
Lord......... my dai-ly guide, Let me ev-er in thy love a-bide.
Be thou, O Lord, my daily guide.

By permission.

No. 183. I've Been Redeemed.

To Rev J. C. Mc Donald.
Plantation Melody.
Arr. by E. O. Excell.
1 There is a fountain fill'd with blood, Drawn from Im-man-uel's veins,
Drawn from Immanuel's, drawn from Immanuel's veins,
2. The dying thief rejoiced to see, That fountain in his day,
That foun - tain in, that foun-tain in his day,
3. E'er since by faith I saw the stream Thy flowing wounds, sup - ply,
Thy flow - ing wounds, thy flowing wounds sup-ply.
And sin-ners plunged beneath that flood, Lose all their guil-ty stains.
Lose all, lose all their guil-ty stains,
And their may I, tho' vile as he, Wash all my sins a - way,
Wash all, wash all my sins a - way,
Re - deem - ing love has been my theme, And shall be till, I die,
And shall, and shall be till I die.
Chorus.
I've been redeem'd, I've been redeem'd, I've been redeem'd, I've been redeem d,
I've been redeem'd. I've been redeem'd, I've been redeem'd, I've been redeem'd,
Been wash'd in the blood of the Lamb. Been redeem'd by the blood of the Lamb,
Been wash'd in the blood, in the blood of the Lamb, Been redeem'd by the blood of the Lamb
Fine.

I've Been Redeemed.—Concluded.

D. S. to 𝄋
Been redeem'd by the blood of the Lamb, That flow'd on Cal - va - ry.
Been redeem'd by the blood of the Lamb, That flow'd that flow'd on Calvary.

No. 184. He Loved Me So.

E. O. E. God so loved the world.—John, iii. 16. E. O Excell.

1. By faith the Lamb of God I see. Ex - pir - ing on the cross for me;
2. For me the Fa - ther sent his Son; For me the vic - tor - y he won;
3. So glad I am that he is mine,—So glad that I with him shall shine:
4. O Lamb of God, that made me free, I con - se - crate my all to thee;
5. And when my Lord shall bid me come, To join the loved ones round the throne,

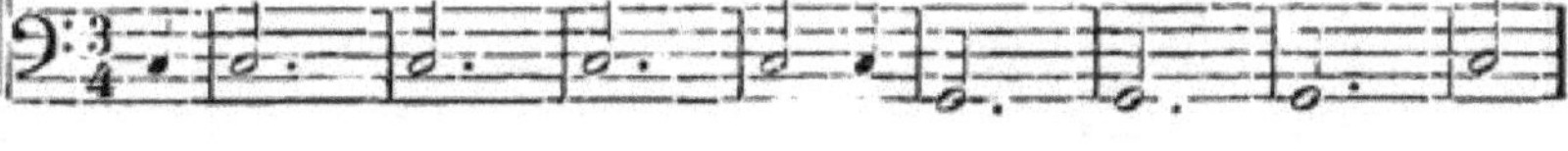

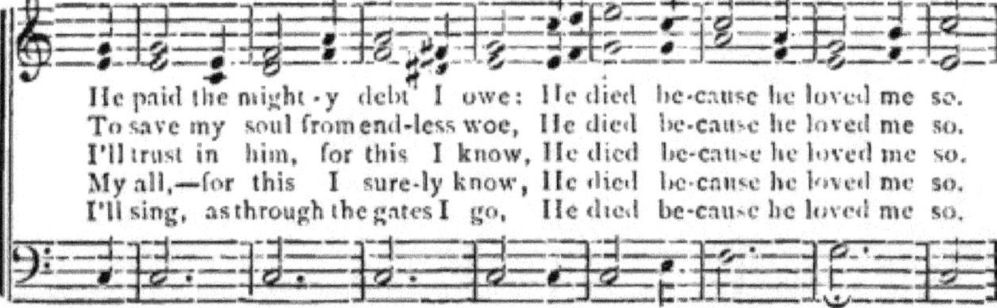
He paid the might - y debt I owe: He died be-cause he loved me so.
To save my soul from end-less woe, He died be-cause he loved me so.
I'll trust in him, for this I know, He died be-cause he loved me so.
My all,—for this I sure-ly know, He died be-cause he loved me so.
I'll sing, as through the gates I go, He died be-cause he loved me so.

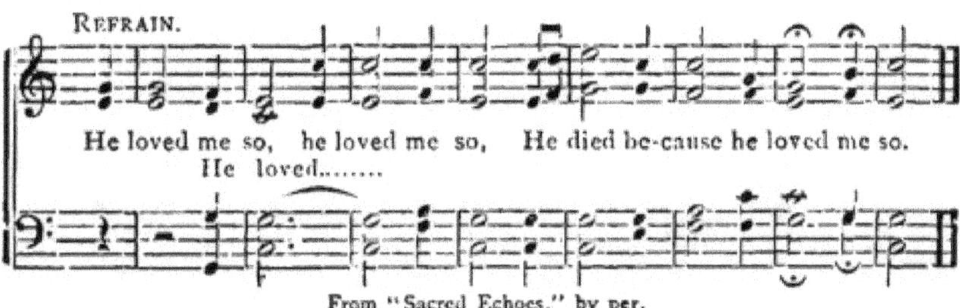
Refrain.
He loved me so, he loved me so, He died be-cause he loved me so.
He loved........

From "Sacred Echoes," by per.

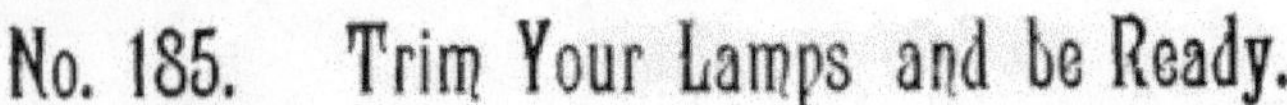
No. 185. Trim Your Lamps and be Ready.

Arr. E. F. Miller.

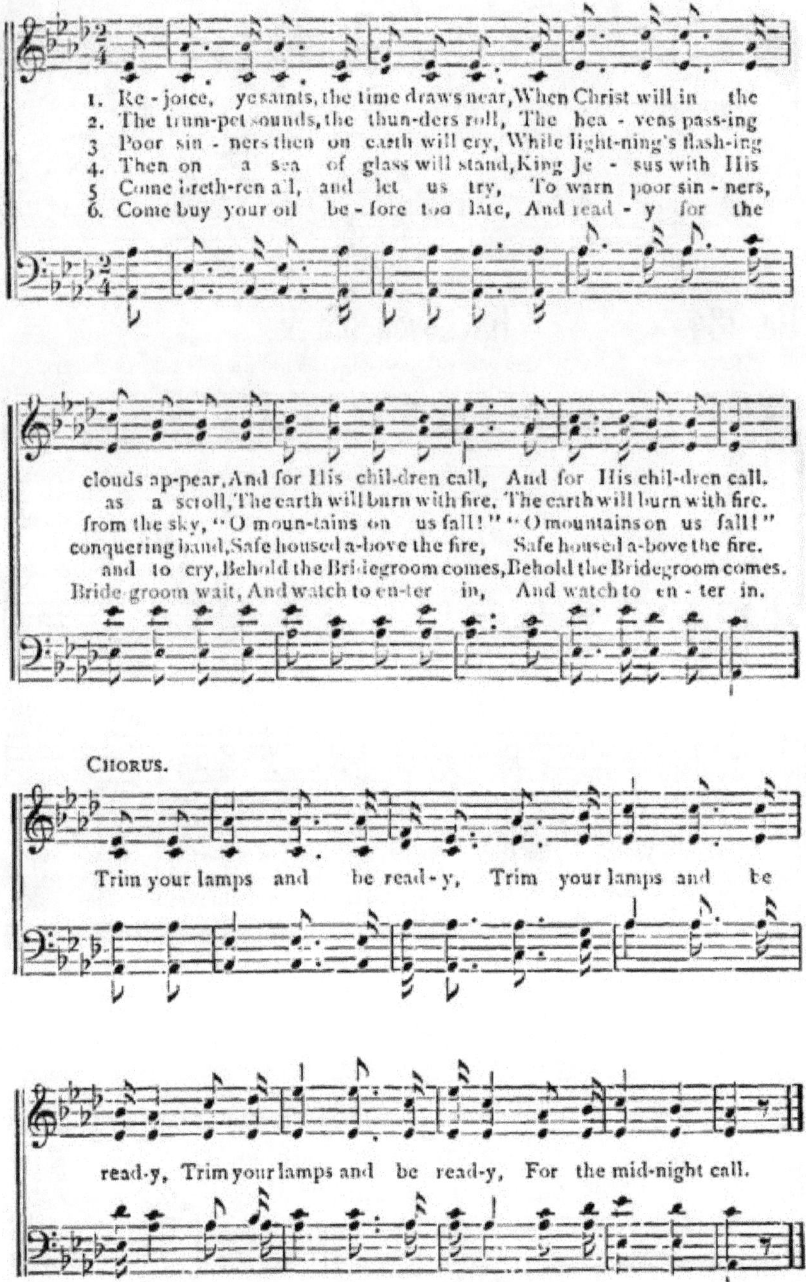

1. Re-joice, ye saints, the time draws near, When Christ will in the clouds ap-pear, And for His chil-dren call, And for His chil-dren call.
2. The trum-pet sounds, the thun-ders roll, The hea-vens pass-ing as a scroll, The earth will burn with fire, The earth will burn with fire.
3. Poor sin-ners then on earth will cry, While light-ning's flash-ing from the sky, "O moun-tains on us fall!" "O mountains on us fall!"
4. Then on a sea of glass will stand, King Je-sus with His conquering band, Safe housed a-bove the fire, Safe housed a-bove the fire.
5. Come breth-ren all, and let us try, To warn poor sin-ners, and to cry, Behold the Bridegroom comes, Behold the Bridegroom comes.
6. Come buy your oil be-fore too late, And read-y for the Bride-groom wait, And watch to en-ter in, And watch to en-ter in.

Chorus.

Trim your lamps and be read-y, Trim your lamps and be read-y, Trim your lamps and be read-y, For the mid-night call.

No. 186. I am Listening.

It is the voice of my beloved that knocketh, saying, Open to me.—Cant. v. 2

W. S. Marshall. W. S. Marshall.

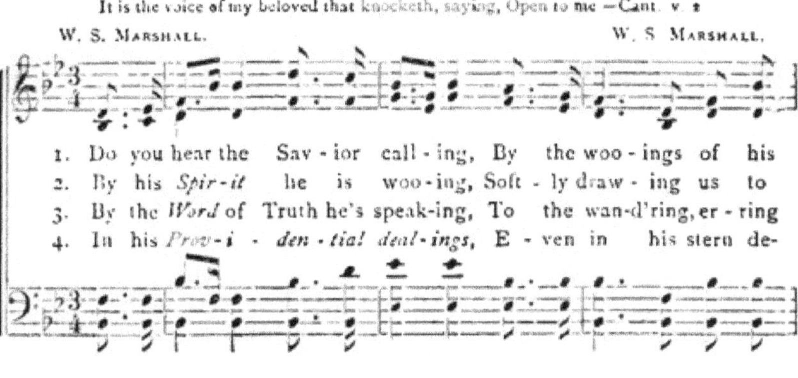
1. Do you hear the Sav - ior call - ing, By the woo - ings of his
2. By his *Spir - it* he is woo - ing, Soft - ly draw - ing us to
3. By the *Word* of Truth he's speak - ing, To the wan - d'ring, er - ring
4. In his *Prov - i - den - tial deal - ings,* E - ven in his stern de-

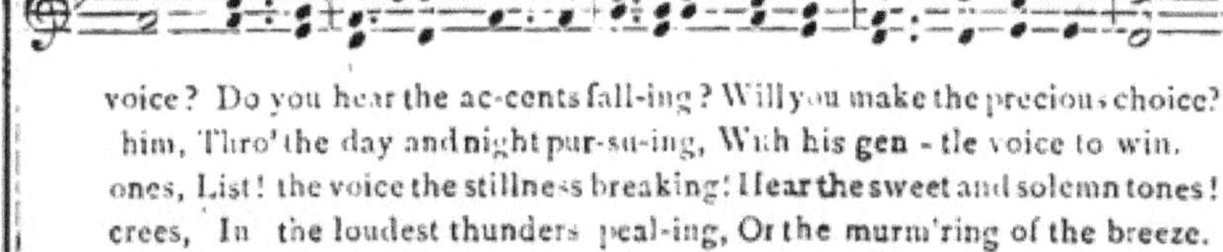
voice? Do you hear the ac - cents fall - ing? Will you make the precious choice?
him, Thro' the day and night pur - su - ing, With his gen - tle voice to win.
ones, List! the voice the stillness breaking! Hear the sweet and solemn tones!
crees, In the loudest thunders peal - ing, Or the murm'ring of the breeze.

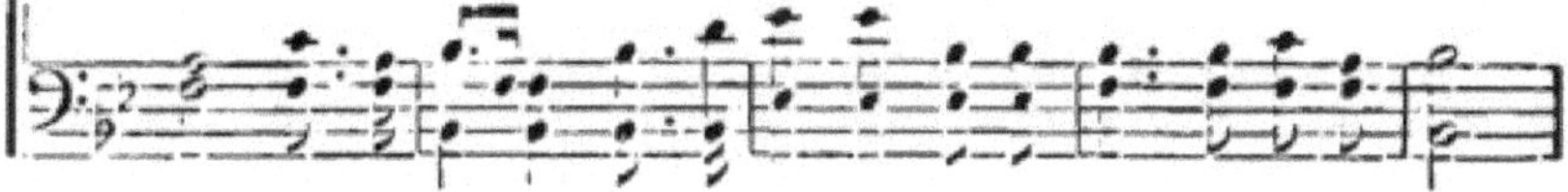

Refrain.
I am list - 'ning, Oh, I'm list - 'ning, Just to hear the ac - cents

Repeat softly
fall; I am list - 'ning, Oh, I'm list - 'ning To the Sav - ior's gen - tle call.

By permission.

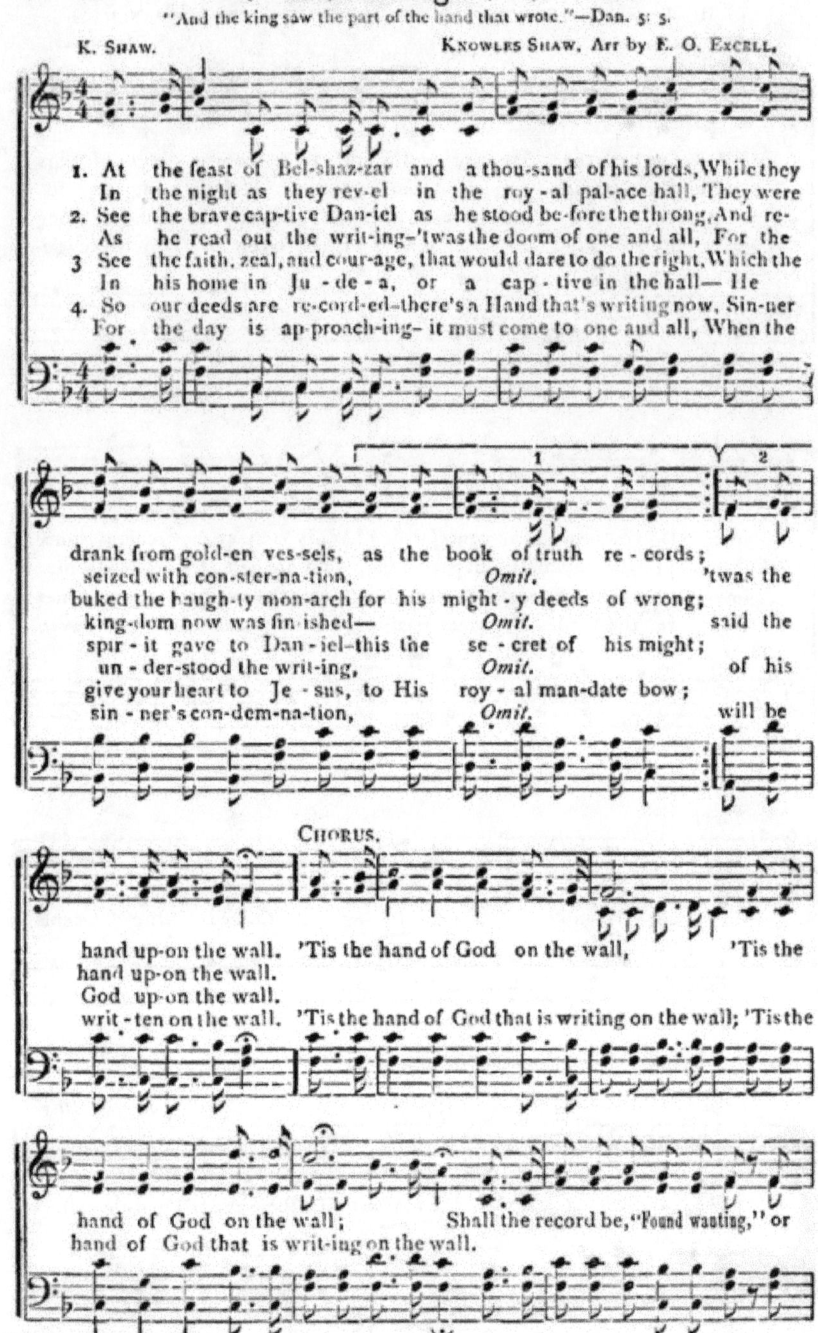

No. 187. The Handwriting on the Wall.
"And the king saw the part of the hand that wrote."—Dan. 5: 5.
K. Shaw.
Knowles Shaw, Arr by E. O. Excell.
1. At the feast of Bel-shaz-zar and a thou-sand of his lords, While they
In the night as they rev-el in the roy - al pal-ace hall, They were
2. See the brave cap-tive Dan-iel as he stood be-fore the throng, And re-
As he read out the writ-ing-'twas the doom of one and all, For the
3 See the faith, zeal, and cour-age, that would dare to do the right, Which the
In his home in Ju - de - a, or a cap - tive in the hall— He
4. So our deeds are re-cord-ed-there's a Hand that's writing now, Sin-ner
For the day is ap-proach-ing- it must come to one and all, When the
drank from gold-en ves-sels, as the book of truth re - cords;
seized with con-ster-na-tion, Omit. 'twas the
buked the haugh-ty mon-arch for his might - y deeds of wrong;
king-dom now was fin-ished— Omit. said the
spir - it gave to Dan - iel-this the se - cret of his might;
un - der-stood the writ-ing, Omit. of his
give your heart to Je - sus, to His roy - al man-date bow;
sin - ner's con-dem-na-tion, Omit. will be
1
2
Chorus.
hand up-on the wall. 'Tis the hand of God on the wall, 'Tis the
hand up-on the wall.
God up-on the wall.
writ - ten on the wall. 'Tis the hand of God that is writing on the wall; 'Tis the
hand of God on the wall; Shall the record be, "Found wanting," or
hand of God that is writ-ing on the wall.

The Handwriting on the Wall.—Concluded.

shall it be, "Found trusting?" While that hand is writing on the wall,
writ-ing on the wall,
No. 188.
Press On.
Mrs E. C. Ellsworth.
L. C. Thayer.
1. Just step be-yond the shad-ows, 'Tis light-er just a - head,
2. Just step be-yond the shad-ows, The tempt-er shuns the light,
3. A few more steps shall take thee Where shad-ows fall no more;
For here the dark-ness gath - ers, But yon-der night has fled
He ne'er thy steps shall fol - low, If Je-sus be in sight.
Then come where gold-en sun - light Re-flects from yon-der shore.
Chorus.
Press on, press on with cour-age, Till shad-ows dis - ap - pear;
Be - yond thee, yes, be - yond thee, The sun is shin-ing clear.

No. 189. Shall I be There?

American "Wesleyan." To E. Harvey, Oil City, Pa. E. O. Excell.

1. When up on the "great white throne" Christ shall stand as judge a-lone,
2. When is closed the judg-ment day, When this earth has passed a-way,
3. When the might-y white-robed throng Swell the all-tri-umph-ant song,
4. If I fol-low Je-sus here, If I hold my trust most dear,

When the "Book of Life" is read, There be-fore the ris-en dead,
When the cit-y new shall come, And the saints be gath-ered home,
Glo-ry to the great "I Am," Glo-ry, glo-ry to the Lamb,
If I plunge be-neath the flood, If I'm washed in Je-sus' blood,

As are turned those pag-es fair, Shall my name be writ-ten there?
Shall I in that tri-umph share? Oh, my Lord, shall I be there?
Ring-ing on the balm-y air; Sav-ior mine, shall I be there?
If for Christ I do and dare, Yes, my Lord, I shall be there,

Interlude.

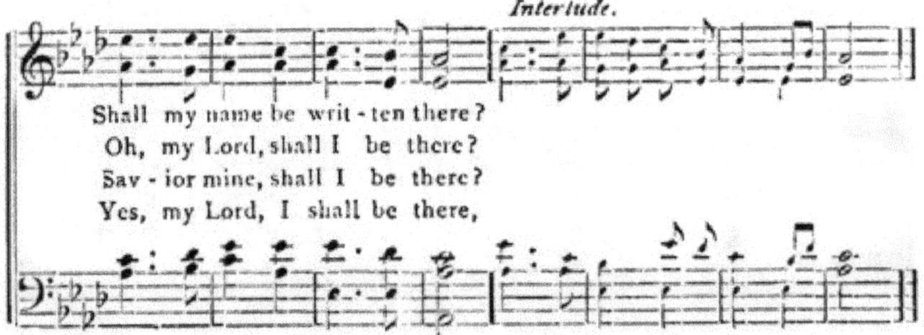

Shall my name be writ-ten there?
Oh, my Lord, shall I be there?
Sav-ior mine, shall I be there?
Yes, my Lord, I shall be there,

No. 190. The Blood is All My Plea.

Rev. F. C. Baker. E. F. Miller.

1. I knew that God in his Word had spoken, The pow'r of sin can all be brok-en, The heart held cap-tive yet be free, Lord, is this bless-ing not for me? The blood, the blood is

2. Must I go on in sin and sor-row, To-day in sun-shine, clouds to-mor-row? First I'm sin-ning, then re-pent-ing, Now I'm stub-born, then re-lenting The blood, etc.

3. With an-guish wrung, I cried, My Lord, Is there not pow'r in Je-sus' blood To make in me a per-fect cure? To cleanse my heart and keep it pure? The blood, etc.

4. Oh, yes, my love will take you in, The blood will cleanse you from all sin, Will wash a-way your guilt-y stains, And cleanse, till not one spot re-mains. The blood, etc.

5. And there I stand this ver-y hour, Kept by Al-might-y keep-ing pow'r, Temp-ta-tions come, the blood's my plea, The pre-cious blood now cleans-es me. The blood, etc.

CHORUS.

The blood, the blood is all my plea, Hal-le-lu-jah! it cleans-eth me; The blood, the blood is all my plea, Hal-le-lu-jah! it cleanseth me.

No. 191.
Glorious Things.
FOR MALE VOICES.
T. C. O'Kane by per.
1. Glo-rious things of thee are spok-en, Zi - on, ci - ty of our God;
2. Sav-iour, if in Zi - on's ci - ty I thro' grace a mem-ber am,
He whose word can-not be brok-en Form'd thee for his own a - bode.
Let the world de - ride or pit - y I will glo - ry in thy name.
On the Rock.................................. of A - ges
Chorus.
On the Rock of A - ges found - ed, On the
On the Rock.................................. of A - ges
On the rock of A - ges found - ed, On the
found - ed,
Rock of A - ges founded, What can shake.................... thy sure re-
found - ed what can shake thy sure re-pose what can
Rock of A - ges founded,
With sal - va - - - tion's walls sur-
pose? With sal - va - tion's walls surrounded, With sal-
shake thy sure re-pose? With sal - va - - - tion's walls sur-
With sal - va-tion's walls sur-round-ed, With sal-

Glorious Things.—Concluded.

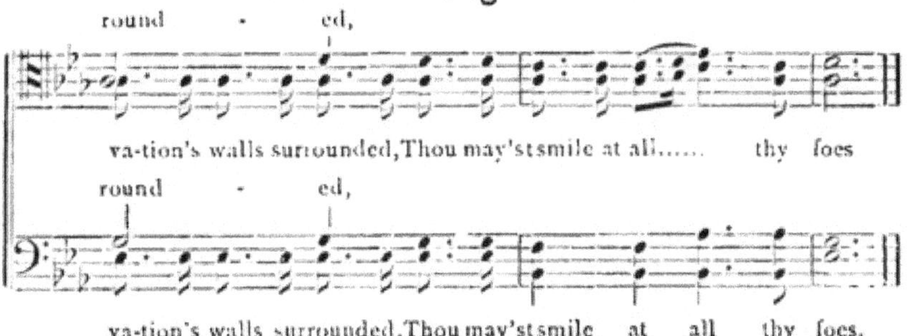
round - ed,
va-tion's walls surrounded, Thou may'st smile at all...... thy foes
round - ed,
va-tion's walls surrounded, Thou may'st smile at all thy foes.

No. 192. Lost, but Jesus Saved Me.

Mrs. Emma Pitt. E. O. Excell.

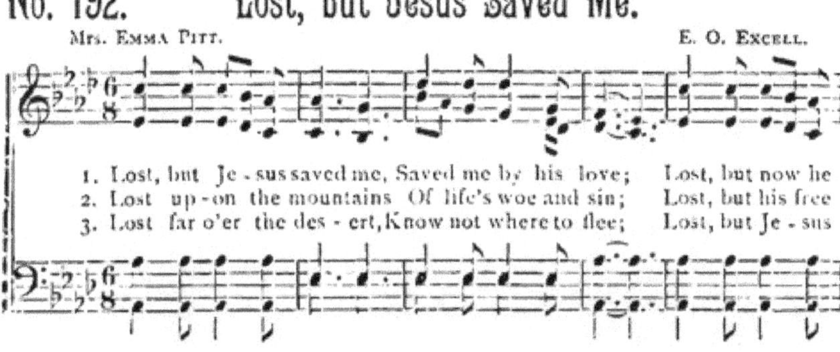
1. Lost, but Je - sus saved me, Saved me by his love; Lost, but now he
2. Lost up - on the mountains Of life's woe and sin; Lost, but his free
3. Lost far o'er the des - ert, Know not where to flee; Lost, but Je - sus

keeps me For my rest a - bove. Lost, but Je - sus found me
par - don Safe - ly took me in: Lost, but Je - sus bought me,
loved me, Kind-ly pit - ied me; Lost, but Je - sus brought me

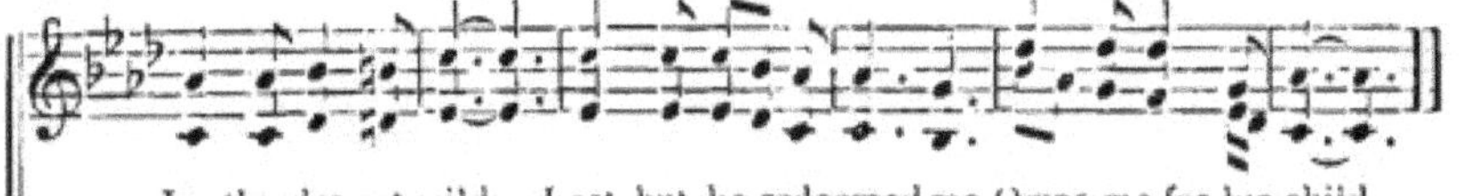
In the des-ert wild; Lost, but he redeemed me, Owns me for his child.
Bought me with his blood; Lost, but Je - sus keeps me In the nar-row road.
Out in - to the light; Lost, but still he saves me, Guards me by his might.

No. 193. I Shall See Jesus as He Is.

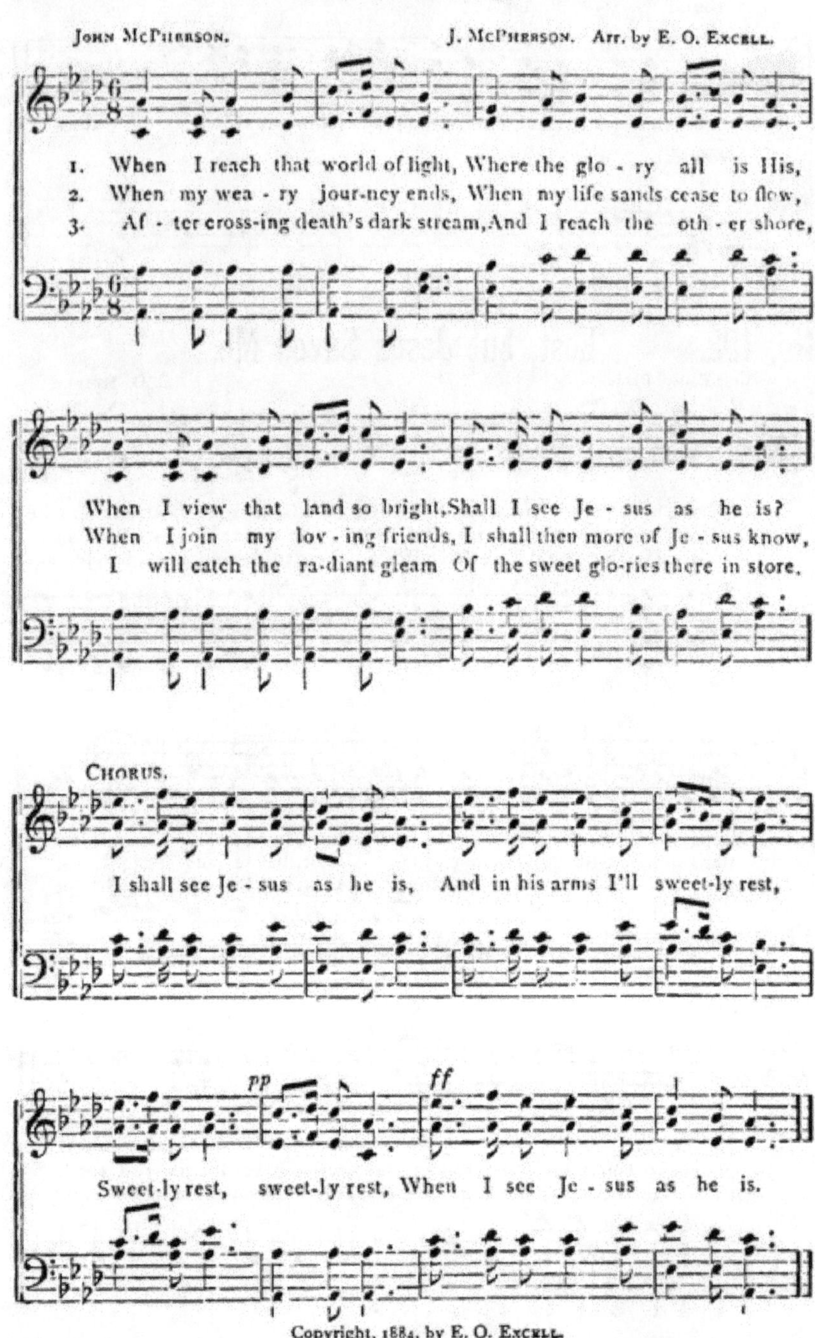
John McPherson.
J. McPherson. Arr. by E. O. Excell.
1. When I reach that world of light, Where the glo - ry all is His,
2. When my wea - ry jour-ney ends, When my life sands cease to flow,
3. Af - ter cross-ing death's dark stream, And I reach the oth - er shore,
When I view that land so bright, Shall I see Je - sus as he is?
When I join my lov - ing friends, I shall then more of Je - sus know,
I will catch the ra-diant gleam Of the sweet glo-ries there in store.
Chorus.
I shall see Je - sus as he is, And in his arms I'll sweet-ly rest,
pp
ff
Sweet-ly rest, sweet-ly rest, When I see Je - sus as he is.

No. 194. Anywhere With Thee.

Mrs. E. C. Ellsworth. Frederic W. Root.

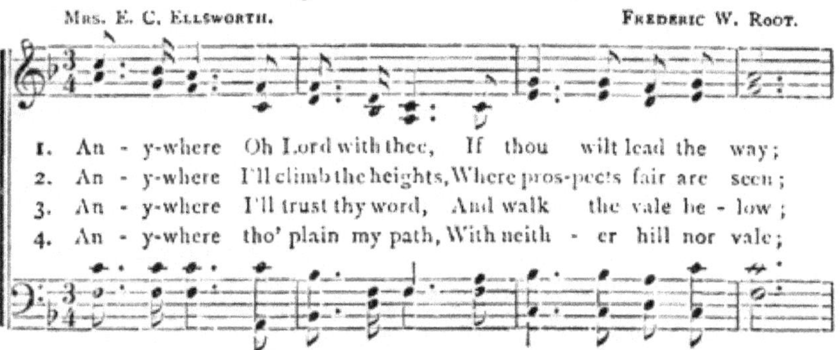

1. An - y-where Oh Lord with thee, If thou wilt lead the way;
2. An - y-where I'll climb the heights, Where pros-pects fair are seen;
3. An - y-where I'll trust thy word, And walk the vale be - low;
4. An - y-where tho' plain my path, With neith - er hill nor vale;

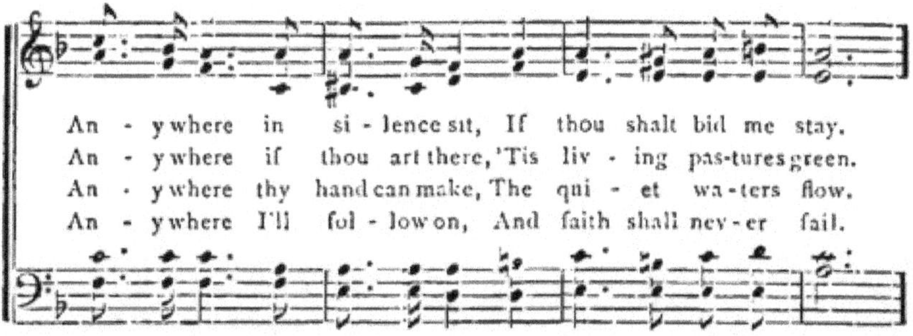

An - y where in si - lence sit, If thou shalt bid me stay.
An - y where if thou art there, 'Tis liv - ing pas-tures green.
An - y where thy hand can make, The qui - et wa-ters flow.
An - y where I'll fol - low on, And faith shall nev - er fail.

Chorus.

An - y where, yes, An - y where, If thou, Oh Lord, if thou art near, My

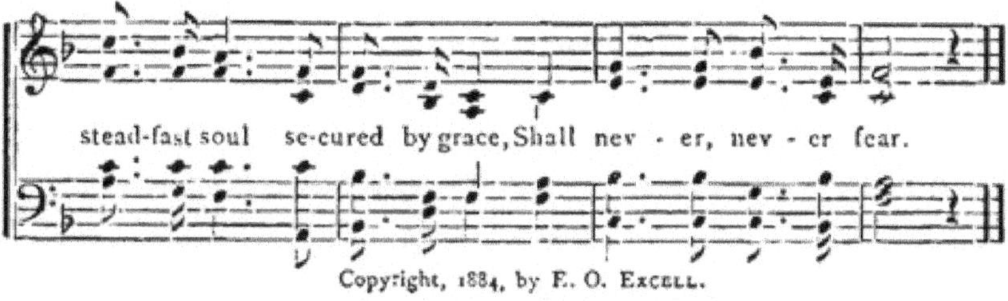

stead-fast soul se-cured by grace, Shall nev - er, nev - er fear.

No. 195. Better Than Gold.

Rev. Frank Pollock. Chas. Edw. Pollock.

"My fruit is better than gold".—Prov. viii 19.

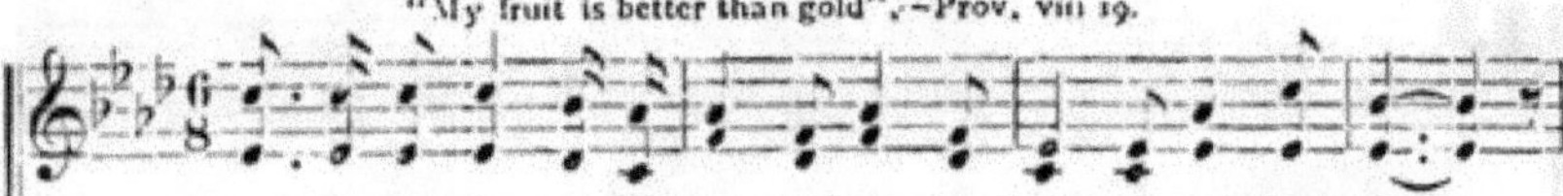

1. Bet - ter than gold is the love of God, Unchanging, rich and free;
2. Bet - ter than gold is the precious blood That cleanseth us from sin;
3. Bet - ter than gold is the precious faith—Than gold ore from the mine;
4. Bet - ter than gold is a home in heav'n Where skies are ever fair;

Flow-ing thro' Je - sus, the sac - ri-fice, To ran-som you and me.
Bless-ed are they who are clean in heart, His blood hath made them clean.
When it is tried, it will come forth pure, And brighter than gold will shine.
Where the dear Lord will for - ev - er keep The pure who en - ter there.

Chorus.

Bet-ter than gold, or wealth untold, Is the love of God to me;
4th V. Bet-ter than gold, or wealth untold, Is a home in heav'n for me,

Thro' the preci us blood of his own dear Son I am saved e-ter - nal - ly.
In a mansion bright, with the sons of light, I shall live e-ter - nal - ly.

No. 196. Delay Not.

Thomas Hastings. Lucy J. Rider.

1. { De - lay not, de - lay not, O sin - ner draw near, The waters of life are now flow - ing for thee, No
price is de - mand - ed, The Sav - ior is here, Re - demp - tion is pur - chased, sal-
2. { De - lay not, de - lay not, Why long - er a - buse, The love and com - pas - sion of Je - sus thy God? A
foun - tain is o - pen'd. How can'st thou re - fuse, To wash and be saved in the
D. C. Come, tho' but faint - ly the voice you may hear, It may be the last time 'twill
va - tion is free. fall on your ear.
par - don - ing blood;
Refrain.
De - lay not, de - lay not, O how can you stay, And thro' all love's bar-riers to death force your way; O
D. C.

3. Delay not, delay not, O sinner to come,
For mercy still lingers and calls thee to day;
Her voice is not heard in the vale of the tomb,
Her message, unheeded, will soon pass away.

4. Delay not, delay not, the spirit of grace,
Long grieved and resisted may take His sad flight
And leave thee in darkness to finish thy race,
And sink in the vale of eternity's night.

No. 197. Acceptance.
Isaac Watts.
Sep. Winner.
1. When I can read my title clear, To mansions in the skies,
2. Should earth against my soul engage, And fi-'ry darts be hurled,
3. Let cares like a wild deluge come, And storms of sorrow fall;
4. There I shall bathe my weary soul, In seas of heav'n-ly rest;
I'll bid farewell to ev-'ry fear, And wipe my weeping eyes,
Then I can smile at Satan's rage, And face a frowning world,
So I but safely reach my home, My God, my heav'n, my all!—
And not a wave of trouble roll, Across my peaceful breast,
I'll bid farewell to ev-'ry fear, And wipe my weeping eyes,
Then I can smile at Satan's rage, And face a frowning world,
So I but safely reach my home. My God, my heav'n my all!—
And not a wave of trouble roll, Across my peaceful breast,
I'll bid fare-well,
Then I can smile,
So I but reach,
And not a wave,
I'll bid farewell to ev-'ry fear, And wipe my weeping eyes.
Then I can smile at Satan's rage, And face a frowning world.
So I but safely reach my home, My God, my heav'n, my all!—
And not a wave of trouble roll, Across my peaceful breast.
I'll bid fare-well.

By permission.

No. 198. My Grace is Sufficient.

JULIA H. JOHNSTON.
II. Cor. 12: 9.
LUCY J. RIDER.
1. O match-less marvelous *grace* of God! O roy-al king-ly Word!
2. "*Suf-fi-cient* grace," the record stands, Hast thou thine own re-ceived?
3. *For thee*, for thee, O wond'rous Word! Thy ut-most need sup-plied,
4. The wit-ness of ten thou-sand saints, Con-firms the prom-ise blest,
In toil and tri-al, grief and loss, This prom-ise sweet is heard.
Thy faith shall measure thy sup-ply, Hast thou in-deed, be-lieved?
Tho' thou-sand oth-ers claim the boon, Thou shalt be sat-is-fied.
Let now, the pow'r of this same word, In me be man-i-fest!
REFRAIN.
My grace, is suf-fi-cient for thee, my
My grace is suf-fi-cient for thee,— suf-fi-cient for, thee, for thee,
grace, is suf-fi-cient for thee. Oh, pre-cious, pre-cious
grace is suf-fi-cient for thee, suf-fi-cient for thee, for thee,
grace of God, My grace is suf-fi-cient for thee.
My grace is suf-fi-cient for thee, suf-fi-cient for thee, suf-fi-cient for thee.

No. 199. Let Him In.

Rev. J. B. Atchinson. FOR MALE VOICES. E. O. Excell.

Melody in Second Tenor.

Let the Sav-ior in, Oh, let the Sav-ior in,

1. There's a strang-er at the door, Let him in,
2. O - pen now to him your heart, Let him in,
3. Hear you now his lov - ing voice? Let him in,
4. Now ad-mit the heav'n-ly Guest, Let him in,

Let the Sav-ior in, Oh, let the Sav-ior in,

Let him in,

Let the Sav-ior in, Oh, let the Sav-ior in,

He has been there oft be - fore, Let him in,
If you wait he will de - part, Let him in,
Now, oh, now make him your choice, Let him in,
He will make for you a feast, Let him in,

Let the Sav-ior in, Oh, let the Sav-ior in,

Let him in,

Let him in ere he is gone, Let him in, the Ho - ly One, Je-sus
Let him in, He is your Friend, He your soul will sure de-fend, He will
He is stand-ing at the door, Joy to you he will re - store, And his
He will speak your sins for-given, And when earth ties all are riven, He will

Let the Sav-ior in, Oh, let the Sav-ior in.
Christ, the Fa-ther's Son, Let him in.
keep you to the end, Let him in.
name you will a - dore, Let him in.
take you home to heav'n, Let him in.
Let the Sav-ior in, Oh, let the Sav-ior in.
Let him in.

No. 200. Great Deliverer.
J. E. H
Acts. 12: 7.
J. E. Hall.
1. Now to thee, who fast in prison, And enchained by bands of sin,
2. He can make thy keep-ers si-lent; He will ope the bol - ted gate;
3. Now there's room and friends a-waiting, In the place of peace and love,
4. Then when all this life is o-ver, And we've reached the far-ther shore,
Je - sus comes to burst thy fet-ters, Glad - ly bid him en - ter in.
Now a-rise, and make thy ex-it, For it may be, soon too late.
Join the ranks of Je - sus' arm-y, March-ing up to realms a - bove.
We will join the song of an-gels, And go out, no, nev - er more.
Chorus.
Je - sus comes the great Deliverer! Comes to burst the Sa - tan band,
Soul a-rise! he'll lead you forward, Through the gates to Canaan Land.

No. 201.
My Tongue Can Tell.
J. E. H.
J. E Hall.
1. I once was blind and could not see, That Je - sus came to res-cue me,
2. That once I lov'd the ways of sin; But now Christ's love has en-ter'd in,
3. How I a sin-ner lost, un-done, And know-ing not God's on-ly son,
4. My tongue can tell how love di-vine, Found out and filled this soul of mine,
And from my sins to set me free, This now my tongue can tell.
And made for me, a crown to win, All this my tongue can tell.
Was by his grace to hea-ven won, Yea this my tongue can tell.
And fitted me blood-washed, to shine With all the hosts on high.
Chorus.
With joy! with joy! my tongue can tell, That Je - sus loves me O! so well,
Can tell,
so well,
Then I his praise would ev-er swell, Both now and ev - er - more.

No. 202. All My Class for Jesus.

JULIA H. JOHNSON. LUCY J. RIDER.

1. My schol-ars all for Je-sus! This be my earn-est pray'r. For they are souls im-
2. My girls, light hearted, thoughtless, On trifling thing in-tent, These cost a price-less
3. My boys I want for Je-sus, My way-ward wand'ring boys, So full of life and
4. Lord, be in ev-'ry les-son, Bless ev-'ry falt'ring word My trembling lips may
mor-tal, En-trust-ed to my care; For each, the mas-ter careth, I
ran-som, On these my care be spent, That each a will-ing hand maid, Be
beau-ty, So charm'd by earth-ly joys. For them the Sav-ior suffer'd, For
ut-ter, To bring them to the Lord, So fleeting are the mom-ents, Of
long, I long for each, Grant, Lord, the heav'n-ly wis-dom, These way-ward hearts to reach.
brought to own her Lord, "What-e'er He saith" to "do it," O-be-dient to His word.
them, His life was giv'n, Lord, by that ran-som, help me. Bring all my boys to heav'n.
op-por-tu-ni-ty! Oh, Je-sus, Master, help me. Bring all my class to thee.
All, all my class for Je-sus, Oh, which one could I spare
All, all my class in heav-en, Let none be miss-ing there!

No. 203. The Bible.

Thy word is a lamp unto my feet. and a light unto my path. Ps. 119: 105.

AMELIA M. STARKWEATHER. H. A. LEWIS.

1. I'd rath-er have that no-ble guide, Which Je - sus Christ hath giv'n, Than
2. I'd rath-er search for hid-den gems, With un - re - mit-ting toil, To
3. For he who delves this mine of wealth, Its treas - ures to un-fold, Shall

8va

own the glitt'ring world be-side, And miss the road to heav'n, My mind with truths I'd
wreathe my brow with di-a-dems, From out its precious soil, Than wear the rich-est
find true hap-pi-ness and health, That's bet-ter far than gold, With-in that Ho - ly

8va

ra-ther store, On which my God may look, Than garner all the wealth of love, That's
king-ly gowns, Pur-chas-ed at any price, Or all the roy-al robes and crowns, This
Book, is found A balm for ev-'ry pain; And he who reads it, shall a-bound, In

8va

CHORUS.

found in ev - 'ry book. With - in that ho - ly book is found, A
side of Par - a - dise.
ev - er-last - ing gain.

8va

The Bible.—Concluded.
balm for ev-'ry pain, And he who reads it shall a-bound In ev-er-last-ing gain.
No. 204. Refuge in Christ.
Mrs. S. E. Gilbert.
A. E. Bowser.
1. There is re-fuge in Christ, In the fold of His love, Which the
2. He will lead them near by, Where the still wa-ters lie, He will
3. Tho' he lead thro' death's vale, Where the shad-ows pre-vail, Yet no
Shep-herd is guard-ing with care, And the lov'd of his choice, Who e'er
fold them with care to his breast, And in pas-tures made bright, By the
e-vil shall com-pass the way, For the light of his love, Will il-
D. S. home with the blest, Thro' his
Fine. Chorus.
list to his voice, He will lead from each dan-ger and snare. He will
pow'r of his might, He will lead his be-lov-ed to rest. He will
lume from a-bove, Lead-ing us to the man-sions of day. He will
own righteousness, For his loved he has gone to pre-pare.
D. S.
lead, He will lead, He will lead from each dan-ger and snare, And a
He will lead He will lead.
Copyright, 1884, by E. O. Excell

No. 205. Oh, The Joy that Awaits Me.
Geo. R. Clarke.
E. F. Miller.
1. Be-yond the si - lent riv - er, In the glo - ry sum-merlands, In the
2. And when I cross that riv - er, The first I will a-dore, The
3. The next one who will greet me, In the mansions fair and bright. Will
4 Then cur - ly headed broth-er And lit - tle ba - by dear, And
beau-ti-ful for-ev-er, Where the jeweled cit - y stands, Where ever blooming
first to bid me wel-come, Up - on that gold-en shore, Will be my lov-ing
be my saint-ed moth-er, Ar-rayed in garments white, And then that gray haired
bright eyed lit - tle sis-ter, With mer - ry laugh and cheer, Will all clus-ter
flow-ers, Send forth their sweet per-fume, My heart's most loved and cherished
Sav-ior, The one who died for me, That in the long for - ev - er,
fa-ther, Close press-ing by her side, Will grasp my hand with fer-vor,
round me, To bid me welcome home, And watch with me the gathering,
Chorus.
In heav'n-ly beau-ty bloom. Oh, the joy that there a-waits me When I
From sin I might be free. Oh, the joy, etc.
Just o'er the swell-ing tide. Oh, the joy, etc.
Of loved ones yet to come. Oh, the joy, etc.
reach that golden shore, When I grasp the hands of loved ones, To part with them no more.
Copyright, 1884, by E. F. Miller.

No. 206. Whosoever Means Me.

J. E. H. *Tenderly.* J. E. Hall.

1. Tho' I'm un-worth-y His love or His care, Je-sus the Sav-ior my soul will pre-pare, Here for His work, then for rest o-ver there, If I will on-ly be-lieve Him.

2. I am as-sured, for the Bi-ble is true, My sin-ful heart He will cleanse and re-new, And He will fit me, and so He will you, If we will on-ly be-lieve Him.

3. Yes, it is true, tho' it seems, oh! so grand! That I may live ev-er-more in that land, Where are the white-robed and star-crown-ed band, If we will on-ly be-lieve Him.

CHORUS.

For "who-so-ev-er" it sure-ly means me, Tho' I am guilt-y and vile as can be, Je-sus will save and will cleanse e-ven me, If I will on-ly believe Him;

No. 207. The Laurels of Victory.

M. E. Servoss. H. A. Lewis.

"It never is wrong to do right: it never is right to do wrong."
Life motto of Frances Power Cobb.

1. What-ev - er the bat-tles of life, What-ev - er temp-ta-tions we meet,
2. It nev - er is wrong to do right, Though none with our ac-tions ac-cord;
3. Then fine-ly we'll stand for the right, For all that is no-ble and good,

If du-ty's clear call we o - bey, We nev-er shall suf-fer de - feat.
It nev-er is right to do wrong, What-ev-er the seem-ing re - ward.
For hon-or, and jus-tice and truth, As brave ones be-fore us have stood.

Chorus.

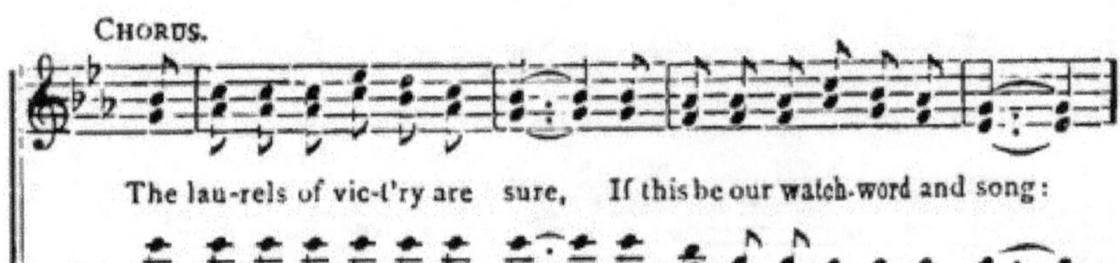
The lau-rels of vic-t'ry are sure, If this be our watch-word and song:

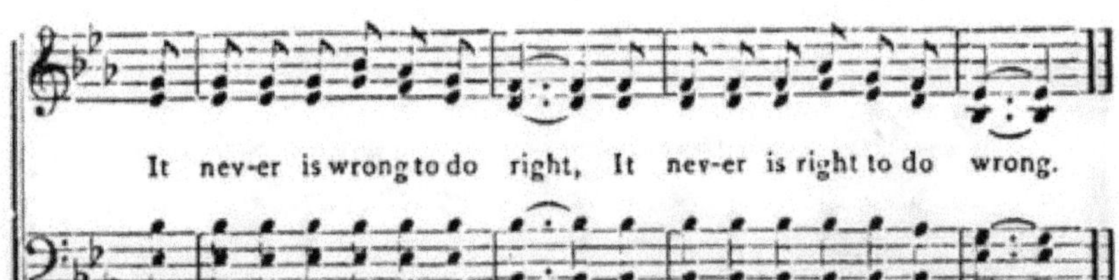
It nev-er is wrong to do right, It nev-er is right to do wrong.

No. 208. Hast Thou Heard of Jesus?

Mrs. E. C. Ellsworth.
J. H. Tenny.
1. Hast thou heard of that won-der-ful Je-sus, Who dwelt among sinners, a God? Who in pu - ri - ty walked with the vil-est, Dis-pens-ing his fa-vors a-broad?
2. Hast thou heard of that won-der-ful Je-sus, Re - ject - ed by sinners of old? He is wait - ing to-day to be gra-cious, Yet slight-ed by num-bers un-told.
3. Hast thou heard that this won-der-ful Je-sus, Dwells now with the low-ly in heart? With the hum - ble he walks in com-mun-ion, And grace he will free-ly im - part.
Chorus.
Oh, that won-der-ful, won-der-ful Je-sus! He left the bright glo-ry a-bove, On a world in its sin and its ru-in, To pour out his in-fi-nite love.

No. 209. Christmas.
E. H. Sears.
CAROL,
R. S. Willis.
Joyful.
1. It came up-on the mid-night clear, That glo-rious song of old,
2. Still thro' the clo-ven skies they come, With peace-ful wings un-furl'd,
3. O ye be-neath life's crush-ing load, Whose forms are bend-ing low,
4. For lo, the days are hast-'ning on, By pro-phets seen of old,
From an-gels bend-ing near the earth, To touch their harps of gold;
And still their heav'n-ly mu-sic floats, O'er all the wea-ry world:
Who toil a-round the climb-ing way, With pain-ful steps and slow!
When with the ev-er-cir-cling years, Shall come the time fore-told,
"Peace on the earth, good-will to men, From heav'n's all gra-cious King,"
A-bove its sad and lone-ly plains, They bend on hov-'ring wing,
Look now, for glad and gold-en hours, Come swift-ly on the wing;
When the new heav'n and earth shall own, The Prince of Peace their King,
The world in sol-emn still-ness lay, To hear the an-gels sing.
And ev-er o'er the Ba-bel sounds, The bless-ed an-gels sing.
Oh, rest be-side the wea-ry road, And hear the an-gels sing.
And the whole world send back the song, Which now the an-gels sing. A-men.

No. 210. Sing Hosanna.

Fredric W. Root.
1. Sing Ho-san - nas loud and clear, David's Son doth now ap-pear;
2. Sing Ho-san - nas loud and clear, David's Lord doth now ap-pear:
3. Sing Ho-san - nas loud and clear, David's King doth now ap-pear,
In a man - ger low He lies, Though the Lord of earth and skies,
Shep-herds and Wise Men from far, Led by Bethle'em's guiding star,
An-gel choirs announce His birth, Singing, "Peace, good will on earth."
Songs of joy we'll raise to-day, Join-ing in the an-gel's lay;
Join to raise in sweet ac-cord, Songs of praise to David's Lord.
Earth-ly choirs re-spon'd, and sing, "Hail to David's Lord and King."
Chorus.
"Ho - san - na, Ho - san - na, Ho-san-na in the highest, in the
high-est!" Sing Ho-san-nas loud and clear, Davids { Son, Lord, King, } doth now ap-pear.

No. 211. Welcome Happy Morning.
J. Ellerton.
EASTER SONG.
Arthur Sullivan.
1. Welcome, hap-py morn - ing! Age to age shall say; Hell to-day is
2. Earth with joy con - fess - es, Clothing her for spring, All good gifts re-
3 Mak-er and Re - deem - er, life and health of all, Thou from heav'n be-
4. Thou, of life the au - thor; death didst un-der - go. Tread the path of
5. Loose the souls long prisoned, bound with Sa-tan's chain; All that now is
van-quished, heav'n is won to - day! Lo, the dead is liv - ing,
turned with her re - turn-ing King; Bloom in ev-'ry mead-ow,
hold - ing hu - man na-tures fall, Of the Father's God - head
dark - ness, saving strength to show; Come, then, true and faith - ful,
fal - len raise to life a - gain, Show thy face in bright - ness,
God for-ev - ermore! Him, their true Cre - a - tor, all his works a-dore.
leaves on ev-'ry bough, Speak His sorrows end - ed, hail his triumph now.
true and on - ly Son, Manhood to de - liv - er, Manhood didst put on.
now ful - fill thy word, 'Tis thine own third morn-ing, rise, my bur-ied Lord!
bid the nations see, Bring a-gain our day - light; day returns with thee!
Chorus.
Wel-come hap-py morn - ing! age to age shall say,
say, hell to-
Hell to - day is van - quished, heav'n is won to - day.
day is

No. 212. There's a Beautiful Land on High.

1. There's a beautiful land on high,
To its glories I fain would fly,—
When by sorrows pressed down,
I long for a crown,
In that beautiful land on high.

Cho.—In that beautiful land I'll be,
From earth and its cares set free;
My Jesus is there,
He's gone to prepare
A place in that land for me.

2. There's a beautiful land on high,
I shall enter it by and by;
There, with friends, hand in hand,
I shall walk on the strand,
In that beautiful land on high.—Cho.

3. There's a beautiful land on high,
Then why should I fear to die,
When death is the way
To the realms of day,
In that beautiful land on high.—Cho.

4. There's a beautiful land on high.
And my kindred its bliss enjoy;
Methinks I now see
How they're waiting for me,
In that beautiful land on high.—Cho.

5. There's a beautiful land on high,
Where we never shall say "good-bye!"
When over the river
We're happy forever,
In that beautiful land on high.—Cho.

No. 213. Jesus Bids Us Shine.

E. O. Excell.

1. Je - sus bids us shine, With a clear pure light, Like a lit - tle can - dle
2 Je - sus bids us shine, First of all for Him; Well He sees and knows it,
3. Je - sus bids us shine, Then for all a - round, Ma - ny kinds of dark - ness,
Burn - ing in the night, In this world of dark - ness,
If our light is dim; He looks down from hea - ven,
In this world a - bound, Sin and want and sor - row;
We must shine, You in your small cor - ner, And I in mine.
Sees us shine, You in your small cor - ner, And I in mine.
We must shine, You in your small cor - ner, And I in mine.

No. 214. Merry Christmas.

A. M. STARKWEATHER. (To JOHN SIGGINS.) E. O. EXCELL.

(The words, "Come. Thou Fount," may be used to this music, by omitting Chorus.)

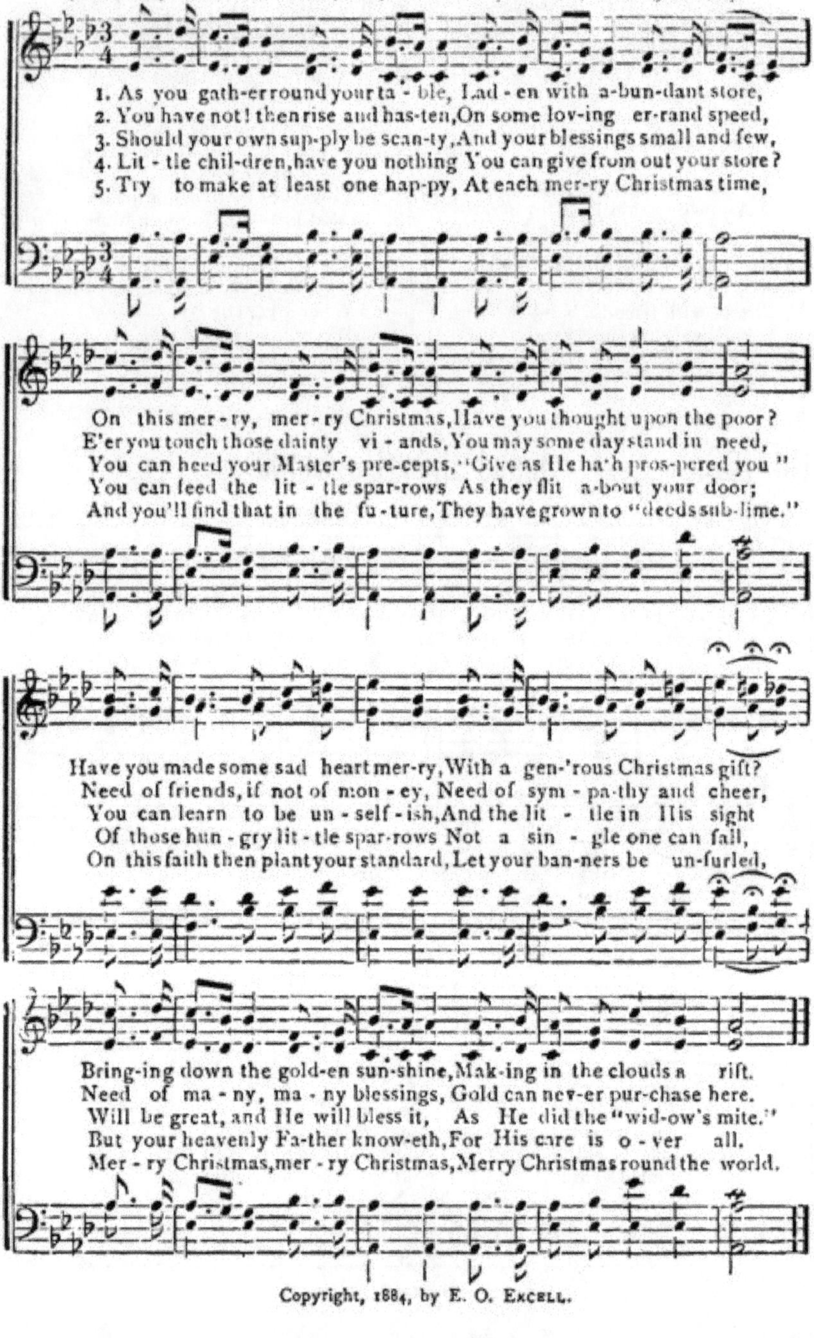

1. As you gath-er round your ta - ble, Lad - en with a-bun-dant store,
2. You have not! then rise and has-ten, On some lov-ing er-rand speed,
3. Should your own sup-ply be scan-ty, And your blessings small and few,
4. Lit - tle chil-dren, have you nothing You can give from out your store?
5. Try to make at least one hap-py, At each mer-ry Christmas time,

On this mer-ry, mer-ry Christmas, Have you thought upon the poor?
E'er you touch those dainty vi - ands, You may some day stand in need,
You can heed your Master's pre-cepts, "Give as He hath pros-pered you"
You can feed the lit - tle spar-rows As they flit a-bout your door;
And you'll find that in the fu - ture, They have grown to "deeds sub-lime."

Have you made some sad heart mer-ry, With a gen-'rous Christmas gift?
Need of friends, if not of mon - ey, Need of sym - pa-thy and cheer,
You can learn to be un - self - ish, And the lit - tle in His sight
Of those hun - gry lit - tle spar-rows Not a sin - gle one can fall,
On this faith then plant your standard, Let your ban-ners be un-furled,

Bring-ing down the gold-en sun-shine, Mak-ing in the clouds a rift.
Need of ma - ny, ma - ny blessings, Gold can nev-er pur-chase here.
Will be great, and He will bless it, As He did the "wid-ow's mite."
But your heavenly Fa-ther know-eth, For His care is o - ver all.
Mer - ry Christmas, mer - ry Christmas, Merry Christmas round the world.

Merry Christmas.—Concluded.
Chorus.
Merry Christmas for the "big folks," Merry Christmas for the small; Christmas for you all.
Merry Christmas,
Merry Christmas,
No. 215.
Come Ye to Bethlehem.
Let us go even unto Bethlehem. Luke. 11: 15.
John Reading.
Oakley.
1. Oh come, all ye faith-ful, Joy-ful and tri-umph-ant, Oh come ye, Oh come ye to Beth - le-hem; Come and be-hold him, Born, the King of an-gels; Oh come, let us a-dore Him, Oh
2. Sing choirs of an-gels, Sing in ex - ul - ta - tion, Sing all ye ci - ti - zens of heaven a - bove, Glo - ry to God.... In ..... the.... high-est; Oh come, etc.
3. Yea, Lord, we greet Thee, Born this hap-py morn ing; Je - sus to Thee be ..... glo - ry given; Word of the Fa - ther, Now in flesh ap-pear-ing; Oh come, etc.
come, let us a-dore Him. Oh come, let us a-dore Him Christ the Lord.

No. 216. Sinner Go, Will You Go?

Unknown. Scotch.

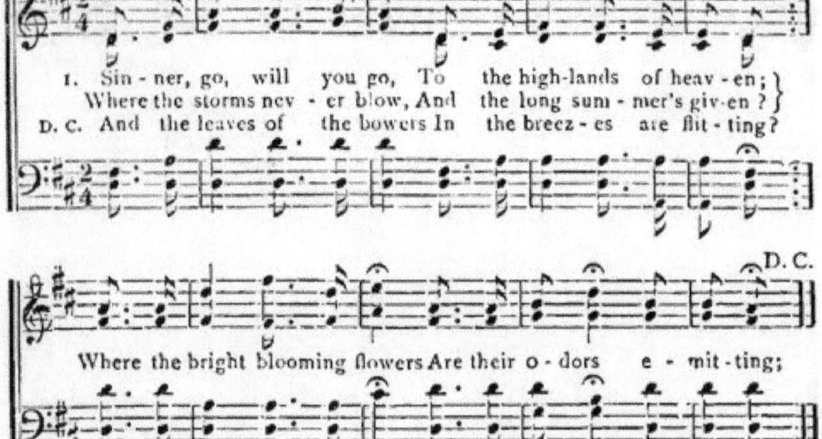
1. Sin - ner, go, will you go, To the high-lands of heav - en;
Where the storms nev - er blow, And the long sum - mer's giv - en?
D. C. And the leaves of the bowers In the breez - es are flit - ting?
D. C.
Where the bright blooming flowers Are their o - dors e - mit - ting;

2. Where the rich golden fruit
Is in bright clusters pending,
And the deep laden boughs
Of life's fair tree are bending;
And where life's crystal stream
Is unceasingly flowing,
And the verdure is green,
And eternally growing?

3. He's prepared thee a home—
Sinner, canst thou believe it?
And invites thee to come—
Sinner, wilt thou receive it?
Oh come, sinner, come,
For the tide is receding,
And the Savior will soon,
And forever, cease pleading.

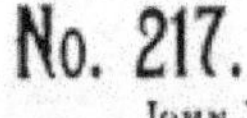

No. 217. The Model Church.

John Yates. E. O. Excell.

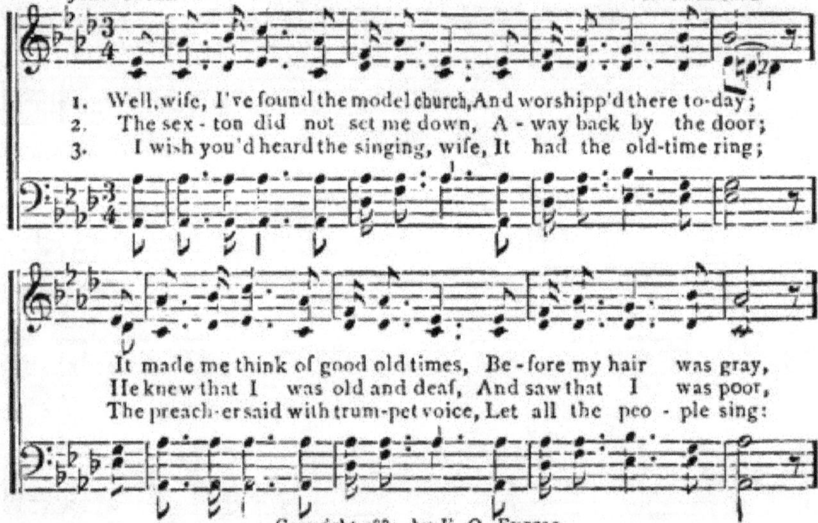
1. Well, wife, I've found the model church, And worshipp'd there to-day;
2. The sex - ton did not set me down, A - way back by the door;
3. I wish you'd heard the singing, wife, It had the old-time ring;
It made me think of good old times, Be - fore my hair was gray,
He knew that I was old and deaf, And saw that I was poor,
The preach - er said with trum - pet voice, Let all the peo - ple sing:

The Model Church.—Concluded.

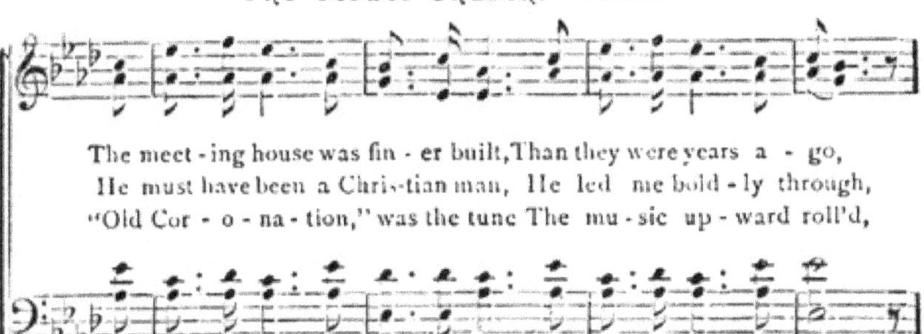

The meet - ing house was fin - er built, Than they were years a - go,
He must have been a Chris-tian man, He led me bold - ly through,
"Old Cor - o - na - tion," was the tune The mu - sic up - ward roll'd,

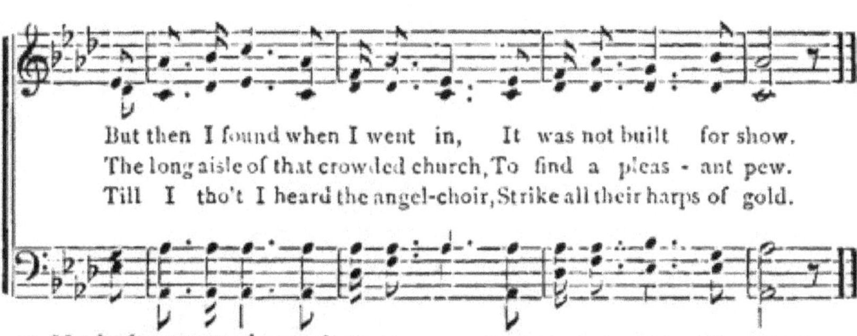

But then I found when I went in, It was not built for show.
The long aisle of that crowded church, To find a pleas - ant pew.
Till I tho't I heard the angel-choir, Strike all their harps of gold.

4. My deafness seemed to melt away,
   My spirit caught the fire;
   I joined my feeble, trembling voice,
   With that melodious choir;
   And sang, as in my youthful days,
   "Let angel's prostrate fall;

Bring forth the roy-al di - a-dem,

And crown him Lord of all."

5. I tell you, wife, it did me good
   To sing that hymn once more;
   I felt like some wrecked mariner
   Who gets a glimpse of shore.
   I almost want to lay aside
   This weather-beaten form,
   And anchor in the blessed port,
   Forever from the storm.

6. 'Twas not a flowery sermon, wife.
   But simple gospel truth;
   It fitted humble men like me;
   It suited hopeful youth,
   To win immortal souls to Christ,
   The earnest preacher tried;
   He talked not of himself, or creed,
   But Jesus crucified.

7. Dear wife, the toil will soon be o'er,
   The victory soon be won;
   The shining land is just ahead,
   Our race is nearly run;
   We're nearing Canaan's happy shore,
   Our home so bright and fair:
   Thank God, we'll never sin again;

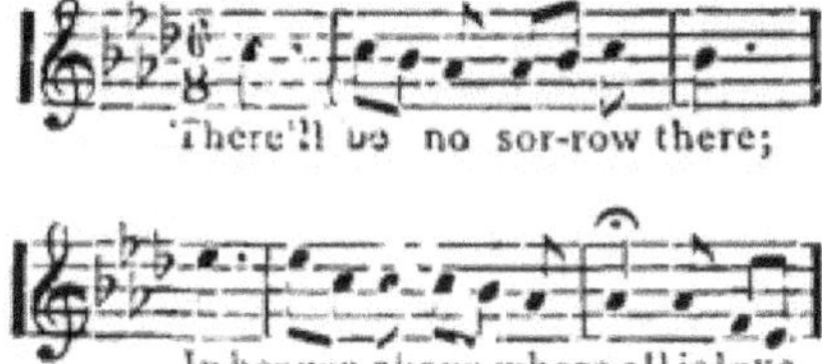

There'll be no sor-row there;
In heaven above where all is love,

There'll be no sor - row there.

No. 218. Work Song.
Sidney Dyer.
Lowell Mason.
1
2
1. Work, for the night is com-ing, Work thro' the morn-ing hours;
Work while the dew is spark ling, Omit Work 'mid springing
D. C. Work, for the night is com-ing, Omit. When man's work is
Fine.
cres.
D. C.
flow'rs; Work, when the day grows bright-er Work in the glow-ing sun;
done.
2. Work, for the night is coming,
Work through the sunny noon;
Fill brightest hours with labor,
Rest comes sure and soon,
Give every flying minute,
Something to keep in store;
Work, for the night is coming,
When man works no more.
3. Work, for the night is coming,
Under the sunset skies;
While their bright tints are glowing,
Work, for daylight flies.
Work till the last beam fadeth,
Fadeth to shine no more;
Work while the night is darkening,
When man's work is o'er.
No. 219. I Am Coming to the Cross.
Wm. McDonald.
W. G. Fischer, by per.
1. I am com - ing to the cross; I am poor, and weak, and blind;
2. Long my heart has sighed for thee, Long has e - vil reigned with-in;
3. Here I give my all to thee, Friends, and time, and earth - ly store;
Chorus. I am trust - ing, Lord, in thee; Blest Lamb of Cal - va - ry;
I am count-ing all but dross, I shall full sal - va - tion find.
Je - sus sweet-ly speaks to me,— "I will cleanse you from all sin."
Soul and bo - dy thine to be, Whol - ly thine for - ev - er - more.
Hum-bly at thy cross I bow, Save me, Je - sus, save me now.

No. 220. In the Cross of Christ I Glory.

Sir. J. Bowring. RATHBUN. 8s. 7s. J. Conkey.

1. In the cross of Christ I glo-ry, Tow'ring o'er the wrecks of time;

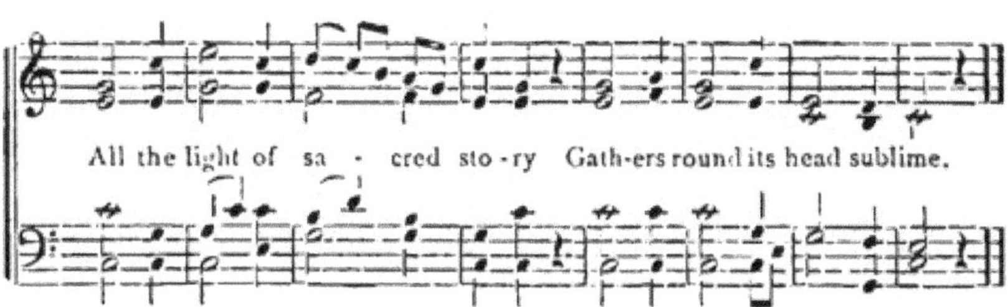
All the light of sa - cred sto-ry Gath-ers round its head sublime.

2. When the woes of life o'ertake me,
Hopes deceive, and fears annoy,
Never shall the cross forsake me;
Lo! it glows with peace and joy.

3. When the sun of bliss is beaming
Light and love upon my way,
From the cross the radiance streaming
Adds more lu-tre to the day.

4. Bane and blessing, pain and pleasure,
By the cross are sanctified;
Peace is there, that knows no measure,
Joys that through all time abide.

No. 221. HARK! WHAT MEAN THOSE HOLY VOICES?

Caswood. Tune—RATHBUN. 8s. 7s.

Hark! what mean those holy voices,
Sweetly sounding through the skies?
Lo! the angelic host rejoices;
Heavenly hallelujahs rise.

2 Hear them tell the wondrous story,
Hear them chant in hymns of joy:—
"Glory in the highest, glory!
Glory be to God most high!

3. "Peace on earth, good-will from heaven,
Reaching far as man is found;
Souls redeemed, and sins forgiven!
Loud our golden harps shall sound.

4. "Christ is born, the great Anointed!
Heaven and earth His praises sing;
Oh, receive whom God appointed,
For your Prophet, Priest, and King.

5. "Haste, ye mortals, to adore him;
Learn his name and taste his joy;
Till in heaven ye sing before him—
'Glory be to God most high!'"

No. 222. THERE'S A WIDENESS IN GOD'S MERCY.

F. W. Faber. Tune—RATHBUN. 8s. 7s.

1. There's a wideness in God's mercy,
Like the wideness of the sea:
There's a kindness in His justice,
Which is more than liberty.

2. There is welcome for the sinner,
And more graces for the good;
There is mercy with the Savior;
There is healing in his blood.

3. For the love of God is broader
Than the measure of man's mind;
And the heart of the Eternal
Is most wonderfully kind.

4. If our love were but more simple,
We should take him at his word;
And our lives would be all sunshine
In the sweetness of our Lord.

No. 223. Come, Thou Almighty King.

CHARLES WESLEY. ITALIAN HYMN. 6s, 4s. FELICE GIARDINI.

Come, thou al - might - y King, Help us thy name to sing,
Help us to praise! Fa - ther all glo - ri - ous, O'er all vic-
to - ri - ous, Come, and reign ov - er us, An-cient of days.

2. Come, holy Comforter,
Thy sacred witness bear,
In this glad hour;
Thou, who almighty art,
Now rule in every heart,
And ne'er from us depart,
Spirit of pow'r.

3. To Thee, great One in Three,
The highest praises be,
Hence, evermore;
Thy sovereign majesty
May we in glory see,
And to eternity
Love and adore.

No. 224. CHRIST FOR THE WORLD WE SING.

SAMUEL WOLCOTT. Tune—ITALIAN HYMN. 6s. 4s.

1. Christ for the world we sing,
The world to Christ we bring,
With love and zeal,
The poor and them that mourn,
The faint and overborne,
Sin sick and sorrow worn,
Whom Christ doth heal.

2. Christ for the world we sing,
The world to Christ we bring,
With fervent prayer;
The way ward and the lost,
By restless passion tossed,
Redeemed at countless cost,
From dark despair.

3. Christ for the world we sing,
The world to Christ we bring,
With one accord:
With us the work to share,
With us reproach to dare,
With us the cross to bear,
For Christ our Lord.

No. 225. GOD BLESS OUR NATIVE LAND.

JOHN DWIGHT. Tune—ITALIAN HYMN. 6s. 4s.

1. God bless our native land!
Firm may she ever stand,
Through storm and night:
When the wild tempests rave,
Ruler of wind and wave,
Do thou our country save
By thy great might!

2. For her our prayers shall rise
To God, above the skies;
On him we wait:
Thou who art ever nigh,
Guarding with watchful eye,
To thee aloud we cry,
God save the State!

No. 226. The Morning Light is Breaking.

SAMUEL F. SMITH — WEBB. 7s, 6s. — GEO. WEBB.

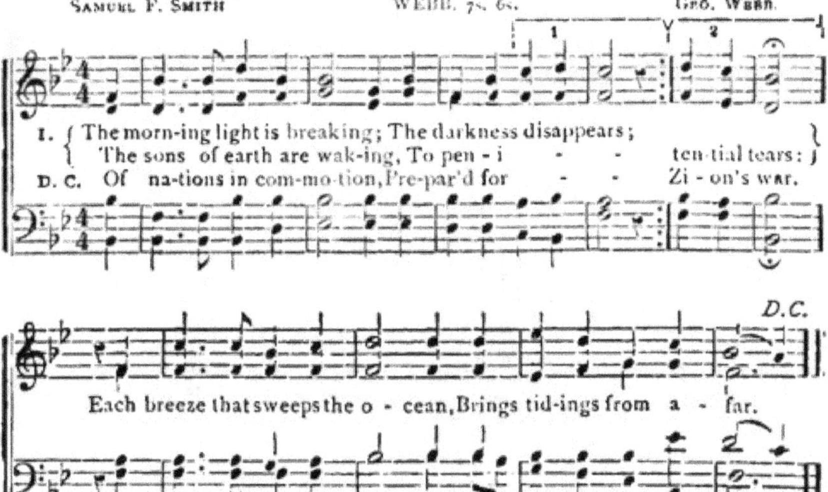
1 2
1. { The morn-ing light is break-ing; The dark-ness dis-ap-pears;
The sons of earth are wak-ing, To pen - i - - ten-tial tears: }
D. C. Of na-tions in com-mo-tion, Pre-par'd for - - Zi - on's war.
D.C.
Each breeze that sweeps the o - cean, Brings tid-ings from a - far.

2. See heathen nations bending,
Before the God of love,
And thousand hearts ascending,
In gratitude above;
While sinners, now confessing,
The gospel's call obey,
And seek a Savior's blessing,
A nation in a day.

3. Blest river of salvation,
Pursue thy onward way;
Flow thou to every nation,
Nor in thy richness stay:
Stay not till all the lowly,
Triumphant reach their home:
Stay not till all the holy
Proclaim, "The Lord is come!"

No. 227. STAND UP, STAND UP FOR JESUS.

GEO. DUFFIELD. — Tune.—WEBB 7s. 8s.

1. Stand up, stand up for Jesus,
Ye soldiers of the cross;
Lift high your royal banner,
It must not suffer loss:
From victory unto victory,
His army shall he lead,
Till every foe is vanquished,
And Christ is Lord indeed.

2. Stand up, stand up for Jesus,
The trumpet call obey;
Forth to the mighty conflict,
In this his glorious day:
"Ye that are men, now serve him,"
Against unnumbered foes;
Your courage rise with danger,
And strength to strength oppose.

3. Stand up, stand up for Jesus,
Stand in his strength alone;
The arm of flesh will fail you;
Ye dare not trust your own;
Put on the gospel armor,
Each piece put on with prayer,
Where duty calls, or danger,
Be never wanting there.

No. 228. OUR COUNTRY'S VOICE IS PLEADING.

MRS. ANDERSON. — Tune.—WEBB, 7s. 8s.

1. Our country's voice is pleading,
Ye men of God, arise!
His providence is leading,
The land before you lies;
Day-gleams are o'er it brightening,
And promise clothes the soil;
Wide fields, for harvest whitening,
Invite the reaper's toil.

2. The love of Christ unfolding,
Speed on from east to west,
Till all, his cross beholding,
In him are fully blest,
Great Author of salvation,
Haste, haste the glorious day,
When we, a ransomed nation,
Thy scepter shall obey!

No. 229 All Hail the Power of Jesus' Name.

PERONET. CORONATION. C. M. OLIVER HOLDEN.

1. All hail the pow'r of Je - sus' name! Let an - gels prostrate fall;
Bring forth the roy - al di - a - dem, And crown Him Lord of all;

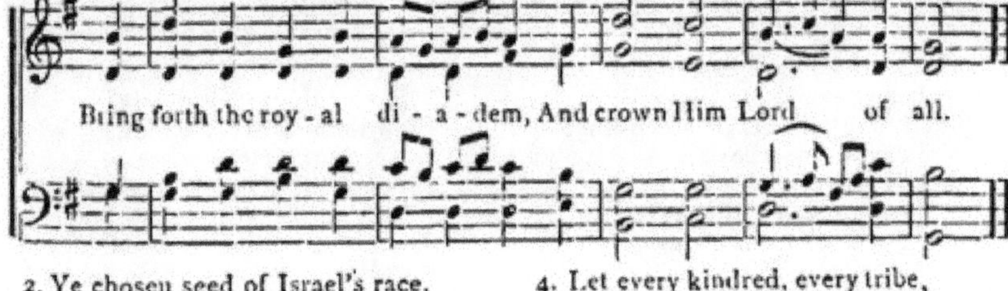
Bring forth the roy - al di - a - dem, And crown Him Lord of all.

2. Ye chosen seed of Israel's race,
Ye ransomed from the fall,
Hail Him who saves you by His grace,
And crown Him Lord of all.

3. Sinners, whose love can ne'er forget
The wormwood and the gall,
Go, spread your trophies at His feet,
And crown Him Lord of all.

4. Let every kindred, every tribe,
On this terrestrial ball,
To Him all majesty ascribe,
And crown Him Lord of all.

5. Oh, that with yonder sacred throng
We at his feet may fall;
We'll join the everlasting song,
And crown him Lord of all.

No. 230. OH, FOR A THOUSAND TONGUES TO SING.

CHARLES WESLEY. Tune—CORONATION. C. M.

1. Oh, for a thousand tongues to sing
My great Redeemer's praise;
The glories of my God and King,
The triumphs of his grace.

2. My gracious Master, and my God,
Assist me to proclaim
To spread thro' all the earth abroad,
The honors of thy name.

3. Jesus! the name that charms our fears,
That bids our sorrows cease;
'Tis music in the sinner's ears,
'Tis life, and health, and peace.

No. 231. I WAITED FOR THE LORD.

Unknown. Tune—CORONATION. C. M.

1. I waited for the Lord my God,
And patiently did bear;
At length to me He did incline
My voice and cry to hear.

2. He took me from a fearful pit,
And from the miry clay;
And on a rock He set my feet,
Establishing my way.

3. He put a new song in my mouth,
Our God to magnify;
Many shall see it, and shall fear,
And on the Lord rely.

No. 232. From Greenland's Icy Mountain.

Heber. MISSIONARY HYMN. 7s, 6s. Mason.

1. From Greenland's i - cy mountains, From In - dia's cor - al strand;
Where Af-ric's sun-ny foun-tains, (Omit)
Roll down their golden sand; From many an an-cient riv-er, From many a palm-y
plain, They call us to de - liv - er, Their land from er-ror's chain.

2. Shall we, whose souls are lighted,
With wisdom from on high,
Shall we, to men benighted,
The lamp of life deny?
Salvation! oh, salvation!
The joyful sound proclaim,
Till earth's remotest nation
Has learned Messiah's name.

3. Waft, waft, ye winds, his story,
And you, ye waters, roll,
Till, like a sea of glory,
It spreads from pole to pole;
Till o'er our ransomed nature,
The Lamb for sinners slain,
Redeemer, King, Creator,
In bliss returns to reign.

No. 233. WHEN SHALL THE VOICE OF SINGING?

James Edmeston. Tune.—MISSIONARY HYMN. 7s. 6s.

1. When shall the voice of singing
Flow joyfully along,
When hill and valley ringing,
With one triumphant song,
Proclaim the contest ended,
And Him who once was slain,
Again to earth descended
In righteousness to reign?

2. Then from the craggy mountains,
The sacred shout shall fly;
And shady vales and fountains,
Shall echo the reply,
High tower and lowly dwelling.
Shall send the chorus round,
All hallelujah's swelling,
In one eternal sound!

No. 234. ROLL ON THOU MIGHTY OCEAN.

James Edmeston. Tune.—MISSIONARY HYMN. 7s, 6s.

1. Roll on, thou mighty ocean!
And, as thy billows flow,
Bear messengers of mercy
To every land below.
Arise, ye gales, and waft them
Safe to the destined shore;
That man may sit in darkness,
And death's black shade, no more.

2. O thou eternal Ruler,
Who holdest in thine arm
The tempests of the ocean,
Protect them, from all harm!
Thy presence, Lord, be with them,
Where ever they may be;
Though far from us who love them
Still let them be with thee.

No. 235. On the Mountain's Top Appearing.

Thomas Kelly. ZION. 8, 7, 4. Thomas Hastings.

1. On the moun-tain's top ap-pear-ing, Lo! the sa-cred her-ald stands, } Mourn-ing cap-tive! God him-self shall loose thy bands;
Wel-come news to Zi-on bear-ing, Zi-on, long in hos-tile lands; }
Mourn-ing cap-tive! God him-self shall loose thy bands.

2. God, thy God, will now restore thee;
He himself appears thy Friend;
All thy foes shall flee before thee;
Hear their boasts and triumphs end;
‖: Great deliverance
Zion's King will surely send. :‖

3. Peace and joy shall now attend thee;
All thy warfare now is past;
God thy Saviour will defend thee;
Victory is thine at last;
‖: All thy conflicts
End in everlasting rest. :‖

No. 236. ZION STANDS WITH HILLS SURROUNDED.

Thomas Kelly. Tune—ZION. 8, 7, 4.

1 Zion stands with hills surrounded,
Zion, kept by power divine;
All her foes shall be confounded,
Though the world in arms combine;
‖: Happy Zion,
What a favored lot is thine! :‖

2. Every human tie may perish;
Friend to friend unfaithful prove;
Mothers cease their own to cherish;
Heaven and earth at last remove;
‖: But no changes
Can attend Jehovah's love. :‖

3. In the furnace God may prove thee,
Thence to bring thee forth more bright,
But can never cease to love thee;
Thou art precious in his sight;
‖: God is with thee,
God, thine everlasting light. :‖

No. 237. O'ER THE GLOOMY HILLS OF DARKNESS.

Williams. Tune—ZION. 8, 7, 4.

1. O'er the gloomy hills of darkness,
Cheered by no celestial ray,
Sun of righteousness! arising,
Bring the bright, the glorious day;
‖: Send the gospel
To the earth's remotest bound. :‖

2. Kingdoms wide that sit in darkness,—
Grant them, Lord! the glorious light;
And, from eastern coast to western,
May the morning chase the night,
‖: And redemption,
Freely purchased, win the day. :‖

3. Fly abroad, thou mighty gospel!
Win and conquer, never cease;
May thy lasting, wide dominion
Multiply and still increase;
‖: Sway the sceptre,
Saviour! all the world around. :‖

No. 238. Blow Ye the Trumpet.

CHARLES WESLEY. LENOX. H. M. LEWIS EDSON.

1. Blow ye the trumpet, blow The gladly solemn sound; Let all the nations
know, To earth's remotest bound, The year of ju - bi - lee is come; The
year of ju - bi - lee is come; Re - turn, ye ransomed sin - ners, home.

2. Jesus, our great High priest;
Has full atonement made;
Ye weary spirits, rest;
Ye mourning souls be glad;
‖: The year of jubilee is come; :‖
Return, ye ransomed sinners, home.

3. Exalt the Lamb of God,
The sin atoning Lamb;
Redemption by His blood
Through all the world proclaim;
‖: The year of jubilee is come; :‖
Return, ye ransomed sinners, home.

No. 239. ARISE, MY SOUL, ARISE.

CHARLES WESLEY. Tune—LENOX. H. M.

1. Arise, my soul, arise;
Shake off thy guilty fears;
The bleeding sacrifice
In my behalf appears:
‖: Before the throne my surety stands, :‖
My name is written on his hands.

2. He ever lives above
For me to intercede,
His all redeeming love,
His precious blood to plead;
‖: His blood atoned for all our race, :‖
And sprinkles now the throne of grace.

3. The Father hears him pray,
His dear anointed one;
He can not turn away
The presence of his Son;
‖: His Spirit answers to the blood, :‖
And tells me I am born of God.

No. 240. LET EARTH AND HEAVEN AGREE.

CHARLES WESLEY. Tune—LENOX. H. M.

1. Let earth and heaven agree,
Angels and men be joined,
To celebrate with me
The Savior of mankind;
‖: T' adore the all-atoning Lamb. :‖
And bless the sound of Jesus' name.

2. Jesus! transporting sound!
The joy of earth and heaven;
No other help is found,
No other name is given,
‖: By which we can salvation have; :‖
But Jesus came the world to save.

3. Oh, for a trumpet voice!
On all the world to call,—
To bid their hearts rejoice
In him who died for all:
‖: For all, my Lord was crucified; :‖
For all, for all, my Savior died.

No. 241. Sun of My Soul.

JOHN KEBLE. HURSLEY. L. M. ART. by HENRY MONK.

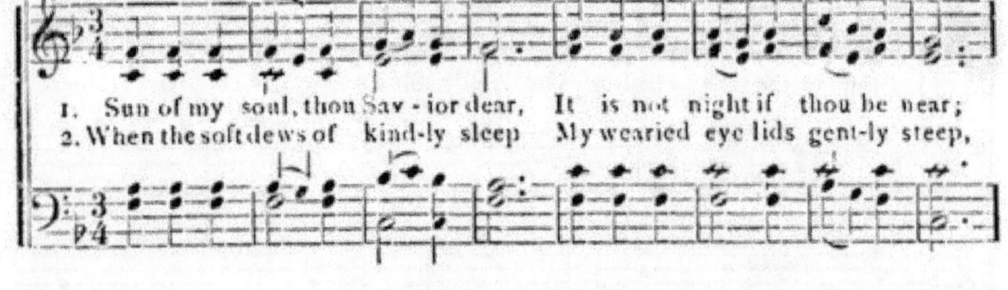

1. Sun of my soul, thou Sav - ior dear, It is not night if thou be near;
2. When the soft dews of kind-ly sleep My wearied eye lids gent-ly steep,

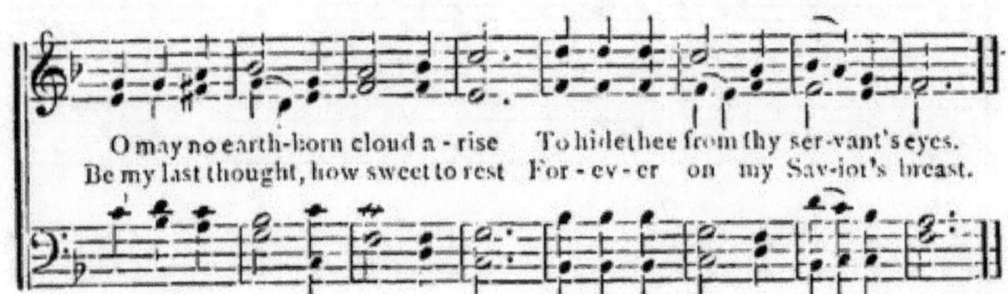

O may no earth-born cloud a - rise To hide thee from thy ser-vant's eyes.
Be my last thought, how sweet to rest For - ev - er on my Sav-ior's breast.

3. Abide with me from morn till eve
For without thee I cannot live;
Abide with me when night is nigh,
For without thee I dare not die.

4. If some poor wandering child of thine
Have spurned to-day the voice divine,
Now, Lord, the gracious work begin;
Let him no more lie down in sin.

5. Watch by the sick; enrich the poor
With blessings from thy boundless store;
Be every mourner's sleep to night,
Like infant's slumbers, pure and light.

6. Come near and bless us when we wake,
Ere thro' the world our way we take,
Till in the ocean of thy love,
We lose ourselves in heaven above.

No. 242. SAY SINNER!

MRS. A. B HYDE. Tune—HURSLEY. L. M.

1. Say, sinner! hath a voice within
Oft whispered to thy secret soul,
Urged thee to leave the ways of sin,
And yield thy heart to God's control?

2. Sinner! it was a heavenly voice—
It was the Spirit's gracious call;
It bade thee make the better choice,
And haste to seek in Christ thine all.

3. Spurn not the call to life and light;
Regard, in time, the warning kind;
That call thou may'st not always slight,
And yet the gate of mercy find.

4. God's Spirit will not always strive
With hardened, self-destroying man;
Ye who persist his love to grieve,
May never hear his voice again.

No. 243. OH, THAT MY LOAD OF SIN WERE GONE.

CHARLES WESLEY. Tune—HURSLEY. L. M.

1. Oh, that my load of sin were gone;
Oh, that I could at last submit
At Jesus' feet to lay it down—
To lay my soul at Jesus' feet.

2. Rest for my soul I long to find;
Saviour of all, if mine thou art,
Give me thy meek and lowly mind,
And stamp thine image on my heart.

3. Break off the yoke of inbred sin,
And fully set my spirit free;
I cannot rest till pure within,
Till I am wholly lost in thee.

4. Fain would I learn of thee, my God,
Thy light and easy burden prove.
The cross all stained with hallowed [blood,
The labor of thy dying love.

No. 244. Oh, For a Heart to Praise My God.

Charles Wesley. AVON. C. M. Hugh Wilson.

Oh, for a heart to praise my God, A heart from sin set free!
A heart that al - ways feels thy blood So free - ly spilt for me!

2. A heart resigned, submissive, meek,
My great Redeemer's throne;
Where only Christ is heard to speak,
Where Jesus reigns alone.

3. Oh, for a lowly, contrite heart,
Believing, true, and clean,
Which neither life nor death can part
From him that dwells within.

4. A heart in every thought renewed,
And full of love divine;
Perfect, and right, and pure, and good,
A copy, Lord, of thine.

5. Thy nature, gracious Lord, impart;
Come quickly from above;
Write thy new name upon my heart,
Thy new, best name of Love.

No. 245. OH, FOR A CLOSER WALK WITH GOD.

Wm. Cowper. Tune—AVON. C. M.

1. Oh, for a closer walk with God—
A calm and heavenly frame;
A light to shine upon the road
That leads me to the Lamb.

2. What peaceful hours I once enjoy'd!
How sweet their mem'ry still!
But they have left an aching void
The world can never fill.

3 Return, O holy Dove, return,
Sweet messenger of rest,
I hate the sins that made thee mourn,
And drove thee from my breast.

4. The dearest idol I have known,
What'er that idol be,
Help me to tear it from thy throne,
And worship only thee.

5. So shall my walk be close with God,
Calm and serene my frame;
So purer light shall mark the road
That leads me to the Lamb.

No. 246. ALAS! AND DID MY SAVIOUR BLEED?

Isaac Watts. Tune—AVON. C. M.

1. Alas! and did my Savior bleed,
And did my Sov'reign die?
Would he devote that sacred head
For such a worm as I?

2. Was it for crimes that I have done
He groan'd upon thee tree?
Amazing pity! grace unknown!
And love beyond degree!

3. Well might the sun in darkness hide,
And shut his glories in,
When Christ, the mighty Maker, died
For man, the creature's sin.

4. Thus might I hide my blushing face
While his dear cross appears;
Dissolve my heart in thankfulness,
And melt mine eyes to tears.

5. But drops of grief can ne'er repay
The debt of love I owe,
Here, Lord, I give myself away,—
'Tis all that I can do.

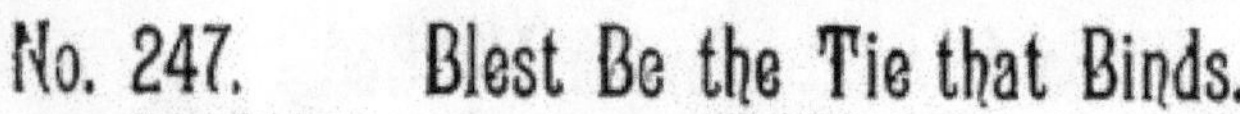
No. 247. Blest Be the Tie that Binds.

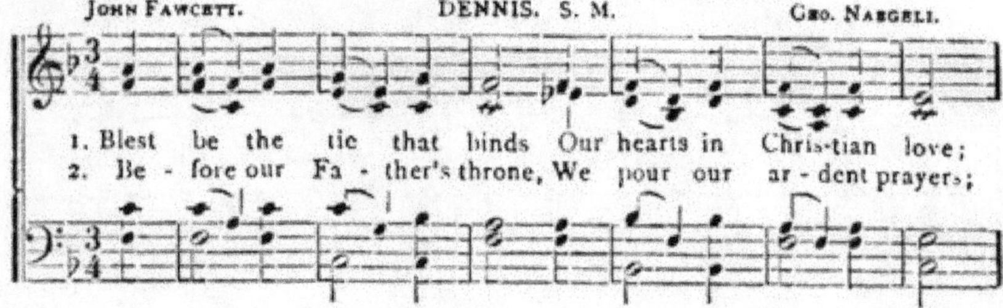
John Fawcett.
DENNIS. S. M.
Geo. Naegeli.
1. Blest be the tie that binds Our hearts in Chris-tian love;
2. Be - fore our Fa - ther's throne, We pour our ar - dent prayers;

The fel - low - ship of kin-dred minds Is like to that a - bove.
Our fears, our hopes, our aims are one Our com-forts and our cares.

3. We share our mutual woes;
Our mutual burdens bear;
And often for each other flows
The sympathising tear.

4. When we asunder part,
It gives us inward pain;
But we shall still be joined in heart,
And hope to meet again.

No. 248. BEHOLD THE THRONE OF GRACE.

Newton.

Tune—DENNIS. S. M.

1. Behold the throne of grace!
The promise calls me near;
There Jesus shows a smiling face,
And waits to answer prayer.

2. That rich atoning blood,
Which sprinkled round I see,
Provides for those who come to God
An all prevailing plea.

3. My soul! ask what thou wilt;
Thou canst not be too bold;
Since his own blood for thee he spilt,
What else can he withhold?

4. Thine image, Lord, bestow,
Thy presence and thy love;
I ask to serve thee here below,
And reign with thee above.

5. Teach me to live by faith;
Conform my will to thine,
Let me victorious be in death,
And then in glory shine.

No. 249. I LOVE THY KINGDOM, LORD.

Dwight.

Tune—DENNIS. S. M.

1. I love thy kingdom, Lord—
The house of thine abode,
The church our blest Redeemer saved
With his own precious blood.

2. I love thy church, O God!
Her walls before thee stand,
Dear as the apple of thine eye,
And graven on thy hand.

3. For her my tears shall fall,
For her my prayers ascend;
To her my cares and toils be given,
Till toils and cares shall end.

4. Beyond my highest joy
I prize her heavenly ways,
Her sweet communion, solemn vows,
Her hymns of love and praise.

5. Jesus, thou Friend divine,
Our Savior and our King,
Thy hand from every snare and foe
Shall great deliverance bring.

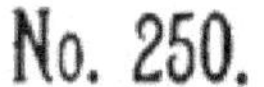

What a Friend.

H. Bonar.
8s, 7s, D.
C. C. Converse. By per.
1. What a friend we have in Je - sus, All our sins and griefs to bear!
Fine.
What a priv-il-ege to car - ry Ev - 'ry thing to God in prayer!
D.S. All because we do not car - ry Ev - 'ry thing to God in prayer!
D. S.
Oh, what peace we of-ten for - feit, Oh, what needless pain we bear.

2. Have we trials and temptations?
Is there trouble anywhere?
We should never be discouraged,
Take it to the Lord in prayer.
Can we find a friend so faithful,
Who will all our sorrows share?
Jesus knows our every weakness,
Take it to the Lord in prayer.

3. Are we weak and heavy laden,
Cumbered with a load of care?
Precious Saviour, still our refuge,—
Take it to the Lord in prayer.
Do thy friends despise, forsake thee?
Take it to the Lord in prayer;
In His arms He'll take and shield thee
Thou wilt find a solace there.

No. 251. SAVIOUR, LIKE A SHEPHERD LEAD US.

Anon.
Tune—WHAT A FRIEND. 8s. 7s. D.

1. Savior, like a shepherd lead us,
Much we need Thy tend'rest care,
In Thy pleasant pastures feed us,
For our use Thy folds prepare;
We are Thine, do Thou befriend us,
Be the Guardian of our way;
Keep Thy flock, from sin defend us,
Seek us when we go astray.

2. Thou hast promised to receive us,
Poor and sinful though we be;
Thou hast mercy to relieve us,
Grace to cleanse and power to free;
Early let us seek Thy favor,
Early let us do Thy will;
Blessed Lord and only Savior,
With Thy love our bosoms fill.

No. 252. GENTLY, LORD, OH, GENTLY LEAD US.

Hastings.
Tune—WHAT A FRIEND. 8s, 7s. D.

1. Gently, Lord, oh, gently lead us
Through this lonely vale of tears;
Thro' the changes thou'st decreed us,
Till our last great change appears.
When temptation's darts assail us,
When in devious paths we stray,
Let thy goodness never fail us,
Lead us in thy perfect way.

2. In the hour of pain and anguish,
In the hour when death draws near,
Suffer not our hearts to languish,—
Suffer not our souls to fear.
And, when mortal life is ended,
Bid us on thy bosom rest,
Till, by angel-bands attended,
We awake among the blest.

No. 253. Jesus, Lover of My Soul.

"The Lord will be a refuge . . . . in times of trouble."—Psalm x. 9.

Charles Wesley. MARTYN 7s, D. S. B. Marsh.

Fine
1. { Je - sus, lov - er of my soul, Let me to Thy bo - som fly,
{ While the nearer wa - ters roll, While the tem - pest still is high!
D. C. Safe in - to the ha - ven guide, Oh, re - ceive my soul at last.

D. C.
Hide me, O my Sav - ior, hide, Till the storm of life is past;

2. Other refuge have I none,
Hangs my helpless soul on Thee;
Leave, oh leave me not alone,
Still support and comfort me.
All my trust on Thee is stayed,
All my help from Thee I bring;
Cover my defenseless head
With the shadow of thy wing.

3. Thou, O Christ, art all I want;
More than all in Thee I find:
Raise the fallen! cheer the faint!
Heal the sick! and lead the blind!
Just and holy is Thy Name,
I am all unrighteousness:
Vile and full of sin I am,
Thou art full of truth and grace.

No. 254. SINNER, TURN! WHY WILL YE DIE?

Charles Wesley. Tune—MARTYN. 7s. D.

1. Sinners, turn! why will ye die?
God, your Maker, asks you "Why?"
God, who did your being give,
Made you with Himself to live;
He the fatal cause demands;
Asks the work of His own hands!
Why, ye thankless creatures, why
Will ye cross His love, and die?

2. Sinners, turn! why will ye die?
God, your Saviour, asks you "Why?"
He, who did your soul retrieve,
Died Himself, that ye might live.
Will you let him die in vain?—
Crucify your Lord again?
Why, ye ransomed sinners, why
Will ye slight His grace, and die?

3. Sinners, turn! why will ye die?
God, the Spirit, asks you "Why?"—
He, who all your lives hath strove,
Urged you to embrace His love.
Will ye not His grace receive?
Will ye still refuse to live?
O ye dying sinners, why?—
Why will ye forever die?

No. 255. WE ARE WAITING, BLESSED LORD.

Unknown. Tune—MARTYN. 7s. D.

1. We are waiting, blessed Lord,
In thy courts with one accord;
At thine altars bending low,
Kindred souls together flow;
Yearing love and strong desire
To thy throne of grace aspire,
And with kindling faith we pray—
Holy Spirit, come to-day.

2. In the closet all alone,
Help us, Christ, to touch thy throne!
As we walk, and talk, and sigh,
Hear, oh, hear thy people's cry;
Bring us nearer to thy heart—
We would dwell no more apart;
Sweep the barriers all away—
Holy Spirit, come to-day.

No. 256. Rock of Ages.

A. M. Toplady. TOPLADY 7s, 6 lines. Thos. Hastings.

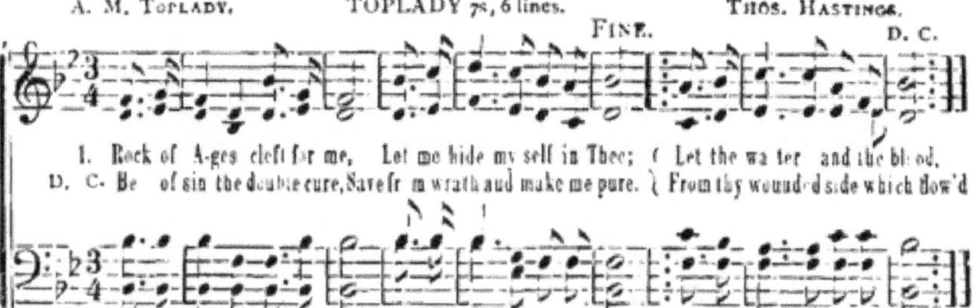
Fine.
D. C.
1. Rock of Ages cleft for me, Let me hide myself in Thee; Let the water and the blood,
D. C. Be of sin the double cure, Save from wrath and make me pure. From thy wounded side which flow'd

2. Could my tears forever flow,
Could my zeal no languor know,
These for sin could not atone;
Thou must save, and thou alone:
In my hand no price I bring;
Simply to thy cross I cling.

3. While I draw this fleeting breath,
When my eyes shall close in death,
When I rise to worlds unknown,
And behold Thee on Thy throne,
Rock of Ages, cleft for me,
Let me hide myself in Thee.

No. 257. TILL HE COME.

Rev. E H Bickersteth. Tune.—TOPLADY. 7s, 6 lines.

1. "Till He come!"—Oh, let the words
Linger on the trembling chords;
Let the "little while" between
In their golden light be seen;
Let us think, how heaven and home
Lie beyond that "Till He come!"

2. When the weary ones we love
Enter on their rest above,
Seems the earth so poor and vast?—
All our life joy over cast?
Hush! be every murmur dumb,
It is only "Till He come!"

3. Clouds and conflicts round us press;
Would we have one sorrow less?
All the sharpness of the cross,
All that tells the world is loss,
Death, and darkness, and the tomb
Only whisper, "Till He come!"

4. See, the feast of love is spread,
Drink the wine, and eat the bread;
Sweet memorials, till the Lord
Call us round His heavenly board,
Some from earth, from glory some,
Severed only "Till He come!"

No. 258. BLESSED JESUS, THOU ART MINE.

Unknown. Tune.—TOPLADY. 7s, 6 lines.

1. Blessed Jesus, thou art mine,
All I have is wholly thine;
Thou dost dwell within my heart,
Thou dost reign in every part:
Blessed Jesus, keep me white,
Keep me walking in the light.

2. I am safe within the fold,
All my cares on Thee are rolled,
I enjoy the sweetest rest,
For I'm leaning on Thy breast;
Blessed Jesus, keep me white,
Keep me walking in the light.

3. Precious Jesus, day by day,
Keep me in the holy way,
Keep my mind in perfect peace;
Every day my faith increase:
Blessed Jesus, keep me white,
Keep me walking in the light.

No. 259. BY THY BIRTH AND BY THY TEARS.

Robt. Grant. Tune.—TOPLADY. 7s, 6 lines.

1 By thy birth, and by thy tears;
By thy human griefs and fears;
By thy conflicts in the hour
Of the subtle tempter's power—
Savior, look with pitying eye;
Savior, help me, or I die.

2. By thy lonely hour of prayer;
By the fearful conflict there;
By thy cross and dying cries;
By thy one great sacrifice,—
Savior, look with pitying eye;
Savior, help me, or I die.

3. By thy triumph o'er the grave;
By thy power the lost to save;
By thy high, majestic throne;
By the empire all thine own,—
Savior, look with pitying eye;
Savior, help me, or I die.

No. 260. Lord, in the Morning.

WATTS. WARWICK. C. M. SAMUEL STANLEY.

1. Lord, in the morn - ing thou shalt hear My voice as - cend - ing high;

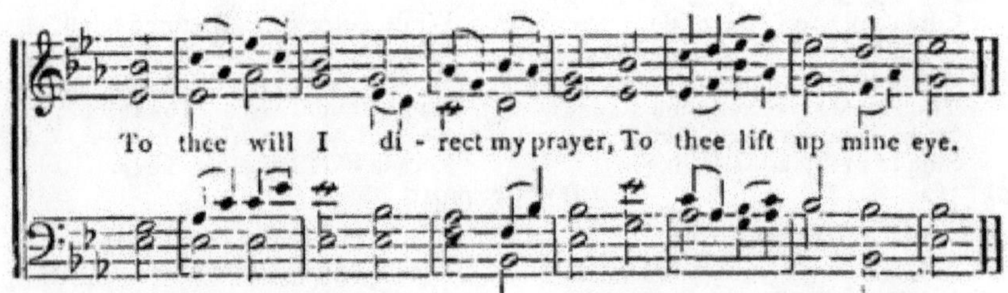
To thee will I di - rect my prayer, To thee lift up mine eye.

2. Up to the hills where Christ is gone,
To plead for all his saints,
Presenting at his Father's throne
Our songs and our complaints.

3. Thou art a God before whose sight
The wicked shall not stand;
Sinners shall ne'er be thy delight,
Nor dwell at thy right hand.

4. But to thy house will I resort
To taste thy mercies there;
I will frequent thy holy court,
And worship in thy fear.

5. Oh, may thy Spirit guide my feet
In ways of righteousness!
Make every path of duty straight,
And plain before my face.

No. 261. JESUS! THE NAME HIGH OVER ALL.

CHARLES WESLEY. Tune—WARWICK. C M.

1. Jesus! the name high over all,
In hell, or earth, or sky;
Angels and men before it fall,
And devils fear and fly.

2. Jesus! the name to sinners dear,
The name to sinners given;
It scatters all their guilty fear;
It turns their hell to heaven.

3. Jesus the prisoner's fetters breaks,
And bruises Satan's head,
Pow'r into strengthless souls he speaks
And life into the dead.

4. O that the world might taste and see
The riches of his grace
The arms of love that compass me
Would all mankind embrace

5. His only righteousness I show,
His saving truth proclaim,
'Tis all my business here below,
To cry, "Behold the Lamb!"

No. 262. JESUS, THE VERY THOUGHT OF THEE.

BERNARD. Tune—WARWICK. C. M.

1. Jesus, the very thought of thee,
With sweetness fills my breast:
But sweeter far thy face to see,
And in thy presence rest.

2. Nor voice can sing, nor heart can [frame,]
Nor can the memory find
A sweeter sound than thy blest name,
O Savior of mankind!

3. O Hope of every contrite heart!
O Joy of all the meek!
To those who fall, how kind thou art!
How good to those who seek!

4. But what to those who find? Ah! this,
Nor tongue nor pen can show;
The love of Jesus, what it is,
None but his loved ones know.

No. 263. Oh, Could I Speak the Matchless Worth.

S. Medley. ARIEL. C. P. M. Dr. Lowell Mason.

1. Oh, could I speak the match-less worth, Oh, could I sound the glo-ries
forth Which in my Sav - ior shine,
I'd soar, and touch the heav'nly strings,
And vie with Ga - briel, while he sings,
In notes almost di-vine, In notes al - most di - vine.

2. I'd sing the precious blood he spilt,
My ransom from the dreadful guilt,
Of sin and wrath divine!
I'd sing his glorious righteousness,
In which all perfect heavenly dress
‖: My soul shall ever shine :‖

3. Well—the delightful day will come,
When my dear Lord will bring me home,
And I shall see his face:
Then with my Savior, Brother, Friend,
A blest eternity I'll spend,
‖: Triumphant in His grace. :‖

No. 264. OH, LET YOUR MINGLING VOICES RISE.

Roscoe. Tune—ARIEL. C. P. M.

1. Oh, let your mingling voices rise
In grateful rapture to the skies,
And hail a Savior's birth;
Let songs of joy the day proclaim
When Jesus all—triumphant came
‖: To bless the sons of earth. :‖

2. He came to bid the weary rest,
To heal the sinner's wounded breast;
To bind the broken heart;
To spread the light of truth around;
And to the world's remotest bound,
‖: The heaven'y gift impart. :‖

3. He came our trembling souls to save,
From sin, from sorrow, and the grave,
And chase our fears away;
Victorious over death and time,
To lead us to a happier clime,
‖: Where reigns eternal day. :‖

No. 265. COME JOIN, YE SAINTS.

Anon. Tune—ARIEL. C. P. M.

1. Come join, ye saints, with heart and voice,
Alone in Jesus to rejoice,
And worship at his feet;
Come take his praises on your tongues,
And raise to him your thankful songs,
‖: "In him ye are complete!" :‖

2. In him, who all our praise excels,
The fullness of the Godhead dwells,
And all perfections meet;
The head of all celestial powers,
Divinely theirs, divinely ours;
‖: "In him ye are complete!" :‖

3. Still onward urge your heavenly way,
Dependent on him day by day,
His presence still entreat;
His precious name forever bless,
Your glory strength and righteousness,
‖: "In him ye are complete!" :‖

No. 266. Come, We Who Love the Lord.

WATTS. ST. THOMAS. S. M. HANDEL.

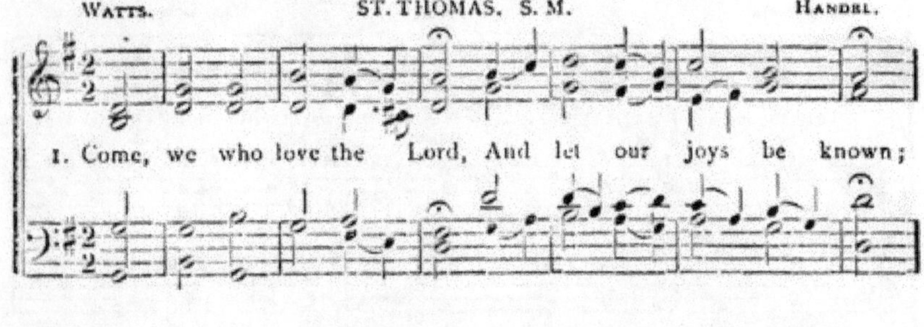
1. Come, we who love the Lord, And let our joys be known;

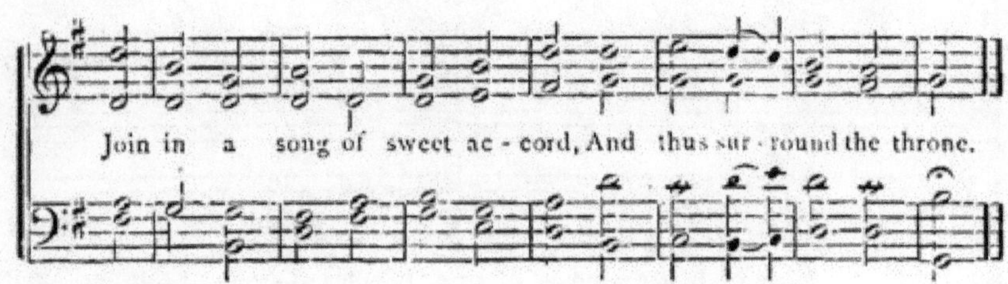
Join in a song of sweet ac - cord, And thus sur - round the throne.

2. Let those refuse to sing
Who never knew our God;
But children of the heavenly King
May speak their joys abroad.

3. The hill of Zion yields
A thousand sacred sweets
Before we reach the heavenly fields,
Or walk the golden streets.

4. Then let our songs abound,
And every tear be dry; [ground
We're marching thro' Immanuel's
To fairer worlds on high.

No. 267. THE LORD MY SHEPHERD IS.

WATTS Tune—ST. THOMAS. S. M.

1. The Lord my Shepherd is,
I shall be well supplied;
Since he is mine, and I am his,
What can I want beside?

2. He leads me to the place
Where heavenly pasture grows,
Where living waters gently pass,
And full salvation flows.

3. If e'er I go astray,
He doth my soul reclaim;
And guides me in his own right way,
For his most holy name.

4. While he affords his aid,
I cannot yield to fear; [shade,
Tho' I should walk thro' death's dark
My Shepherd's with me there.

5. In spite of all my foes,
Thou dost my table spread;
My cup with blessings overflows,
And joy exalts my head.

6. The bounties of thy love
Shall crown my future days;
Nor from thy house will I remove,
Nor cease to speak thy praise.

No. 268. A CHARGE TO KEEP I HAVE.

CHARLES WESLEY. Tune—ST. THOMAS. S. M.

1. A charge to keep I have,
A God to glorify,
A never-dying soul to save,
And fit it for the sky.

2. To serve the present age,
My calling to fulfill;
Oh, may it all my powers engage
To do my Master's will.

3. Arm me with jealous care,
As in thy sight to live;
And oh, thy servant, Lord, prepare
A strict account to give.

4. Help me to watch and pray,
And on thyself rely,
Assured, if I my trust betray,
I shall forever die.

No. 269. Just as I Am.

CHARLOTTE ELLIOT. WOODWORTH. L. M. WM. BRADBURY.

1. Just as I am! with-out one plea, But that Thy blood was shed for me,

And that thou bidd'st me come to Thee, O Lamb of God I come! I come!

2. Just as I am! and waiting not
To rid my soul of one dark blot,
To Thee, whose blood can cleanse each [spot,
O Lamb of God I come! I come!

3. Just as I am! tho' tossed about,
With many a conflict, many a doubt,
Fightings and fears within, without,
O Lamb of God! I come! I come!

4. Just as I am! poor, wretched, blind,
Sight, riches, healing of the mind,
Yea, all I need, in Thee to find,
O Lamb of God! I come! I come!

5. Just as I am! Thou wilt receive,
Wilt welcome, pardon, cleanse, relieve;
Because Thy promise I believe:
O Lamb of God! I come! I come!

No. 270. JESUS, AND SHALL IT EVER BE?

GRIGG. Tune—WOODWORTH. L. M.

1. Jesus, and shall it ever be?
A mortal man ashamed of Thee—
Ashamed of Thee, whom angels praise,
Whose glories shine to endless days?

2. Ashamed of Jesus! that dear Friend,
On whom my hopes of heaven depend?
No! when I blush, be this my shame,
That I no more revere His name.

3. Ashamed of Jesus! Yes, I may,
When I've no guilt to wash away,
No tears to wipe, no good to crave,
No fears to quell, no soul to save.

4. Till then, nor is my boasting vain,
Till then I boast a Savior slain:
And oh, may this my glory be,
That Christ is not ashamed of me!

No. 271. LORD, HEAR MY PRAYER.

Unknown. Tune—WOODWORTH. L. M.

1. Lord, hear my prayer, and let my cry
Have speedy access unto Thee;
In day of my calamity
Oh hide not Thou Thy face from me.

2. Hear when I call to Thee; that day
An answer speedily return:
My days, like smoke, consume away,
And, as an hearth, my bones do burn.

3. My heart is wounded very sore,
And withered, like grass doth fade:
I am forgetful grown therefore
To take and eat my daily bread.

4. By reason of my smart within,
And voice of my most grievous groans,
My flesh consumed is; my skin,
All parched, doth cleave unto my bones.

No. 272. Jesus Shall Reign.

WATTS. DUKE STREET. L. M. JOHN. HATTON.

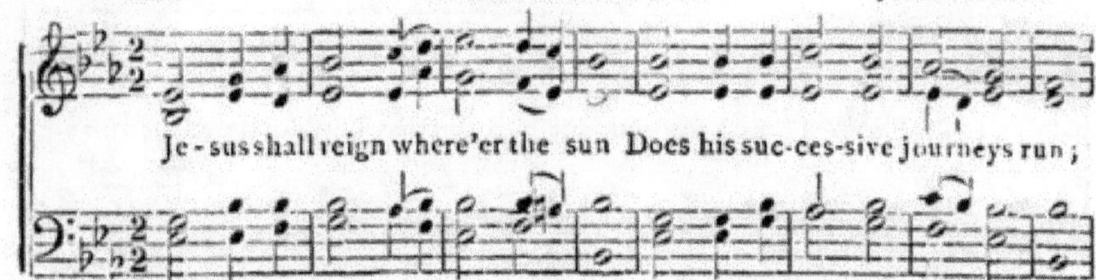
Je - sus shall reign where'er the sun Does his suc-ces-sive journeys run;

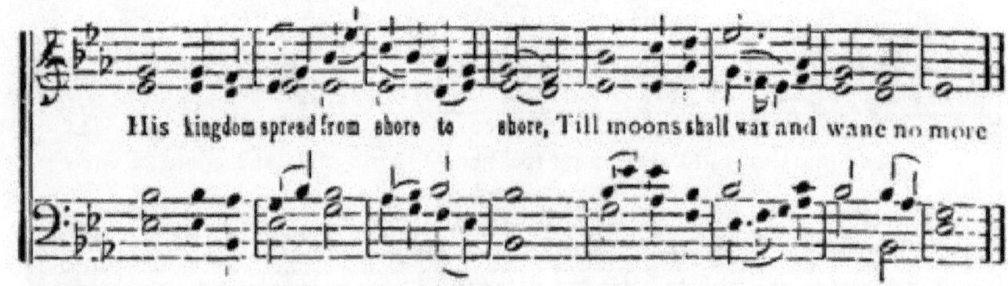
His kingdom spread from shore to shore, Till moons shall wax and wane no more

2. To him shall endless prayer be made,
And praises throng to crown his head:
His name, like sweet perfume, shall rise
With every morning sacrifice.

3. People and realms of every tongue
Dwell on his love with sweetest song;
And infant voices shall proclaim
Their early blessings on his name.

4. Blessings abound where'er he reigns
The prisoner leaps to loose his chains;
The weary find eternal rest,
And all the sons of want are blest.

5. Let every creature rise, and bring
Peculiar honors to our King:
Angels descend with songs again,
And earth repeat the long amen

No. 273. SHOW PITY LORD.

WATTS. Tune—DUKE STREET. L. M.

1. Show pity, Lord! O Lord, forgive;
Let a repenting rebel live;
Are not thy mercies large and free?
May not a sinner trust in thee?

2. Oh, wash my soul from every sin,
And make my guilty conscience clean
Here on my heart the burden lies,
And past offences pain mine eyes.

3. My lips with shame my sins confess,
Against thy law, against thy grace;
Lord, should thy judgment grow severe,
I am condemned, but thou art clear.

4. Should sudden vengeance seize my breath,
I must pronounce thee just in death;
And if my soul were sent to hell,
Thy righteous law approves it well,

5. Yet save a trembling sinner, Lord!
Whose hope, still hovering round thy word,
Would light on some sweet promise [there,]
Some sure support against despair.

No. 274. WITH TEARFUL EYES.

C. ELLIOTT. Tune—DUKE STREET. L. M.

1. With tearful eyes I look around;
Life seems a dark and stormy sea;
Yet, 'mid the gloom, I hear a sound,
A heavenly whisper, "Come to me;"

2. It tells me of a place of rest;
It tells me where my soul may flee:
Oh, to the weary, faint, oppressed,
How sweet the bidding, "Come to me!"

3. "Come for all else must fail and die!
Earth is no resting place for thee;
To heaven direct thy weeping eye,
I am thy portion; Come to me!"

4. O voice of mercy! voice of love!
In conflict, grief, and agony,
Support me, cheer me from above!
And gently whisper, "Come to me!

No. 275. Faith is a Living Power.

A. D 1531. SESSIONS. L. M. L. O. Emerson.

1. Faith is a liv-ing pow'r from heaven Which grasps the promise God has given,
2. Faith finds in Christ whate'er we need To save and strengthen, guide and feed

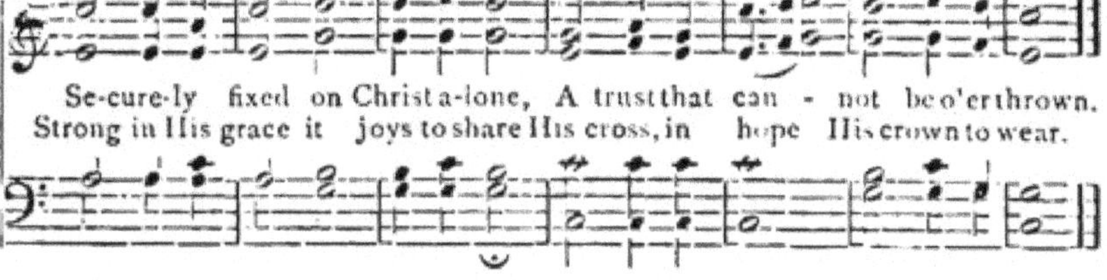
Se-cure-ly fixed on Christ a-lone, A trust that can - not be o'erthrown.
Strong in His grace it joys to share His cross, in hope His crown to wear.

3 Faith to the conscience whispers peace,
And bids the mourner's sighing cease;
By faith the children's right we claim,
And call upon our Father's name,

4. Such faith in us, O God, implant,
And to our prayers Thy favor grant
In Jesus Christ, Thy saving Son,
Who is our fount of health alone.

No. 276. LORD, I AM THINE.

Samuel Davies. Tune—SESSIONS. L. M.

1. Lord, I am thine, entirely thine,
Purchased and saved by blood divine!
With full consent thine I would be,
And own thy sovereign right in me.

2. Grant one poor sinner more a place,
Among the children of thy grace,
A wretched sinner, lost to God,
But ransomed by Immanuel's blood

3. Thine would I live, thine would I die,
Be thine through all eternity;
The vow is passed beyond repeal,
Now will I set the solemn seal.

4. Here at the cross where flows the blood
That bought my guilty soul for God;
Thee, my new Master, now I call,
And consecrate to thee my all

5. Do thou assist a feeble worm,
Thy great engagement to perform;
Thy grace can full assistance lend,
And on that grace I dare depend.

No. 277. GRACE.

Unknown. Tune—SESSIONS. L. M.

(*Before Tea.*)

1. Be present at our table, Lord,—
Be here and everywhere adored.
Thy bounties bless, and grant that we
May feast in Paradise with Thee.

(*After Tea.*)

2. We thank Thee Lord, for this our food
And more because of Jesus' blood
Let manna to our souls be given,
The bread of life, sent down from heaven

No. 278. DOXOLOGY.

Thos. Ken. Tune—SESSIONS L. M.

Praise God, from whom all blessings flow;
Praise Him, all creatures here below;
Praise Him above, ye heavenly host,
Praise Father, Son, and Holy Ghost.

No. 279. Nearer, My God, to Thee.

S. F. Adams. BETHANY. 6s, 4s. Lowell Mason.

1. Near-er, my God to thee, Near-er to thee! E'n tho' it be a cross, That rais-eth me!
Still all my songs shall be, Near-er, my God, to thee, Near-er, my God, to thee, Near-er to thee.

2. Though like the wanderer,
The sun gone down,
Darkness be over me,
My rest a stone,
Yet in my dreams I'd be
‖: Nearer, my God, to thee, :‖
Nearer to thee!

3. There let the way appear,
Steps unto heaven;
All that thou sendest me,
In mercy given;
Angels to beckon me
‖: Nearer, my God, to thee, :‖
Nearer to thee.

No. 280. FADE, FADE, EACH EARTHLY JOY.

Mrs Bonar. Tune—BETHANY. 6s, 4s.

1. Fade, fade, each earthly joy;
Jesus is mine!
Break, every tender tie;
Jesus is mine:
Dark is the wilderness;
Earth has no resting place;
Jesus alone can bless;
Jesus is mine.

2. Tempt not my soul away;
Jesus is mine:
Here would I ever stay;
Jesus is mine:
Perishing things of clay,
Born but for one brief day,
Pass from my heart away,
Jesus is mine.

3. Farewell, mortality;
Jesus is mine:
Welcome, eternity;
Jesus is mine:
Welcome, O loved and blest!
Welcome, sweet scenes of rest;
Welcome, my Savior's breast;
Jesus is mine!

No. 281. MORE LOVE TO THEE.

Mrs Prentis. Tune—BETHANY. 6s 4s.

1. More love to Thee, O Christ!
More love to Thee;
Hear thou the prayer I make
On bended knee;
This is my earnest plea,
‖: More love, O Christ, to Thee, :‖
More love to Thee!

2. Once earthly joy I craved,
Sought peace and rest;
Now Thee alone I seek,
Give what is best;
This all my prayer shall be,
‖: More love, O Christ, to Thee! :‖
More love to Thee!

3. Then shall my latest breath,
Whisper Thy praise,
This be the parting cry
My heart shall raise;
This still its prayer shall be:
‖: More love, O Christ, to Thee, :‖
More love to thee!

No. 282. Come, Thou Fount.

Geo. Robinson. NETTLETON. 8s, 7s. D. Anon.

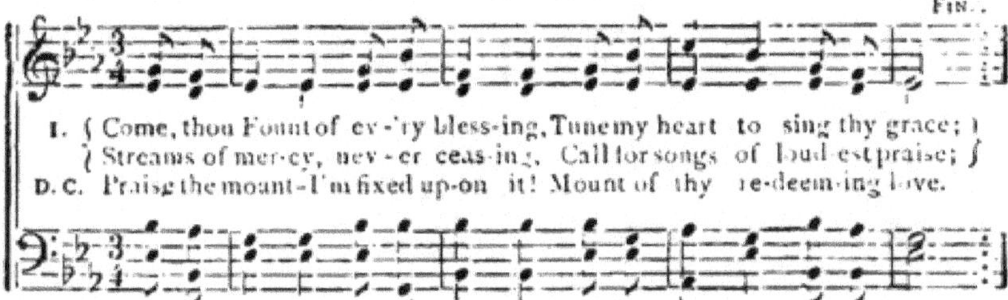
Fine.
1. { Come, thou Fount of ev-'ry bless-ing, Tune my heart to sing thy grace; }
{ Streams of mer-cy, nev-er ceas-ing, Call for songs of loud-est praise; }
D. C. Praise the mount-I'm fixed up-on it! Mount of thy re-deem-ing love.

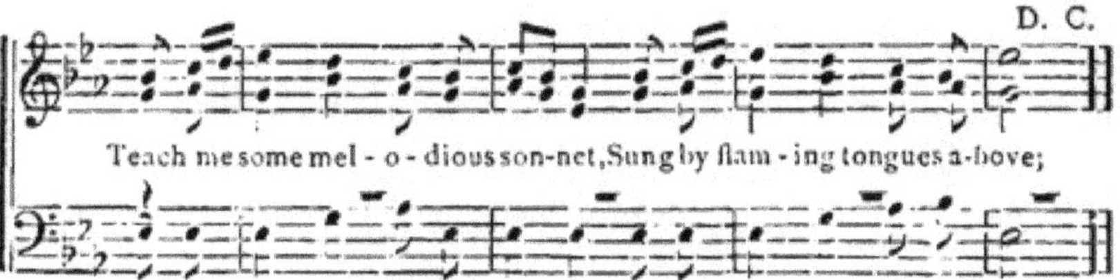
D. C.
Teach me some mel-o-dious son-net, Sung by flam-ing tongues a-bove;

2. Here I raise my Eben-ezer,
Hither by thy help I'm come;
And I hope, by thy good pleasure,
Safely to arrive at home,
Jesus sought me when a stranger,
Wandering from the fold of God;
He to rescue me from danger,
Interposed his precious blood,

3. Oh, to grace how great a debtor,
Daily I'm constrained to be!
Let thy goodness, like a fetter,
Bind my wandering heart to thee;
Prone to wander, Lord, I fe l it—
Prone to leave the God I love—
Here's my heart, oh, take and seal it,
Seal it for thy courts above.

No. 283. COME, YE SINNERS.

Rev. Hart. Tune—NETTLETON. 8s, 7s. D.

1. Come, ye sinners, poor and needy,
Weak and wounded, sick and sore,
Jesus ready stands to save you,
Full of pity love and power:
‖: He is able, He is able,
He is willing, doubt no more. :‖

2. Now ye needy, come and welcome,
God's free bounty glorify:
True belief and true repentance,
Every grace that brings you nigh,
‖: Without money, without money,
Come to Jesus Christ and buy :‖

3. Come, ye weary, heavy-laden,
Bruised and mangled by the fall,
If you tarry till you're better,
You will never come at all;
‖: Not the righteous, not the righteous,
Sinners, Jesus came to call. :‖

No. 284. OH, THOU GOD.

Thomas Olivers. Tune—NETTLETON. 8s, 7s. D.

1. Oh, thou God of my salvation,
My Redeemer from all sin;
Moved by thy divine compassion,
Who hast died my heart to win;
‖: I will praise thee, I will praise thee;
Where shall I thy praise begin? :‖

2. Though unseen, I love the Savior,
He hath brought salvation near;
Manifests his pard'ning favor;
And when Jesus doth appear,
‖: Soul and body, soul and body,
Shall his glorious image bear. :‖

3. Angels now are hov'ring round us,
Unperceived amid the throng;
Wond'ring at the love that crowned us,
Glad to join the holy song;
‖: Hallelujah, hallelujah,
Love and praise to Christ belong. :‖

No. 285. Must Jesus Bear the Cross Alone?

THOS. SHEPHERD. MAITLAND. C. M. GEO. N. ALLEN.

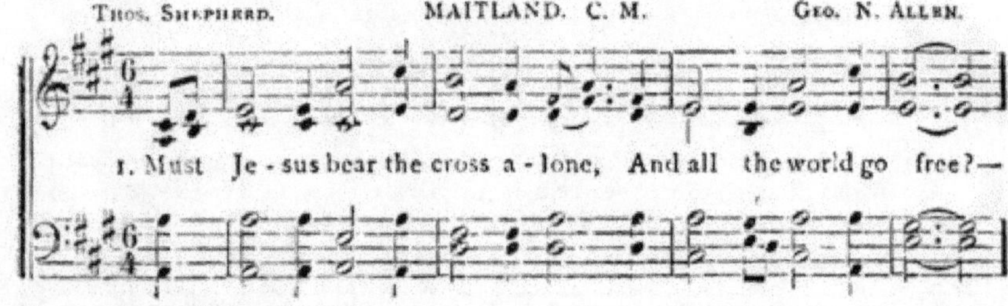
1. Must Je - sus bear the cross a - lone, And all the world go free?—

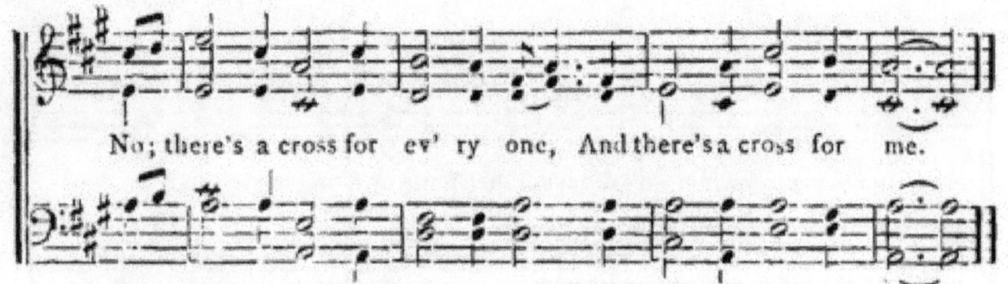
No; there's a cross for ev' ry one, And there's a cross for me.

2. The consecrated cross I'll bear,
Till death shall set me free,
And then go home my crown to wear,
For there's a crown for me.

3. Upon the crystal pavement, down
At Jesus' pierced feet,
Joyful, I'll cast my golden crown,
And his dear name repeat.

4 O, precious cross! O, glorious crown!
O, resurrection day!
Ye angels, from the stars come down,
And bear my soul away.

No. 286. COME, HOLY SPIRIT.

ISAAC WATTS. Tune—MAITLAND. C. M.

1. Come, Holy Spirit, heavenly dove,
With all thy quickening powers;
Kindle a flame of sacred love
In these cold hearts of ours.

2. Look how we grovel here below,
Fond of these earthly toys;
Our souls, how heavily they go,
To reach eternal joys.

3. In vain we tune our formal songs
In vain we strive to rise;
Hosannas languish on our tongues,
And our devotion dies.

4. Father, and shall we ever live
At this poor dying rate,
Our love so faint, so cold to thee,
And thine to us so great?

5. Come, Holy Spirit, heavenly dove
With all thy quickening powers;
Come, shed abroad a Savior's love,
And that shall kindle ours.

No. 287. HOW SWEET THE NAME OF JESUS.

JOHN NEWTON. Tune—MAITLAND. C. M.

1. How sweet the name of Jesus sounds
In a believer's ear;
It soothes his sorrows, heals his wounds,
And drives away his fear.

2. It makes the wounded spirit whole,
And calms the troubled breast;
'Tis manna to the hungry soul,
And to the weary, rest.

3. Dear Name, the Rock on which I build,
My shield and hiding place;
My never failing treasure, filled
With boundless stores of grace.

4. Jesus my Shepherd, Savior, Friend,
My Prophet, Priest and King;
My Lord, my Life, my Way, my End,
Accept the praise I bring.

No. 288. Glorying in the Cross.

Isaac Watts. EUCHARIST. L. M. Isaac Woodbury.

1. When I sur - vey the won - drous cross On which the Prince of Glo - ry died, My rich-est gain I count but loss, And pour con - tempt on all my pride.
2. For - bid it, Lord, that I should boast, Save in the death of Christ, my God; All the vain things that charm me most, I sac - ri - fice them to his blood.

3. See, from his head, his hands, his feet,
Sorrow and love flow mingled down:
Did e'er such love and sorrow meet,
Or thorns compose so rich a crown?

4. Were the whole realm of nature mine,
That were a present far too small;
Love so amazing, so divine,
Demands my soul, my life, my all.

No. 289. FROM EVERY STORMY WIND.

Boehm. Tune—EUCHARIST. L. M.

1. From every stormy wind that blows,
From every swelling tide of woes,
There is a calm, a sure retreat:
'Tis found beneath the mercy seat.

2. There is a place where Jesus sheds
The oil of gladness on our heads;
A place than all besides more sweet:
It is the blood bought mercy seat.

3 Ah! whither could we flee for aid,
When tempted, desolate, dismayed,
Or how the hosts of hell defeat,
Had suffering saints no mercy seat?

4. There, there on eagle wings we soar,
And sin and sense molest no more;
And heav'n comes down our souls to greet,
While glory crowns the mercy seat.

No. 290. OF HIM WHO DID SALVATION BRING.

Hugh Stowell. Tune—EUCHARIST. L. M.

1. Of Him who did salvation bring,
I could forever think and sing;
Arise, ye needy,—he'll relieve;
Arise, ye guilty,—he'll forgive.

2. Ask but his grace, and lo, 'tis given;
Ask, and he turns your hell to heaven,
Though sin and sorrow wound my soul,
Jesus, thy balm will make it whole.

3. To shame our sins he blushed in blood;
He closed his eyes to show us God;
Let all the world fall down and know
That none but God such love can show.

4. 'Tis thee I love, for thee alone
I shed my tears and make my moan;
Where'er I am, where'er I move,
I meet the object of my love.

No. 291. And Can I Yet Delay?

ISAAC WATTS. BOYLSTON. S. M. LOWELL MASON.

1. And can I yet de - lay My lit - tle all to give?

To tear my soul from earth a - way For Je - sus to re - ceive?

2. Nay, but I yield, I yield;
I can hold out no more:
I sink, by dying love compelled,
And own thee conqueror.

3 Though late, I all forsake;
My friends, my all, resign;
Gracious Redeemer, take, O take
And seal me ever thine.

4. Come, and possess me whole,
Nor hence again remove,
Settle and fix my wavering soul
With all thy weight of love.

5. My one desire be this,
Thy only love to know;
To seek and taste no other bliss,
No other good below

No. 292. THE DAY IS PAST AND GONE.

JOHN LELAND. Tune—BOYLSTON. S. M.

1. The day is past and gone,
The evening shades appear;
O may we all remember well
The night of death draws near.

2. We lay our garments by,
Upon our beds to rest,
So death will soon disrobe us all
Of what we've here possessed.

3. Lord, keep us safe this night,
Secure from all our fears;
May angels guard us while we sleep,
Till morning light appears.

4. And when we early rise,
And view the unwearied sun,
May we set out to win the prize,
And after glory run.

5. And when our days are past,
And we from time remove,
O may we in thy bosom rest,
The bosom of thy love.

No. 293. MY SOUL, BE ON THY GUARD.

GEO. HEATH. Tune—BOYLSTON. S. M.

1. My soul be on thy guard,
Ten thousand foes arise;
The hosts of sin are pressing hard,
To draw thee from the skies.

2. Oh watch, and fight, and pray,
The battle ne'er give o'er;
Renew it boldly every day,
And help divine implore.

3. Ne'er think the vict'ry won,
Nor lay thine armor down;
The work of faith will not be done;
Till thou obtain the crown.

4. Then persevere till death
Shall bring thee to thy God;
He'll take thee at thy parting breath,
To His divine abode.

No. 294. Revive Us Again.

Dr. W. P. Mackay.
English Melody.
1. We praise Thee, O God! for the Son of Thy love, For Je-sus who died, and is now gone a-bove.
2. We praise Thee, O God! for Thy Spir-it of light, Who has shown us our Sav-ior, and scattered our night.
3. All glo-ry and praise to the Lamb that was slain, Who has borne all our sins, and has cleansed ev-'ry stain.
Chorus.
Hal-le-lu-jah! Thine the glo-ry, Hal-le-lu-jah! A-men. Re-vive us a-gain.
Hal-le-lu-jah! etc
Hal-le-lu-jah! etc.
4. All glory and praise to the God of all grace, [and guided our ways.
Who has bought us, and sought us,
5. Revive us again; fill each heart with Thy love; [from above.
May each soul be rekindled with fire
No. 295. Oh, Happy Day.
E. F. Rimbault.
1. O, hap-py day that fixed my choice On Thee, my Sav-ior and my God! Well may this glow-ing heart re-joice, And tell its rap-tures, all a-broad.
2. O hap-py bond, that seals my vows To him who mer-its all my love! Let cheerful an-thems fill his house, While to that sa-cred shrine I move
Chorus.
Fine.
D. S.
Hap-py day, hap-py day, When Jesus washed my sins away { He taught me how to watch and pray, And live rejoicing ev'-ry day, }

3. 'Tis done; the great transaction's done,
I am my Lord's and he is mine;
He drew me, and I followed on,
Charmed to confess the voice divine.

4. Now rest, my long, divided heart!
Fixed on this blissful center rest;
Nor ever from thy Lord depart,
With him,

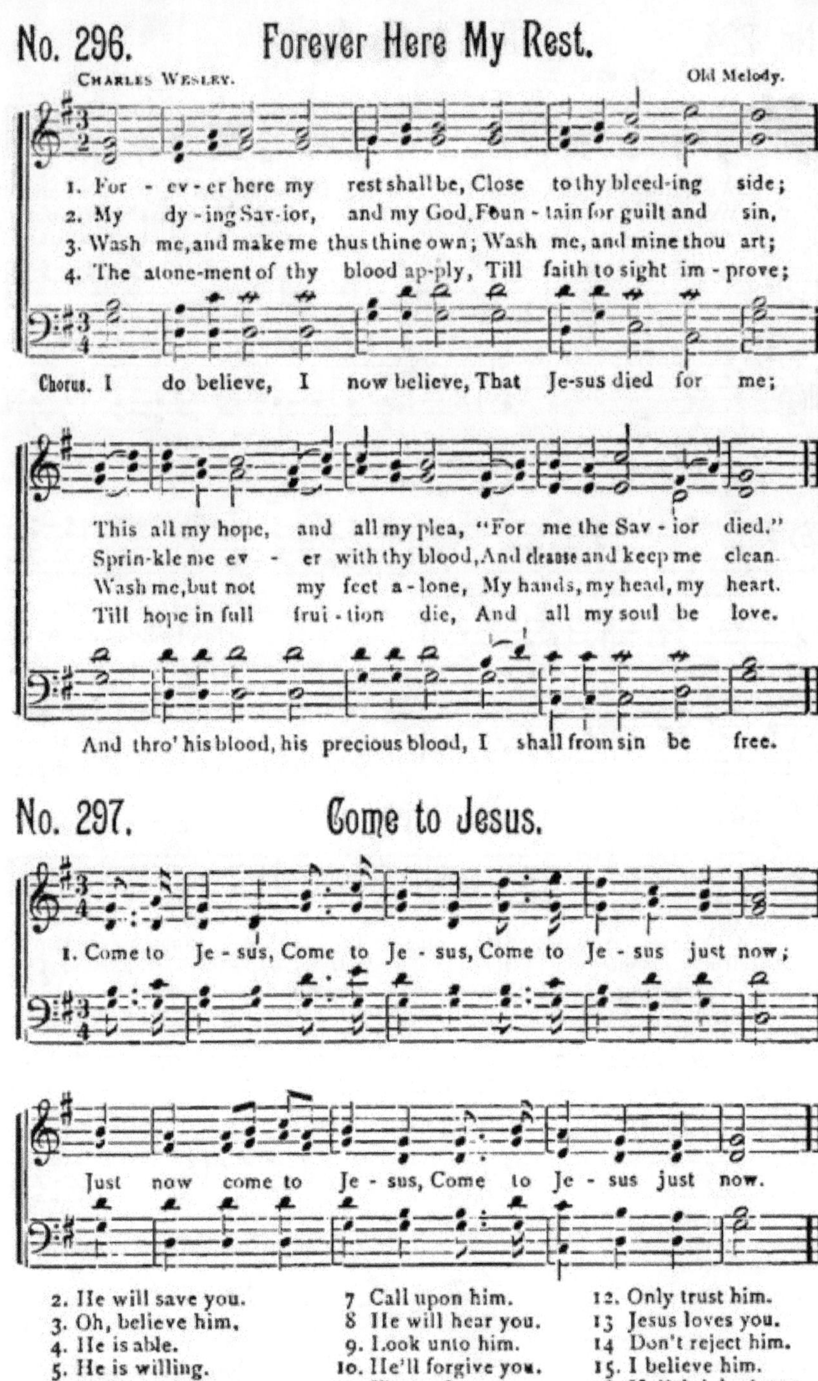
No. 296. Forever Here My Rest.
Charles Wesley.
Old Melody.
1. For - ev - er here my rest shall be, Close to thy bleed-ing side;
2. My dy - ing Sav-ior, and my God, Foun - tain for guilt and sin,
3. Wash me, and make me thus thine own; Wash me, and mine thou art;
4. The atone-ment of thy blood ap-ply, Till faith to sight im - prove;
Chorus. I do believe, I now believe, That Je-sus died for me;
This all my hope, and all my plea, "For me the Sav - ior died."
Sprin-kle me ev - er with thy blood, And cleanse and keep me clean.
Wash me, but not my feet a - lone, My hands, my head, my heart.
Till hope in full frui - tion die, And all my soul be love.
And thro' his blood, his precious blood, I shall from sin be free.
No. 297. Come to Jesus.
1. Come to Je - sus, Come to Je - sus, Come to Je - sus just now;
Just now come to Je - sus, Come to Je - sus just now.
2. He will save you.
3. Oh, believe him.
4. He is able.
5. He is willing.
6. He'll receive you.
7 Call upon him.
8 He will hear you.
9. Look unto him.
10. He'll forgive you.
11. Flee to Jesus.
12. Only trust him.
13 Jesus loves you.
14 Don't reject him.
15. I believe him.
16. Hallelujah, Amen.

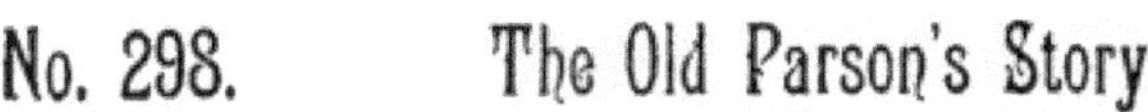
No. 298. The Old Parson's Story.

Eugene J. Hall. (To Mr. and Mrs. J. M. Hitchcock, Chicago, Ill.) E. O. Excell.

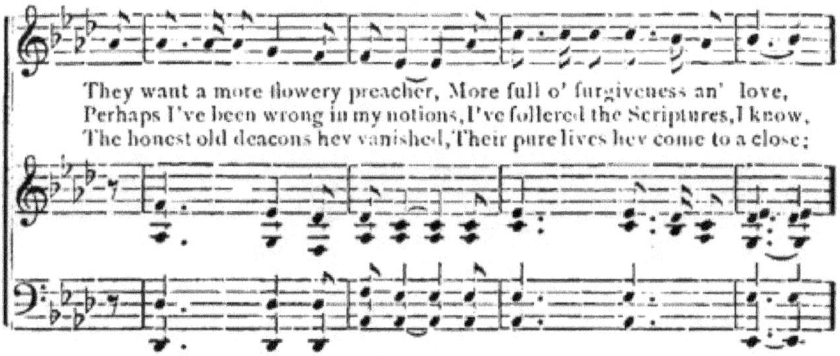

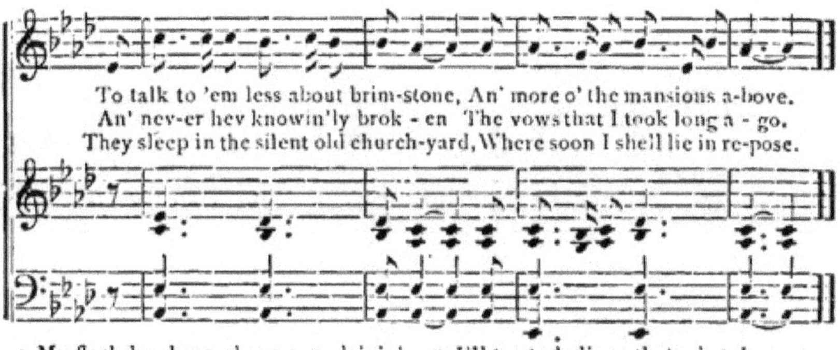

1. They say I am old an' for-get - ful, My style is ez slow ez a snail;
My doctrines are all out o' fash-ion, My mind is be-ginnin' to fail;
They want a more flowery preacher, More full o' furgiveness an' love,
To talk to 'em less about brim-stone, An' more o' the mansions a-bove.

2. Fur fifty long years I've been preachin', I've studied my old Bible well;
I al - wus hev felt it my du - ty To show 'em the horrors o' hell:
Perhaps I've been wrong in my notions, I've follered the Scriptures, I know,
An' nev-er hev knowin'ly brok - en The vows that I took long a - go.

3. I've seen ma-ny tri-als an' chan-ges, I've fit a good fight against wrong;
The gals hev grown up to be wimmin, The boys hev got manly an' strong;
The honest old deacons hev vanished, Their pure lives hev come to a close;
They sleep in the silent old church-yard, Where soon I shell lie in re-pose.

4. My flock hez been alwus complainin',
The church wus not rightly arranged,
They voted to hev a high steeple,
The gallery hed to be changed;
They built up a fanciful vestry,
They bought the best organ in town;
They chopped the old pews into kin-dlin's
An' tumbled the tall pulpit down.

5. I'll try to believe that what happens
Will alwus come out for the best;
They tell me my labor is ended,
'Tis time I wus takin' a rest:
I've leetle o' comfort or riches,
(I'm sartin my conscience is clear);
An' when in the church-yard I'm sleepin',
Perhaps they may wish I was here.

No. 299.

Wine is a Mocker.

Moderato. MALE VOICES. EDWIN SHERRETT.

BASE SOLO.

1. Wine is a mock-er, and strong drink is ra - ging, And who-so-ev-er is de-ceived there by is not wise, And who-so-ev - er, who-so-ev-er, who - so-ev - er is de-ceived there-by is not wise, is not wise,

Rall.

Rall.

QUARTET.

Wine is a mock - er, strong drink is ra - ging, And

Wine is a Mocker.—Continued.

who-so-ev-er is de-ceived there-by is not wise, And
who-so-ev-er is de-ceived there-by is not wise,
They that tar-ry long at the wine,
Who hath woe.
Who hath sor-row, They that tar-ry long at the wine,
who hath con-ten-tions? They that tar-ry long at the wine.

Wine is a Mocker.—Continued.

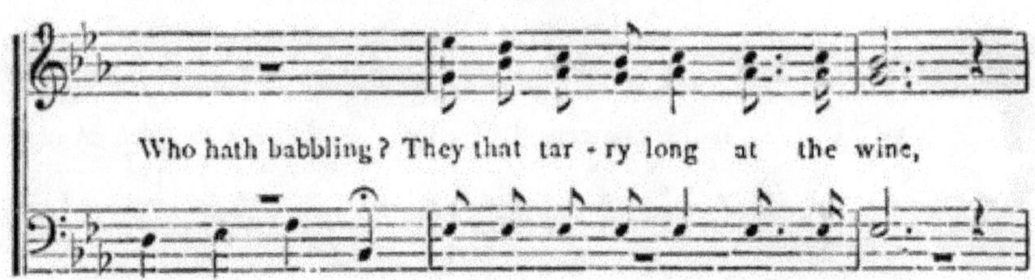
Who hath babbling? They that tar - ry long at the wine,

Who hath wounds without cause? They that tar-ry long at the wine,

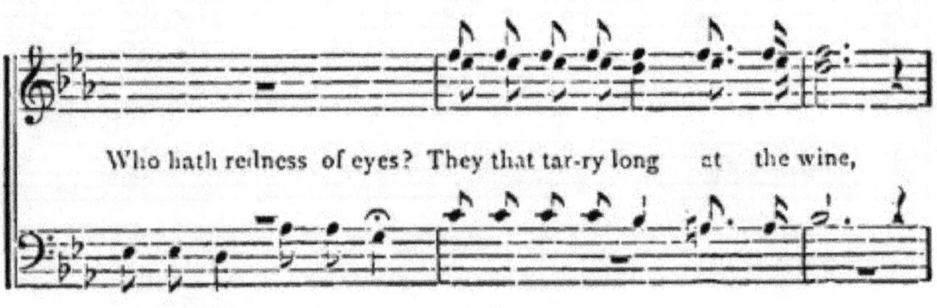
Who hath redness of eyes? They that tar-ry long at the wine,

TENOR SOLO.
Look not thou up-on the wine when it is red, When it

Wine is a Mocker.—Concluded.

mov-eth it-self a-right, Death lurk-eth there, For it bit-eth
2d. Ten.
like a
1st. Base.
2d. Base.

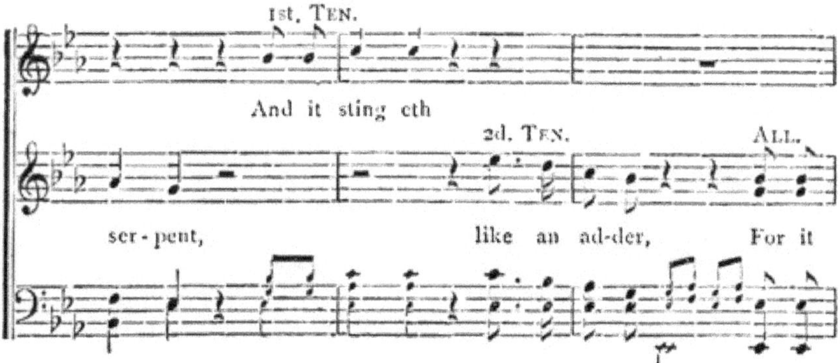

1st. Ten.
And it sting eth
2d. Ten.
All.
ser-pent, like an ad-der, For it

bit-eth like a ser-pent and it sting-eth like an ad-der, And

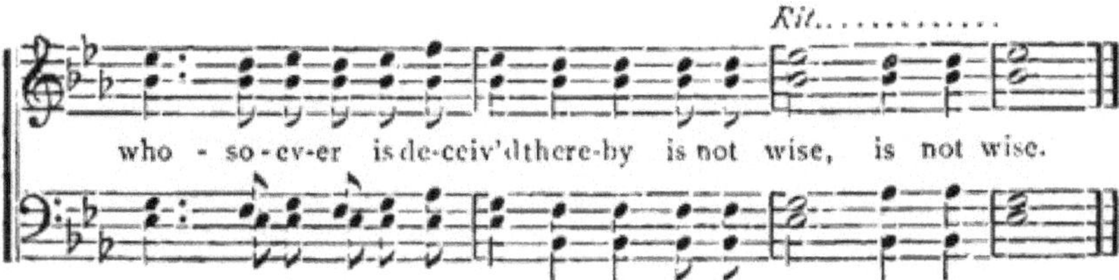

Rit............
who-so-ev-er is de-ceiv'd there-by is not wise, is not wise.

No. 300. Responsive Service.

Psa. xxv. 1—9.

(Note.—The organist should have the music of the following pieces at hand, and the singing should follow *at once* after each reading.)

Leader—1. Unto thee, O Lord, do I lift up my soul.

All Sing. Bethany.

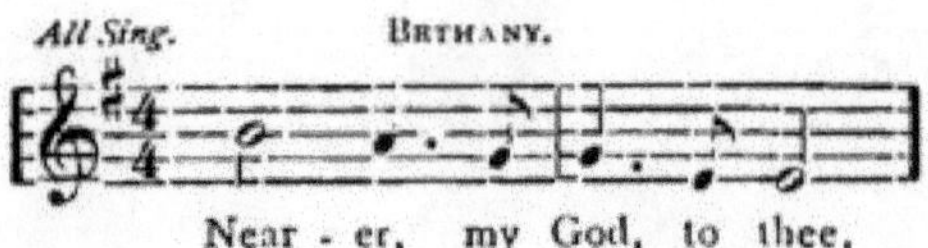

Near - er, my God, to thee,

Nearer to thee;
E'en though it be a cross
That raiseth me:
Still all my song shall be,
Nearer, my God, to thee,
Nearer to thee.

Leader—2. O my God, I trust in thee: let me not be ashamed, let not mine enemies triumph over me.

All Sing. I am Trusting.

Cho.—I am trusting, Lord, in thee,
Dear Lamb of Calvary;
Humbly at thy cross I bow:
Save me, Jesus, save me now.

Leader—3 Yea, let none that wait on thee be ashamed: let them be ashamed which transgress without cause.

All Sing. Woodworth.

Ashamed of Jesus! yes, I may,
When I've no guilt to wash away,
No tear to wipe, no good to crave,
No fear to quell, no soul to save.

Leader. 4. Show me thy ways, O Lord, teach me thy paths.

All Sing. Zion.

Guide me, O Thou great Jehovah.
Pilgrim through this barren land;
I am weak, but Thou art mighty,
Hold me with thy powerful hand:
Bread of heaven,
Feed me till I want no more.

Leader—5. Lead me in thy truth, and teach me: for thou art the God of my salvation; on thee do I wait all the day.

All Sing. What a Friend.

Savior, like a shepherd lead us,
Much we need thy tend'rest care,
In Thy pleasant pastures feed us,
For our use Thy folds prepare;
We are Thine, do Thou befriend us,
Be the Guardian of our way;
Keep Thy flock, from sin defend us,
Seek us when we go astray.

Responsive Service.—Concluded.

Leader—6. Remember, O Lord, thy tender mercies and thy loving kinkness, for they have been ever of old.

All Sing.
LOVING KINDNESS.

Awake, my soul, in joyful lays,
And sing the great Redeemer's praise;
He justly claims a song from me:
His loving kindness, oh, how free,
His loving kindness, loving kindness,
His loving kindness, oh, how free.

Leader—7. Remember not the sins of my youth, nor my transgressions: according to thy mercy remember thou me, for thy goodness sake, O Lord.

All Sing.
MARTYN.

Other refuge have I none,
  Hangs my helpless soul on thee:
Leave, oh, leave me not alone,
  Still support and comfort me.
All my trust on thee is stayed,
  All my help from thee I bring;
Cover my defenceless head,
  With the shadow of thy wing.

Leader—8. Good and upright is the Lord: therefore will he teach sinners in the way.

9. The meek will he guide in judgment; and the meek will he teach his way.

All Sing.
ST. THOMAS.

He leads me to the place,
  Where heavenly pasture grows,
Where living waters gently pass,
  And full salvation flows.
If e'er I go astray,
  He doth my soul reclaim;
And guides me in his own right way,
  For his most holy name.

GLORIA PATRI.
Glory be to the Father, and to the Son, and to the Ho-ly Ghost,
As it was in the beginning, is now, and ever shall be, world without end. A-men.

No. 301. Opening Service, No. 3.

FOR SUNDAY SCHOOLS, AND DIVINE WORSHIP.

Leader.—Praise ye the Lord. Praise God in his sanctuary: praise him in the firmament of his power.

Congregation.—Praise him for his mighty acts: praise him according to his excellent greatness.

All Sing. SESSIONS.

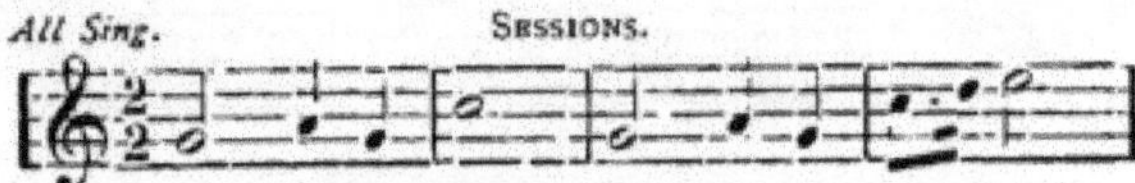

Praise God, from whom all blessings flow
Praise Him, all creatures here below;
Praise Him above, ye heavenly host:
Praise Father, Son, and Holy Ghost.

Leader.—Exalt ye the Lord our God, and worship at his footstool; for he is holy.

Congregation.—Enter into his gates with thanksgiving, and into his courts with praise

All Sing. REVIVE US AGAIN.

We praise thee, O God! for the Son of thy love,
For Jesus who died, and is now gone above!

Cho. Hallelujah! thine the glory, Hallelujah! amen.
Hallelujah! thine the glory, revive us again.

Leader.—It is a good thing to give thanks unto the Lord, and to sing praises unto thy name, O most high.

Congregation.—To show forth thy loving kindness in the morning, and thy faithfulness every night

All Sing. WARWICK.

1. Lord! in the morning Thou shalt hear
My voice ascending high;
To Thee will I direct my prayer,
To Thee lift up mine eye:

Leader.—Blessed is every one that feareth the Lord; that walketh in his ways.

Congregation.—Teach me thy way, O Lord, and lead me in a plain path, because of mine enemies.

All Sing. WHAT A FRIEND.

1. Gently, Lord, oh, gently lead us
Through this lonely vale of tears;
Thro' the changes thou'st decreed us,
Till our last great change appears,
When temptation's darts assail us,
When in devious paths we stray,
Let thy goodness never fail us,
Lead us in thy perfect way.

2. In the hour of pain and anguish,
In the hour when death draws near,
Suffer not our hearts to languish,—
Suffer not our souls to fear,
And, when mortal life is ended,
Bid us on thy bosom rest,
Till, by angel-bands attended
We awake among the blest.

No. 302. Opening Service, No. 4.

By W. B. Jacobs.

Supt.—For God so loved the world, that he gave his only begotten Son, that whosoever believeth in him should not perish, but have everlasting life.—John iii. 16.

Sch.—In this was manifested the love of God toward us, because that God sent his only begotten Son into the world, that we might live through him.—1 John iv. 9.

Supt.—Beloved if God so loved us, we ought also to love one another.—1 John iv. 11.

Revive Us Again.

1. We praise Thee, O God! for the Son of Thy love,
For Jesus who died, and is now gone above.
Cho.—Hallelujah! Thine the glory,
Hallelujah! Amen!
Hallelujah! Thine the glory,
Revive us again.

Supt.—But the comforter, which is the Holy Ghost, whom the Father will send in my name, he shall teach you all things, and bring all things to your remembrance, whatsoever I have said unto you.—John xiv. 26.

Sch.—When he, the Spirit of truth, is come, he will guide you into all truth: for he shall not speak of himself; but whatsoever he shall hear, that shall he speak: and he will show you things to come.—John xvi. 13.

Supt.—He shall glorify me: for he shall receive of mine, and shall show it unto you.—John xvi. 14.

Revive Us Again.

2. We praise Thee, O God! for Thy Spirit of light,
Who has shown us our Savior, and scattered our night.
Cho.—Hallelujah! etc.

Supt.—And I beheld, and I heard the voice of many angels round about the throne, and the living creatures and the elders; and the number of them was ten thousand times ten thousand, and thousands of thousands.—Rev. v. 11.

Sch.—Saying with a loud voice. Worthy is the Lamb that was slain to receive power, and riches, and wisdom, and strength, and honor, and glory, and blessing.—Rev. v. 12.

Revive Us Again.

3. All glory and praise to the Lamb that was slain,
Who has borne all our sins, and has cleansed every stain.
Cho.—Hallelujah! etc.

Supt.—Blessed be the God and Father of our Lord Jesus Christ, which according to his abundant mercy hath begotten us again unto a lively hope by the resurrection of Jesus Christ from the dead.—1 Peter i. 3.

Sch.—To an inheritance incorruptible, and undefiled, and that fadeth not away, reserved in heaven for you.—1 Peter i. 4.

Revive Us Again.

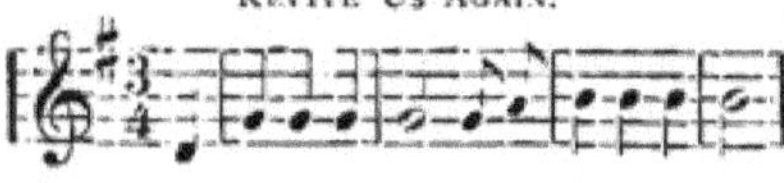

4. All glory and praise to the God of all grace,
Who has brought us, and sought us and guided our ways.
Cho.—Hallelujah! etc.

Supt.—And suddenly there came a sound from heaven as of a rushing mighty wind and it filled all the house where they were sitting.—Acts ii. 2.

Sch.—And there appeared unto them cloven tongues like as of fire, and it sat upon each of them.—Acts ii. 3.

Revive Us Again.

5. Revive us again; fill each heart with Thy love;
May each soul be rekindled with fire from above.
Cho.—Hallelujah! etc.

No. 303. Closing Service.

(SCHOOL STANDING)

Supt.—If my people, which are called by my name, shall humble themselves, and pray, and seek my face, and turn from their wicked ways; then will I hear from heaven, and will forgive their sin. 2 Chron. vii. 14.

Sch.—And whatsoever ye shall ask in my name, that will I do, that the Father may be glorified in the Son. John xiv. 13.

ALL SING: WHAT A FRIEND.

What a Friend we have in Jesus,
All our sins and griefs to bear!
What a privilege to carry
Everything to God in prayer!
O what peace we often forfeit,
O what needless pain we bear,
All because we do not carry
Everything to God in prayer.

Supt.—In everything by prayer and supplication with thanksgiving let your requests be made known unto God. Phil. iv. 6.

Sch.—The Spirit also helpeth our infirmities: for we know not what we should pray for as we ought: but the Spirit itself maketh intercession for us with groanings which cannot be uttered. Rom. viii. 26.

ALL SING:

Have we trials and temptations?
Is there trouble anywhere?
We should never be discouraged,
Take it to the Lord in prayer.
Can we find a friend so faithful
Who will all our sorrows share?
Jesus knows our every weakness,
Take it to the Lord in prayer.

Supt.—Confess your faults one to another, and pray one for another, that ye may be healed. The effectual fervent prayer of a righteous man availeth much. James v. 16.

Sch.—The sacrifice of the wicked is an abomination to the Lord: but the prayer of the upright is his delight. Prov. xv. 8.

ALL SING:

Are we weak and heavy laden,
Cumbered with a load of care?—
Precious Saviour, still our refuge,—
Take it to the Lord in prayer.
Do thy friends despise, forsake thee?
Take it to the Lord in prayer:
In his arms he'll take and shield thee,
Thou wilt find a solace there.

Supt.—After this manner therefore pray ye:

All.—Our Father which art in heaven, Hallowed be thy name. Thy kingdom come. Thy will be done in earth as it is in heaven. Give us this day our daily bread. And forgive us our debts, as we forgive our debtors. And lead us not into temptation, but deliver us from evil. For thine is the kingdom, and the power, and the glory, for ever. Amen. Matt. vi. 9-13.

→INDEX.←

Titles in SMALL CAPS—First Lines in Roman.

	No.
ABUNDANTLY ABLE TO SAVE....	62
ACCEPTANCE	197
A CHARGE TO KEEP I HAVE....	268
ALAS, AND DID MY SAVIOR....	246
A LITTLE TALK WITH JESUS...	150
ALL HAIL THE POWER OF JESUS'	229
ALL MY CLASS FOR JESUS	202
AND CAN I YET DELAY?.......	291
ANYWHERE WITH THEE	194
ARE YOU WASHED IN THE.....	177
ARISE, MY SOUL, ARISE.........	239
AROUND THE THRONE OF GOD..	3
A SINNER LIKE ME	13
As you gather round your table..	214
At the Feast of Belshazzar	187
At the feet of Jesus............	168
AT THE FOUNTAIN............	134
AT THE MERCY SEAT.........	116
Awake, my soul, in joyful lays ..	140
AWAKENING HYMN...........	146
BEAUTIFUL ZION BUILT ABOVE .	2
BEFORE THE CROSS	110
BEHOLD THE THRONE OF GRACE	248
Be present at our table, Lord....	277
BETTER THAN GOLD...........	195
BE UP AND DOING..............	154
Beyond the Silent River....	205
BLESSED JESUS THOU ART MINE	258
BLESSED JESUS	106
BLEST BE THE TIE THAT BINDS	247
BLOW YE THE TRUMPET, BLOW..	238
BRIGHT HOME................	96
BRINGING IN THE SHEAVES	147
Busy Servants in the Vineyard..	167
By Faith the Lamb of God I See	184
BY THY BIRTH, AND BY THY	259
CALL THEM IN...............	141
Children of the Heavenly King..	129
CHILDREN'S DAY..............	9
CHRIST FOR THE WORLD WE SING	224
Christian, wake, be up and doing.	154
CHRIST IS THE DOOR...........	55
CHRISTMAS...................	209
CITY OF BEAUTY	100
CLOSE TO THEE	11
COME AND BE SAVED...........	74
COME, HOLY SPIRIT, HEAVENLY	286
Come, is the Savior's dying word,	157
COME, JOIN YE SAINTS, WITH ...	265
COME, SINNER, COME	56
COME, THOU ALMIGHTY KING ..	223
COME, THOU FOUNT OF EVERY..	282
COME TO JESUS, JUST NOW......	297
COME TO ME.................	103
COME TO THE FOUNT	157
COME WE WHO LOVE THE LORD	113-266
COME YE SINNER.............	112-283
COME YE TO BETHLEHEM	215
CONCERT READING NO. 1.......	138
" " NO. 2.......	139
DELAY NOT, DELAY NOT	196
DELIGHTFUL HOME	53

INDEX.

	No.
Dennis	120-164
Depth of mercy	128
Does life seem sad and gloomy	54
Do you hear the Savior calling	186
Do you know the wondrous	57
Down at the cross where my	170
Doxology	278
Draw near, O Christ, to me	63
Each cooing dove and sighing	162
Even me	114
Fade, Fade, each Earthly	130-280
Faith is a Living Power	275
Far Up in Heaven's Blue	52
Father, Lead Me	144
Fear not, Little Flock	102
Forever here my rest shall	296
For Victorious Faith	121
For You and for Me	27
Fountain	119-160
From Death unto Life	161
From Every Stormy Wind	289
From Greenland's Icy	232
From Mountain Top	99
Gathering Home	76
Gathering Homeward from every	12
Gently, like the Summer	72
Gently, Lord, oh, Gently	252
Give Me Welcome	31
Give to Jesus Glory	99
Gloria	127
Glorious Fountain	15
Glorious Things	191
Glory be to the Father	127
Glory to His Name	170
Go and gather	17
God Bless our Native Land	225
God's almighty arms are round	49
Go Forward	75
Go Tell Them	159
Go, Wash in the Stream	39
Grace	277
Great Deliverer	200
Hail the Great Emancipation	48
Hark! the Voice of Jesus	8

	No.
Hark! What mean those	221
Haste, oh, Haste to Jesus	86
Hast thou Heard of Jesus?	208
Have you been to Jesus?	177
Have you Heard that Sweet,	180
Hear the Gentle Shepherd	108
Hear the Saviour sweetly saying,	141
Hear you not the voice of Jesus?	31
Heaven is my Home	124
He Leadeth me	115
He Loved me so	184
Help Each Other	85
He Saved my Soul	77
Ho! Every One that is Thirsty	175
How gentle God's commands	120-164
How I Wish I Knew	104
How Sweet the Name of	287
I am Coming to the Cross	219
I am just now persuaded	67
I am Listening	186
I am Persuaded	67
I am the Light, says Jesus	28
I am Saved	123
I am waiting for the morning	41
I'd rather have that noble guide	203
If you find yourself insulted	24
I have a song I love to sing	163
I have drank of the water of life	65
I have dream'd sweet dreams	30
I have Work for Thee	168
I Hear Thy Welcome Voice	125
I knew that God in his word	190
I know I love Thee better, Lord	66
I'll sing of that stream	39
I Long to be There	61
I Love Thy Kingdom, Lord	249
I Love you, Mother	25
I'm but a stranger here	124
I'm Coming Back To-night	149
I'm Glad Salvation's Free	133
I'm Nearer my Home	176
I'm Washed in the Blood	58
In a little while	21
In a world so full of weeping	16
In Heavenly Love Abiding	153

INDEX.

	No.
IN THE CROSS OF CHRIST	220
In the land of strangers	23
In the morning fresh and fair	60
In the name of Christ my Savior,	145
IN THE SHADOW OF HIS WINGS,	174
I once was Blind and could not	201
I SHALL SEE JESUS AS HE IS	193
IS IT RIGHT?	24
Is my name on the page?	38
IS MY NAME WRITTEN THERE?	38-166
Is thy brother sad and weary?	85
It came upon the midnight clear	209
I THINK WHEN I READ THAT	105
I've a dear Savior ready to listen,	172
I'VE BEEN REDEEMED	183
I'VE BEEN WASHED	65
I'VE WASHED MY ROBES	44
I WAITED FOR THE LORD	231
I want to be like Jesus	88
I was once far away from the	13
I WILL FOLLOW THEE	178
I WILL SEEK MY FATHER	60
I WILL TELL JESUS	172
I YIELD TO THEE	98
JESUS, AND SHALL IT EVER BE?	270
JESUS BIDS US SHINE	213
JESUS, BLESS THE CHILDREN	107
JESUS' BLOOD	29
JESUS CHRIST IS PASSING BY	145
JESUS IS CALLING FOR THEE	33
Jesus, I my cross have taken	35
JESUS IS MINE	130
Jesus is pleading with my poor	5
JESUS, LOVER OF MY SOUL	90-131-253
JESUS LOVES ME	19
JESUS SHALL REIGN	272
JESUS, THE NAME HIGH OVER ALL	261
JESUS, THE VERY THOUGHT OF	262
Jesus, thine all victorious love	116
JUST AS I AM WITHOUT ONE	269
Just step beyond the shadows	188
Lead me forth, O blessed Jesus	178
LEAVING ALL	35
LET EARTH AND HEAVEN	240
LET HIM IN	40-199
LET THEM COME TO ME	108
Let the nations awake	146
LIKE THE RAIN	72
List, the Spirit calls to thee	43
Little stars that twinkle	104
Look, ye saints, and see the light	142
LORD, HEAR MY PRAYER	271
LORD, I AM THINE	276
Lord, I care not for riches	166
Lord, I hear of showers of blessing	114
LORD, IN THE MORNING THOU	260
LOST, BUT JESUS FOUND ME	192
LOVE TO JESUS	69
LOVING KINDNESS	140
MARCHING HOME	10
MARCHING TO ZION	113
MEMORIES OF GALILEE	162
MERRY CHRISTMAS	214
MODEL CHURCH	217
MORE LOVE TO THEE, O CHRIST	281
MORE LIKE JESUS	88
MUST JESUS BEAR THE CROSS	285
MUSIC OVER YONDER	84
My days are gliding swiftly by	117
MY FAITH LOOKS UP TO THEE	110-156
My Father is rich in houses and	68
MY GOD WILL SEND HIS ANGELS	87
MY GRACE IS SUFFICIENT FOR	198
My Heavenly home is bright and	61
MY JESUS, I LOVE THEE	152
My robes were once all stained	44
My scholars all for Jesus	202
MY SOUL BE ON THY GUARD	293
MY SOUL DOTH MAGNIFY THE	50
MY TONGUE CAN TELL	201
NEARER HOME	4
NEARER, MY GOD, TO THEE	279
NEARER TO ME	63
Never mind your earthly	36
NO MATTER	101
NOW BE THE GOSPEL BANNER	148
Now to thee who fast in prison	200
O brother, you are helpless	86
O CITY OF BEAUTY	100
O'er the hills the sun is setting	4

INDEX.

	No.
O'ER THE GLOOMY HILLS OF	237
OF HIM WHO DID SALVATION, .135-290	
O for a faith that will not shrink.	121
Oh, come all ye faithful.........	215
OH, COULD I SPEAK THE........	263
Oh, fear not the waters	75
OH, FOR A CLOSER WALK WITH..	245
OH, FOR A HEART TO PRAISE MY,	244
OH, FOR A THOUSAND TONGUES .	230
OH, HAPPY DAY................	294
Oh, have you not heard.........	14
Oh, joyful is the tribute..........	32
OH, LET YOUR MINGLING VOICES,	264
Oh sing me a song of the better .	97
OH, TELL IT ALL ABROAD.......	158
OH, THAT MY LOAD OF SIN WERE.	243
Oh, the joy that awaits me	205
Oh, think of a home over there...	111
OH, THOU GOD OF MY..........	284
Oh, ye who follow Jesus.........	159
O LOOK ABOVE.................	54
O matchless, marvelous grace of.	198
ONE BY ONE..................	12
One sweetly solemn thought	176
ONLY WAITING	41
ON THE MOUNTAIN TOP	235
ON THE OTHER SIDE	169
ONWARD CHISTIAN SOLDIERS...	151
Opening service, No. 1..........	135
" " " 2..........	136
" " " 3..........	301
" " " 4..........	302
OPEN THE DOOR FOR THE	18
OUR COUNTRY'S VOICE IS.......	228
OUR FATHER 95-171	
OUT WITH THE LIFE BOATS	181
OVER ON THE HILLS OF GLORY..	142
OVER THE RIVER	89
O ZION, ZION................	7
Poor sinner, where art thou	55
Praise God, from whom all......	278
PRAISE SERVICE..............	137
PRESS ON..................	188
REFUGE....................	59
REFUGE IN CHRIST...........	204
Rejoice ye saints the time draws.	185
Resist not the spirit............	94
RESPONSIVE SERVICE..........	300
Return, O wand'rer..	91
REVIVE US AGAIN.............	294
Ring on, ring on, ye bells........	173
ROCK OF AGES CLEFT FOR ME..143-256	
ROLL ON, THOU MIGHTY OCEAN..	234
SAILING O'ER LIFE'S OCEAN.....	81
SAILING O'ER THE SEA..........	165
SAVIOR, LIKE A SHEPHERD LEAD	251
SAY IS YOUR LAMP BURNING?...	22
SAY SINNER HATH A VOICE.....	242
SEEK A SAVIOUR'S BLESSING...	93
SHALL I BE SAVED TO-NIGHT?...	5
SHALL I BE THERE?...........	189
SHOW PITY, LORD, O LORD.....	273
SINCE I HAVE BEEN REDEEMED.	163
SINFUL, WEARY, HEAVY LADEN.	6
SING HOSANNA................	210
SINGING WITH THE ANGELS.....	30
SINNER GO, WILL YOU GO?......	216
Sinner, press your way to Jesus..	78
SINNER, TURN ,WHY WILL YE....	254
Softly and tenderly Jesus is calling	27
SONG OF PEACE...............	49
Sowing in the morning.........	147
STAND UP, STAND UP FOR JESUS.	227
STAY, WEARY CHILD...........	64
STEAL AWAY TO JESUS.........	91
SUN OF MY SOUL, THOU SAVIOUR	241
SWEET HOUR OF PRAYER.......	118
TAKE YOUR SINS TO JESUS......	83
THAT SWEET STORY...........	105
THE BEACON LIGHT............	155
THE BIBLE..................	203
THE BLOOD IS ALL MY PLEA.....	190
THE CHILD OF A KING..........	68
The children's Sabbath comes...	9
THE DAY IS PAST AND GONE....	292
THE HALF HAS NEVER BEEN....	66
THE HAND WRITING ON THE....	187
THE HAPPY LAND.............	109
THE HOME OVER THERE........	111
THE LAURELS OF VICTORY......	207

INDEX.

	No.
The Lord may come to-day...	167
The Lord my shepherd is....	267
The Lord's prayer...........	171
The mansions of love........	82
The master hath need of....	80
The morning light is breaking	226
The old parson's story	298
The one thing needful......	73
The promised land.	97
There are mansions of love......	82
There comes a time, a happy time	52
There is a country pure and bright	53
There is a fountain filled 15-119.160-183	
There is a habitation............	7
There is a happy land...........	109
There is music over yonder......	84
There is refuge in Christ........	204
There's a beautiful land on high..	212
There's a crown in heaven	182
There's a land of wondrous beauty	96
There's a wideness in God's.	222
There's a wonderful........	42
There's a stranger at the door...40-199	
There's much we can do......	20
The road to heaven..........	132
The shining shore...........	117
The song of jubilee..........	1
The true easter..............	173
They say I am old and forgetful.	298
They say there's a land.....	37
Tho' I'm unworthy his love.....	206
Though trials oft beset me.......	87
Three warnings...............	94
Throw the door wide open...	92
Till he come, O let the word	257
Till I learned to love thy name..	161
Title clear.................	122
Touch the hem of his garment	78
Treasures of heaven.........	182
Trim your lamps and be ready	185
Waiting by the river........	79
Wake the song of jubilee........	1
Walk in the light...	129
Watch and pray...............	179
We are marching homeward....	10

	No
We are waiting, blessed Lord	255
We are waiting by the river	79
Weary soul, by care oppressed...	103
We come to Thee, dear Savior...	158
We know there's a bright and ...	34
Welcome happy morning.....	211
Welcome, wanderer, welcome,	23
We'll sing the gospel.........	32
We'll soon be at home.........	76
Well, wife, I've found the model.	217
We praise thee, O God..........	294
We're a faithful, pilgrim band....	81
We're a happy pilgrim band......	165
We're over on the stormy side...	169
We shall walk...............	126
We speak of the realms of the blest	46
What a friend we have in...	250
Whatever the battles of life......	207
What must it be to be there?	46
What tho' the path be rugged....	101
When as of old in her sadness...	33
When I can read my title clear.122-197	
When I reach the world of light.	193
When I survey the wondrous	288
When I think of Jesus' love.....	69
When I tune my harp in glory	26
Wehn shall the voice of.....	233
When the harvest is past....	51
When the shadows round you...	179
When upon the great white throne	189
When with clouds the sky is filling	59
Where art thou steering, brother?	155
Which loved mother best?...	25
While Jesus whispers to you....	56
While the years are rolling	16
While upon the earthly journey.	73
Whiter than the snow.......	102
Whoever receiveth the crucified.	62
Whosoever believeth........	45
Whosoever means me.........	206
Who was in a manger laid?......	106
Why I love my Jesus..........	47
Will you and I be there?....	34
Will you be washed in the...	43
Will you meet me?...........	70

INDEX.

	No.
Will you not come to him for life?	74
Wine is a mocker	299
With Jesus by and by	36
With tearful eyes I look	274
Wonderful fountain	42
Wonderful love	14
Wonderful Savior	28
Work for the night is coming	218
Would you have a Savior near?	93
Would you know why I love Jesus?	47
Yield so meekly	71
You ask me, brethren, how I	77
Yonder a vessel is breasting the	181
Zion stands with hills	235

www.ingramcontent.com/pod-product-compliance
Lightning Source LLC
Chambersburg PA
CBHW030405270326
41926CB00009B/1280
* 9 7 8 3 3 3 7 1 8 1 7 2 7 *